# GERMAN-JEWISH THOU
## AND ITS AFTERLIFE

JEWISH LITERATURE AND CULTURE

Alvin H. Rosenfeld, editor

# GERMAN-JEWISH THOUGHT AND ITS AFTERLIFE

*A Tenuous Legacy*

Vivian Liska

Indiana University Press

This book is a publication of

Indiana University Press
Office of Scholarly Publishing
Herman B Wells Library 350
1320 East 10th Street
Bloomington, Indiana 47405 USA

iupress.indiana.edu

Uitgegeven met steun van de Universitaire Stichting van België

Manufactured in the United States of America

Library of Congress Cataloging-in-Publication Data

Names: Liska, Vivian, author.
Title: German-Jewish thought and its afterlife : a tenuous legacy /
    Vivian Liska.
Description: Bloomington : Indiana University Press, 2017. | Series:
    Jewish literature and culture | Includes bibliographical references
    and index.
Identifiers: LCCN 2016041008 (print) | LCCN 2016046902 (ebook) |
    ISBN 9780253024688 (cloth : alk. paper) | ISBN 9780253024855
    (pbk. : alk. paper) | ISBN 9780253025005 (ebook)
Subjects: LCSH: Jews—Germany—Intellectual life. |
    Jews—Germany—Civilization.
Classification: LCC DS113 .L65 2017 (print) | LCC DS113 (ebook) |
    DDC 943/.004924—dc23
LC record available at https://lccn.loc.gov/2016041008

1 2 3 4 5  22 21 20 19 18 17

*In memoriam* Geoffrey Hartman
(1929–2016)

.

# Contents

# Acknowledgments

ONE OF THE joys of finishing this book is the realization that so many precious moments shared with others in discussion and debate are now safely ensconced within its pages. The book cover features a painting by the US artist Rebecca H. Quaytman that evokes Paul Klee's *Angelus Novus* and, with it, the ultimate icon of German-Jewish thought, Walter Benjamin's Angel of History. The background of Klee's *Angelus* is still recognizable in Quaytman's painting, but the angel has vanished. The painting jolts our visual memory into projecting the angelic figure onto the voided surface and invites us to imagine the angel's flight. Like the departure of the owl of Minerva, the absent angel indicates that a form of life— in Hegel's words *eine Gestalt des Lebens*—is about to disappear. I am grateful to Rebecca H. Quaytman for the generous permission to reproduce her painting and to Sylvia Liska and Daniel Heller-Roazen for putting me in touch with her. Seeing it for the first time at an exhibit of Quaytman's work in the Tel Aviv Museum of Art in fall 2015, I realized that I had arrived at the end of a journey of which this book is the record.

Numerous colleagues and friends accompanied me on my way, and many inspiring conversations and discussions about intellectual, political and existential questions are woven into the scholarly texture of this book. I wish to express my gratitude to all those interlocutors who offered insight and advice on different parts and aspects of this book. Some of them have been friends for decades; others became friends at an age when one no longer expects to form such life-changing relationships: Steven and Hannah Aschheim, Dennis Baert, Leora Batnitzky, Michal Ben Naftali, Alfred Bodenheimer, Richard I. Cohen, Yves Kohn, Arthur Cools, Georges Didi-Huberman, Sergey Dolgopolski, Theodor Dunkelgrün, Amir Eschel, Sidra DeKoven Ezrahi, Michael Fagenblat, Mark Gelber, Eckart Goebel, Moshe Halbertal, Sarah Hammerschlag, Carola Hilfrich, Eric Hoppenot, Moshe Idel, Nitzan Lebovic, Eva Meyer, Nancy K. Miller, the late John Neubauer, Ashraf Noor, Paul North, Ilana Pardes, Amnon Raz-Krakotzkin, Elchanan Reiner, Yoav Rinon, David B. Ruderman, Eli Schönfeld, Jeremy Schreiber, Paula Schwebel, Galili Shahar, Bernd Witte, Irving Wohlfarth, and Shira Wolosky. I am particularly grateful to Katrien Vloeberghs and Stanley Corngold, who generously commented on my manuscript at a stage when it barely deserved that name and who contributed greatly to making it a better book. I am deeply indebted to Stefani Hoffman for far more than her ingenious editing of the manuscript; with stunning expertise and soothing serenity, she turned my Teutonic formulations into proper English and cleared the fog of many a thought. I also want to thank Jan Morrens, Rachel Rosolina, and Paige Rasmussen for their help with technical matters big and small. I am most grateful to Alvin H. Rosenfeld for his trust and loyalty and for including this book in his series. Dee Mortensen, the editorial director of Indiana University Press, appeared magically in the midst of a conference at a crucial moment and played a decisive role in the completion of this book. I had the privilege of enjoying the friendship of Geoffrey Hartman for two decades. I shall miss him. Throughout these years he was a model and inspiration for my work and gave me guidance and counsel in the early stages of writing this book.

Nathalie, Jacques, Tamara, and Daphne, their spouses, and their children are the joy of my life that I share with Charles for more than four decades in gratitude, admiration, and love.

SOME OF THE material in this book has been published in earlier versions. Wherever it was necessary, the author has obtained permission to use this material. Parts of chapter 1 were published in *Jewish Culture in Early Modern Europe. Essays in Honor of David B. Ruderman,* ed. Richard I. Cohen, Natalie B. Dohrmann, Adam Shear, and Elchanan Reiner (Pittsburgh, Pennsylvania: University of Pittsburgh Press, 2014), 344–55. An earlier version of chapter 2 appeared in *Secularism in Question: Jews and Judaism in Modern Times,* ed. Ari Joskowicz and Ethan B. Katz (Pennsylvania: University of Pennsylvania Press, 2015), 65–76. A shorter version of chapter 4 appeared in *Messianism and Politics: Kabbalah, Benjamin, Agamben,* ed. Vivian Liska, Bernd Witte, and Karl Solibakke (Würzburg: Königshausen and Neumann, 2010), 159–74. Chapter 5 appeared in an earlier version in *Naharaim* 6, no. 2 (2013), 175–94, reprinted with permission of Walter De Gruyter. A shorter version of chapter 6 was published in *The Book of Job,* ed. Leora Batnitzky and Ilana Pardes (Berlin: Walter De Gruyter, 2014), 121–43, reprinted with permission of Walter De Gruyter. Chapter 7 was published in parts in *The German Quarterly* 87, no. 2 (2014; copyright Wiley-Blackwell, 2014, American Association of Teachers of German), 229–45. A shorter version of chapter 8 was published in *Messianic Thought outside Theology,* ed. Anna Glazova and Paul North (New York: Fordham University Press, 2014),

93–104. Chapter 9 was published in *Das Dämonische: Schicksale einer Kategorie der Zwei-deutigkeit nach Goethe*, ed. Lars Friedrich, Eva Geulen, and Kirk Wetters (Paderborn: Fink, 2014), 311–25. Parts of chapter 10 were published in *Die Waffen nieder! Lay Down Your Weapons! Ingeborg Bachmanns Schreiben gegen den Krieg*, ed. Karl Ivan Solibakke and Karina von Tippelskirch (Würzburg: Königshausen and Neumann, 2012), 95–103. An earlier version of chapter 11 was published in *Against the Grain: Jewish Intellectu-als in Hard Times*, ed. Ezra Mendelsohn, Stefani Hoffman, and Richard I. Cohen (New York: Berghahn, 2014), 198–210. A part of chapter 13 was published as "Winged Words and Wounded Voices: Geoffrey Hartman on Midrash and Testimony," in *The Jewish Quar-terly Review* 103, no. 2 (2013), ed. Elliott Horowitz and David N. Myers, 133–40, Copyright University of Pennsylvania Press and the Herbert D. Katz Center for Advanced Judaic Studies.

The artist R. H. Quaytman has given permission to use her painting on the cover.

# GERMAN-JEWISH THOUGHT
## AND ITS AFTERLIFE

# Introduction

"The Emperor—so it is said—has sent a message to you, the one individual, his puny subject, a tiny shadow who has fled from the imperial sun into the most distant of distances, to you alone, the emperor has sent a message from his death-bed."[1] Thus begins Franz Kafka's short text, "An Imperial Message" [Eine kaiserliche Botschaft], published in 1917 in the Prague Jewish periodical *Selbstwehr*. Although the story never reveals the contents of the imperial message, we may assume that it conveys the dying emperor's final testament. Surely, the emperor would not have placed such emphasis on conveying the message accurately had it concerned anything less important than the transmission of his legacy. The emperor, having ensured, in the presence of the most distinguished witnesses, that the messenger has recorded the correct wording, thence dispatches him. This strong and tireless man cleaves his way through the crowd, but he encounters mounting obstacles: stairs, courtyards, palaces, "and more stairs and courtyards, and another palace, and so on through the millennia; and if he did finally crash out of the outmost gate—but that can never, never happen—the imperial capital would now lie before him, the center of the world, heaped to the top with its sediment."[2] Ultimately, this message does not reach the individual for whom it was intended. In the final sentence of the text, the addressee sits expectantly at the window and envisions the message "as in a dream when the evening comes" [Du erträumst sie dir wenn der Abend kommt].[3]

Kafka's parable describes the fate of tradition in modernity.[4] Thousands of years, an intractable distance, and insurmountable obstacles lie between the modern individual and the source of an authoritative, perhaps divine, message. At the conclusion of the text, the increasingly impeded transmission comes to a halt at the moment of the emperor's death. At this point, instead of a diminished yet nonetheless continuous passing of the message from generation to generation, only the longing gaze of the individual at the window crosses the divide separating him from his origins, from the emperor and his message. We are not explicitly told whether the Jewish tradition is at issue; nor is the addressee clearly identified as the modern individual; nevertheless, there are compelling reasons for exploring the story in these terms. The mighty emperor who, thousands of years ago, publicly conveyed a private message destined for a singular subject evokes the revelation of a monotheistic, personal God who, in Kafka's time, is dying, or, perhaps, is already dead. The emperor's emphasis on an accurate and spoken, rather than written, transmission could refer to the *Torah she be'al peh*, the oral Torah.[5] The emperor's legacy, which he himself communicated and which has traveled through millennia and past mounting obstacles before coming to a standstill, is addressed to an individual subject who has fled into the remotest distance, into godless modernity. This individual thus finds himself in both physical and metaphysical exile from the divine realm. The content of the imperial message remains unknown, both to him and to us, the story's readers. We learn only of its origin—itself no more than a rumor, of the increasing difficulties and ultimate rupture of its transmission, and, finally, of the intended recipient's longing anticipation of this message in the evening, the twilight of history. History itself appears in this story as an impenetrable labyrinth filled with "sediment," that is, as a ruin or, in Walter Benjamin's words, as a desolate "heap of rubble" [*Trümmerhaufen*].

An eagerly anticipated message of uncertain content, thus open to all conceivable interpretations; a message dispatched from the highest authority and borne across millennia that can no longer actually be heard; an individual who dwells at an insuperable distance from his origins and dreams of a message from the emperor. Revealed law and its transmission, election, exile, and the anticipation of redemption: Each evokes elements of the Jewish tradition, understood here as the body of texts, themes, and motifs that constitute Judaism. As the text's initial "so it is said" suggests, these elements have, in modernity, become mere hearsay. They have faded into what Benjamin, in a letter about Kafka to Gershom Scholem, calls "rumor[s] of the true things."[6] Benjamin's oxymoronic expression perfectly renders a central ambiguity in the final sentence of Kafka's story. As Benjamin's formulation suggests, the modern individual cannot know whether the emperor's message—"the true things"—indeed exists but can no longer reach us or whether the message's very existence is nothing but rumor, a vision that arose in a dream—or in a work of fiction.

Benjamin's description of this rumor as "a sort of theology passed on by whispers dealing with matters discredited and obsolete"[7] does not resolve the uncertainty about the existence of an original message. It suggests, however, that earlier theological certainties, which may originally have been legends, appear to modern humanity only as remnants, as fragments of uncertain value and authenticity. The game of relayed whispers, nevertheless, continues apace, both in Benjamin's time and in ours. Starting from the historical moment when Kafka wrote his parable and Benjamin coined his metaphor, it continues, with exponential unreliability. The uncertainties generated by this disrupted transmission of residues from the Jewish tradition not only arouse melancholic longing but also spur the major modernist German-Jewish authors discussed here: Franz Kafka, Walter Benjamin, Gershom Scholem, Hannah Arendt, and Paul Celan.[8] This work traces how these thinkers and writers address remnants of the Jewish tradition, and it examines their interlocutors and successors' attitudes toward the recovery of these residues.

This book explores the changing form, fate, and function of several key concepts of the Jewish tradition—law, messianism, exile, election, remembrance, and the transmission of tradition itself—in three temporal and intellectual frameworks: German-Jewish modernism; postmodernism, in its deconstructive variant; and the current period, sometimes called "theory after theory," but which does not yet have a name.[9] My underlying argument is that the Jewish dimension in the works of major modernist German-Jewish writers and thinkers is crucial to their approach to modernity; that this dimension is transformed, but remains significant in postmodernist theory; and that it is appropriated, dismissed or denied by some of the most acclaimed intellectuals and philosophers at the turn of the twenty-first century.

Kafka, Benjamin, Scholem, Arendt, and Celan[10] belong to what Stéphane Mosès, in his typology of twentieth-century Jewish thinkers, terms "critical modernity," which he distinguishes from the "normative modernity" of Hermann Cohen, Franz Rosenzweig, and Emmanuel Lévinas.[11] The concept normative modernity applies to thinkers who consider the Jewish scriptures as endowed with the authority of truth even while they recast them in a modern idiom. By contrast, the critical modernity of the German-Jewish authors discussed in this book conceives of modernity in the light of a Jewish tradition that it revises in its awareness of the very rupture constituted by modernity. For these authors, the Jewish tradition has "lost its validity"; all that remains of it "in a world without God" are mere scattered shreds—"textual fragments, categories of thought, modes of argumentation and sensibility"[12]—that stand in a charged relationship with the modern values and ideas that these thinkers have helped to shape.

The German-Jewish authors whom I discuss spoke of their Jewishness as a *"Selbstverständlichkeit"* [self-evident matter]. Arendt, in her famous epistolary exchange with Scholem, writes, "I have always regarded my Jewishness as one of the indisputable factual data of my life."[13] In a letter to his friend Ludwig Strauss, Benjamin declares, *"Das Jüdische* is always self-understood. . . . Everything Jewish that goes beyond this self-evidence seems dangerous to me."[14] Kafka, replying to his non-Jewish lover, Milena Jeszenska, states, "Then there is the question of being Jewish. You are asking me if I'm a Jew. Maybe that's just a joke."[15] Celan, in a letter to his last lover, Ilana Shmueli, writes, "The self-evidence of my Jewishness in the midst of it all, you, Ilana, understand it, even as I now—no longer?—know how to formulate it."[16]

Little of this *Selbstverständlichkeit*, however, translates into a straightforward or simple relationship to the Jewish tradition. Much of these writers' shared interest in things Jewish derived partly from their critical attitude to the assimilation of their bourgeois fathers. This association of assimilation and bourgeoisie, a mode of life they despised, led them in very different ways to establish links with the Judaism largely abandoned by their parents' generation. With the exception of Scholem, however, such interest rarely sprang from deep familiarity with the Jewish textual tradition. These thinkers' limited Jewish knowledge justifies the widespread focus on their Jewishness, rather than on the traces of the Jewish tradition in their writings.[17] This circumstance, however, arguably renders their actual references to Jewish motifs, genres, and texts all the more intriguing. Furthermore, aspects of their writings—such as a temporality of deferral or concern with worldly, everyday life rather than with theological speculation—can be traced to the Jewish tradition. Finally, and most important for this book, the juxtaposition and comparison with subsequent readings of their work reveal differences that illuminate the importance of the Jewish tradition in their thought.

In the works of these German-Jewish authors, the impact of references to the Jewish tradition comes to light as a complex questioning of the Enlightenment. Their critique is neither reactionary nor conservative nor progressive; rather, it generates, via these references, alternative ideas of the modern subject in its apprehension of itself, of others, of history, of transcendence, and of the transmission of tradition. Beyond the conflicts about identity and belonging and the ambivalences about Jewishness and the "Jewish community" that permeate their work (a subject I address elsewhere, in relation to Kafka and other twentieth-century literary authors),[18] the visions of modernity of these German-Jewish thinkers manifest a paradoxical dynamic, namely, the attempt to conceptualize the break with tradition that constitutes modernity by using figures of thought derived from Jewish tradition. They conceive of the Jewish references they draw upon as interferences, countermovements, and interruptions of dominant ideas that underpin the still-reigning presumptions and values of the Enlightenment. For the notion of a linear, progressive march of history, they substitute a politically and theologically envisioned redemptive interruption of homogeneous time. Rejecting the individualism and belief in the self-enclosed subject of the Enlightenment, they posit uncommon communities based on a fractured and variously reconfigured tradition.

Both the power and the fragility of these reconfigurations ensue from the effort to reconcile Jewish tradition with the Western philosophical tradition. The task is fraught with difficulty: Jewish references conflict with Kafka's nihilist Gnosticism, Scholem's antinomian anarchism, Benjamin's historical materialism, Arendt's commitment to Enlightenment values, and Celan's poetics of crossing through and carrying ad absurdum the conventional tropes and metaphors that have lost their validity after the catastrophe.

From the 1970s through the 1990s, postmodernist critics elaborated the connections between the Jewish tradition and modernity found in the work of these modernist German-Jewish authors. In their reception of this legacy, Jewish and non-Jewish thinkers of the late twentieth century such as Maurice Blanchot, Jean-François Lyotard, and Jacques Derrida both radicalized the tensions in this thought and made it more abstract.[19] There are significant affinities between these later thinkers and the earlier German-Jewish writers, but important shifts have occurred.[20] In short, whereas the former authors' invocation of Jewish tradition evinces an unresolved tension between Jewish particularism and modern universalism, postmodernist thinkers thematize and regard this unresolvedness as a constitutive impossibility characteristic of modernity.

The postmodernist approach creates an astonishing web of indeterminacies, paradoxes, and aporias. It relies on a performative use of language reminiscent of literary *écriture*: the law that abolishes itself; Jewish exile as exile from Judaism; "the messianic without messianism"[21] and certainly without a Messiah; election as universal; and a ubiquitous textuality that is understood in Jewish terms yet conceived as subversion of a Jewish (and ultimately every potential) identity. Arguably, literature plays an even greater role in the writings of postmodernist thinkers than it did in the works of their German-Jewish predecessors, although it serves a different function. The unresolved tensions that literature helps to sustain in the works of the modernist thinkers are both absorbed and dissolved by the pervasive literariness of postmodernists' deconstructive writings. In light of their all-encompassing fictionalization, the uncertainty about whether an original imperial message ever existed—whether there were ever "true things"—paradoxically attains a resolution in the consistent trope of aporia. Considering this aporetic thinking as a source of political and philosophical paralysis, some theorists at the dawn of the twenty-first century viewed it as a dead end that needed to be overcome. This brings us to the present.

Whereas it cannot be denied that these German-Jewish figures' "resonance has increased rather than diminished,"[22] this assertion holds true mainly for their academic and popularizing reception. It is less valid for their legacy among the current generation of thinkers who occupy a leading role in the intellectual imagination of the present. In recent years, thinkers who continue to invoke these earlier figures considerably alter or dismiss the Jewish dimension of their writings, mounting critical challenges to this approach that embraces the unresolved tension between Jewish tradition and modernity.

The first, and arguably most profound and subtle, of these challenges consists of a selective Paulinian rereading of some of the German-Jewish modernists—primarily Kafka and Benjamin—along with a rejection of others whose work resists such revision. The main representative of such a selective rereading is the Italian philosopher Giorgio Agamben, who has dealt extensively with each of the German-Jewish authors discussed here and whose remarkable but also questionable readings of their work I explore in depth. The second challenge consists of the outright rejection of both the Jewish tradition and its manifestation in

German-Jewish thought, as well as its postmodernist and deconstructionist interpretations. The challenge issues from thinkers who call for a radical universalism
and deplore what they consider the twentieth century's loss of philosophical and
political acumen. The primary proponents of this position are Alain Badiou and
Slavoj Žižek. Like Agamben, these two thinkers have devoted elaborate studies to
the apostle Paul, in which context they advert to the Jewish tradition.[23]

Despite major differences among Agamben, Žižek, and Badiou, especially
in their conception of universalism, all three claim to generate a new mode of
thinking that differs from the approaches of their modernist and postmodernist precursors.[24] Their implicit, and sometimes explicit, claims of newness, however, represent more than a simple philosophical innovation. The "new" refers,
in fact, to a very old distinction between the Jewish tradition as one that must be
superseded and the "new tidings" of a politically reconfigured, largely (and often
emphatically) atheist Christianity.

A third challenge—this one from a different direction—proceeds by nar-
rowing the definition of what is "genuinely" Jewish and thereby questions the
Jewishness of the modernist and postmodernist thinkers under discussion. This
tendency finds adherents mainly among scholars of Jewish studies who seek to
restore an authentically Jewish tradition that they consider to have been obscured
by the canonization of thinkers such as Benjamin or authors such as Kafka.[25]
Despite clear differences among these lines of thought, these scholars question
the relevance of the Jewish tradition to the manner in which these German-
Jewish thinkers have conceptualized modernity.

Historical events, undoubtedly, affected the formation of these challenges:
the premonition, caesura, aftershock, and fading impact of the Holocaust; the
founding of the State of Israel; the attraction and ambivalence toward Zionism
and its increasingly negative reception among Western intellectuals; the seduction, consolidation, and decline of Western Marxism, and the search for a surrogate ideology. The present book, however, intends to support its claims via
close, sometimes minutely exacting readings of texts—mostly essays, letters, diaries, theoretical treatises, poems, parables, and translations—that reveal crucial
moments in this phase of intellectual history.

The structure of this book is thematic rather than diachronic. Each of its
sections is organized around an element of Jewish tradition that originates in
scriptures, came to define Judaism as it developed as an exilic community, and
persists in modernity. These elements—the transmission of tradition, the relation
between law and narrative, messianism—particularly messianic language—and
the interconnection between exile, remembrance, and exemplarity (which can be
regarded as a modern version of the theological term "election") are arguably the
most prominent aspects of Judaism that inspired German-Jewish thought. Those
thinkers conceptualized transmission together with the rupture of modernity,

Jewish law with modernist anarchism, Jewish messianism with modernist politics, exile with the alienation of modern man, remembrance with modernist antihistoricism and Jewish exemplarity with universalism. As this book will show, the balancing act between modernity and elements of the Jewish tradition also constitute its most tenuous dimension in recent theoretical debates, particularly in the context of the Pauline turn.

Each section highlights a German-Jewish author's approach to the topic: the transmission of tradition focuses on Arendt; the interaction between law and narrative on Kafka; the conception of a messianic language on Benjamin; and the interrelated notions of exile, remembrance, and exemplarity on Celan. The chapters in each section explore various voices from different phases in the reception of the particular thinker's writings related to the topic under discussion. Some chapters focus on an exchange between contemporaries such as Arendt and Scholem, Benjamin and Scholem, and Celan and Ingeborg Bachmann. This emphasis on diachronic and synchronic dialogues and conversations enables one to trace the whispered transmission—often minute, elusive, or implicit shifts, correlations, echoes, distortions, and disjunctions—of visions of modernity seen in light of the Jewish tradition and its contemporary challenges.

PART I

# TRADITION AND TRANSMISSION

# 1 Early Jewish Modernity and Arendt's Rahel

THE BEGINNINGS OF German-Jewish thought, generally associated with Moses Mendelssohn (1729–86), date back to the last decades of the eighteenth century. Although critics traditionally pointed to the Enlightenment as the starting point of German-Jewish thought, its source may lie in Early Modernity, a term in scholarly use since the 1970s. This term has become a battleground for historians of Jewish modernization. On one side are scholars who consider the period a mere—and insubstantial—precursor of a genuine, enlightened modernity, a "halfway house of the modern spirit";[1] opposing them are those who, refusing to "accept modernity's own narratives about itself,"[2] regard it as a distinct and praiseworthy epoch in its own right. This construction of an Early Modernity entails both a questioning of Enlightenment narratives of linear progress leading toward emancipation, integration, assimilation, and homogenization and an affirmation of the preceding era's discontinuities and disparities, its mixing and mingling of identities, its contradictions, incongruities, and collisions, and the mutually inspiring simultaneity of incompatible, even incommensurable, cultural, social, and religious entities and endeavors. Whereas historians who affirm the Early Modern paradigm appraise the coexistence of tradition and modernity without harmonization, those who reject it see only "debris of the collapsed breakthroughs to modernity that had not quite come about."[3]

The dispute between these two narratives is particularly significant in the Jewish context. The first believes in a progressive and teleological development and assumes a dichotomy between traditional and modern society. It implies the backwardness of religious Judaism and its eventual dissolution into a radically secular mainstream modernity or, alternatively, a dilution of both modernity and Judaism as embodied in proponents of a Jewish Enlightenment, who attempt to harmonize their faith and the benefits of modernity. From this perspective, Jewish modernity begins in the late eighteenth century; everything that preceded it belongs to a premodern era, in which Jewish life existed mainly inside a closed community that hardly participated in or interacted with the surrounding modern world.

Historians who consider the Early Modern period in Jewish history as an independent moment oppose this narrative and its belief in a teleological process from the ghetto to modernity. They see an opportunity for revaluing the praiseworthy aspects of modernity—mobility, creativity, heterogeneity, and flexibility—precisely in the Early Modern period, with its incoherencies, overlapping, and mixed identities, when elements of the premodern world coexisted with anticipatory visions of a new one. Advocates of this perspective view the Early Modern period as a model for situations, figures, and modes of life that affirm the possibility of being consciously, even traditionally Jewish, yet at the same time eager to participate in modernity and engage in the exploration of an ever-expanding world.

Embracing the contradictions, conflicts, and disparities that ensue from these multiple and potentially clashing worlds, this view lends visibility to a period that allows for a simultaneous perception of the multifarious possibilities of Jewish modernization. Soon after, both external and internal factors—rising nationalisms, a more rigorous division between traditionalist and modern Jews, and increasingly formalized borders between Jews and non-Jews—defined and consolidated the character of modernity and institutionalized it according to the more starkly contoured categories of the Enlightenment proper. One can thus view the Early Modern period as a reservoir of potentialities inherent in the encounter between Jewish life and the modern world.

The German-Jewish context provides a particularly fertile ground for probing the assumptions and consequences of the two narratives outlined above. The first option equates modernity with emancipation, integration, and assimilation; the second views it as a moment ending in a more clear-cut but also more sterile modernity characterized by "solutions." In her study of German-Jewish life between the seventeenth and early nineteenth centuries, Deborah Hertz succinctly described these "solutions": "Whereas in the seventeenth century one could be either a Christian or a Jew" interacting in the manifold ways described by the historians of early modern Jewry, in the period explored by Hertz—the end of the eighteenth and the first decades of the nineteenth century—Jews "faced three fundamental alternatives: They could remain traditional, commit to the harmonious modernization of Judaism, or try to escape Judaism altogether." Hertz concludes: "The choices which emerged in this era set the terms for the centuries since."[4] Possibly, by invoking the Early Modern period, described by Adam Sutcliffe as this "fascinatingly vivid episode" with "countervailing values" and without "final resolutions,"[5] one can provide an alternative to these three choices, preclude the story of progress from a premodern to a fully enlightened modern world, and recognize a prefiguration of the matrix underlying German-Jewish thought in the early twentieth century.

## Heroine of Jewish Modernity or Herald of Its End?

In the German-Jewish context, the stakes of narrating history as a story of progressive, teleological modernization are especially high because it inevitably has to confront German Jewry's tragic end. A particularly significant case is the reception of Rahel Levin Varnhagen, whose life presents a paradigm for the situation of the privileged class of German Jews at the end of the eighteenth century. Her thousands of letters offer a lively testimony to the exhilarating changes that opened up hitherto unknown horizons for a Jewish woman yet also instilled self-doubts resulting from unfulfilled aspirations and conflicts of loyalty that continued to haunt her throughout her life.

Born in 1771 in Berlin, the daughter of a rich jeweler, she spent most of her life trying to escape what she considered the stigma of her Jewish origins. She finally converted in 1814, when she married the Christian diplomat Karl August Varnhagen von Ense. The conversion and marriage did not end her anxieties, and her increasingly nervous efforts to gain acceptance in the high society of her times marred her existence until her death in 1833. Rahel's life story became an inspiration for many scholars of the history of women, minorities, and intercultural relations but also an object of scrutiny for those who tried to understand the evolution of German-Jewish history up to its cataclysm. Examples from this reception of Rahel's life and writings can illuminate the implications of the positions that scholars have taken in the debates about the beginnings of Jewish modernity; they can also illuminate the temptations, risks of—and possible alternatives to—constructing a linear narrative of German-Jewish modernity. As the following examples show, the perspective of the prevalent teleological model leads to a portrait of Rahel's life in which her assimilation and conversion mark a sharp rupture between old and new. The binary opposition between a backward ghetto and an enlightened modernity is correlated with either a positive or negative appraisal of her assimilation and abandonment of her Jewish origins. These judgments hinder an understanding of Rahel as a figure caught between cultures, religions, and classes who both embraces and doubts her own solution.

The most famous study of Rahel is undoubtedly Hannah Arendt's monograph,[6] largely finished by 1933, completed in exile, and published in 1958. In it, Arendt introduces her famous and controversial distinction between the pariah and the parvenu and describes Rahel's life in terms of the relative success and ultimate questioning of her long and desperate efforts to become a respectable member of the established society. Despite repeated attempts to escape her status as pariah through her marriage to Varnhagen von Ense and her conversion to Christianity, Rahel nevertheless remained, in Arendt's view, a mere parvenu who had given up her freedom and had condemned herself to a life of opportunistic subservience to the powerful. What saves Rahel in Arendt's eyes are faint hints (given great emphasis in the final chapters) that Rahel retrospectively embraced and affirmed her former existence as Jew and pariah.

Critics often disparage Arendt's overemphasis on Rahel's Jewishness at the expense of her challenges as a woman or her achievements as an author. More relevant to the present context, these readers take Arendt to task for the general rejection of Jewish assimilation into German society underlying her portrait of

Rahel, a position she was accused of articulating under the impact of her youthful Zionist leanings. The main criticism leveled against Arendt's portrait was that she made an ahistorical judgment based on the hindsight perspective of the annihilation of German Jewry. One of the harshest of these criticisms came from another German-Jewish intellectual, the important literary theorist Käte Hamburger.

Hamburger expresses her disagreement with Arendt in her essay "Rahel und Goethe,"[7] which ends with an emphatically universalist credo: "The question whether someone is Jewish or German becomes irrelevant, and all that matters is the human being itself, without any concern for race, class, nation, and religion as the Enlightenment and classicism regarded and wanted it."[8] Guided by her Enlightenment ideals of homogeneity and integration, Hamburger polemically attacks Arendt's focus on Rahel's Jewishness, her scornful attitude toward Rahel's conversion, and the continuity she constructs between eighteenth-century assimilation and the catastrophe of Nazi Germany. Hamburger's critique that Arendt projected her own experiences onto a figure from the distant past—a critique that Arendt's dissertation supervisor and friend Karl Jaspers had also expressed years earlier[9]—is plausible from a historicist perspective. Hamburger's own depiction of Rahel, however, also raises questions, but of a different nature. She acknowledges the "yawning abyss" that the Holocaust created between German Jewry (*Deutsches Judentum*) and German culture (*Deutsche Geisteskultur*), but, unlike Arendt, she does not acknowledge the rupture it caused in Arendt's assessment of Rahel. Her Enlightenment-inspired belief in universality and its progressive deployment from the time of Rahel until her own remains unshaken. Numerous scholars and critics from the 1970s onward who rediscovered Rahel as a model of emancipation and adhere to Hamburger's ideals of a coherent and stable self and a homogeneous and integrated public sphere echo her view of Rahel as a classical humanist striving for unity and harmony.[10] Among them is Rahel's biographer Heidi Thomann Tewarson.

Tewarson goes even further than Hamburger in her critique of Arendt's "Zionist-influenced anti-assimilationist" and "anachronistic"[11] judgment of Rahel as a traitor to her people. Rejecting Arendt's (admittedly speculative) belief in Rahel's return to Jewishness toward the end of her life, Tewarson considers her conversion the fulfillment of her desire to "join the large class of enlightened humanity" that, she believes, "has been Rahel's wish almost from the beginning."[12] Projecting her own ideas onto Rahel's final thoughts, she concludes: "her life must have appeared to her as a small token of historical progress. . . . She could at least look with satisfaction upon her own case."[13] Tewarson defines the aim of her own study as a demonstration of Rahel's "prophetic understanding of the forces of history" because "eighteenth century Jews had good reasons to be optimistic."[14] Tewarson accuses Arendt of blindness to the fact that "for Rahel and her generation, history began anew with the Enlightenment."[15] She clearly regards assimilation as the desired culmination of an initial promising "Jewish modernity," whereas Arendt saw it as the beginning of the end.

Although Arendt and Tewarson's interpretations of Rahel's life and its significance could not be more opposed, they share similar assumptions, which they evaluate in different ways. For Tewarson, Rahel is a heroine of emancipation, which she achieved through assimilation; Arendt criticizes Rahel on precisely these grounds and sees her as a social climber who had betrayed her origins and her less privileged, still backward coreligionists "who were still present and geographically close by."[16] Tewarson regarded Rahel as a forerunner of contemporary liberated moderns; Arendt considered her a representative of the "Berlin Jew who looked upon his origins" and incorrectly assumed that he or she was "not one of the last but one of the first."[17] For both, however, Rahel's modernity sharply demarcates her world from the somber and primitive place that preceded it. Even as Arendt criticizes Rahel for her lack of solidarity with her still religious brethren, she describes their world as a "dark stage set of poverty, misery and ignorance."[18] Tewarson could not agree more: For her, there is simply no Jewish history before Rahel's letters. Despite their contrary views, Arendt and Tewarson have little doubt that there is a beginning and an end and that the two can be clearly distinguished.

## Rahel—End or Beginning?

"Early Modern" can be construed to extend beyond its accepted time lines and include the entire period of Rahel's life (1771–1833) by regarding it not only as a circumscribed period that ended in the 1880s but also, as David Ruderman writes, "a condition,"[19] a paradigm characterized by a specific state of mind and mode of being. Her affinities with the Early Modern paradigm are evident where she is described as "a polyphonous and not always harmonious self,"[20] as an outsider striving to be accepted in gentile society without accepting its norms and prejudices, as an author of idiosyncratic letters in which her Yiddish mother tongue lurks behind her High German words,[21] or as a bridge-builder who created a social space in which individuals of the most diverse backgrounds could "mix and mingle with each other," forging "bonds across classes, religious groups and the two sexes."[22]

This view of Rahel derives primarily from scholars who read her letters as literature and, like Arendt, evoke her life and person as a literary text.[23] If one abandons the attempt to pin her down conceptually, Rahel emerges in all her multiple unresolved contradictions, including her equivocal, inconsistent statements about herself. This brings to the foreground how she borrowed contradictory elements of different registers and traditions in her reflections on her existence as well as on the art and society of her times; how she cursed femininity as a personal obstacle, yet in various contexts affirmed the superiority of its ways to the ways of men; how she said of herself that she could write nothing but letters, yet considered her epistolary exchanges worthy of publication and spoke of herself as an artist equal to the greatest in the literary tradition; how she strove with all her means to be accepted in established society, yet repeatedly commented on its worthlessness; and finally, how she struggled with her Jewishness all her life, generally considering it her most painful stigma and doing what she could to escape it, yet never fully freeing herself from it and, in some ways, never wanting to relinquish it entirely.

Her letters testify to the conflicts and the suffering resulting from her contradictions, but she was also highly self-conscious about them and affirmed them as a privilege and strength. Even in her early letters, Rahel repeatedly and proudly praises her own duality and views it as a talent rather than a defect or a plight. In a letter to her close friend David Veit, himself a "successfully assimilated Jew,"[24] she contrasts herself with him and describes herself as "*doppelt organisiert*," explaining: "I have a tremendous power to be double without confusing myself."[25] Her most famous words, which she reportedly said on her deathbed, echo this unruffled lack of coherence: "What a history! A fugitive from Egypt and Palestine, here I am and find help, love, fostering in you people. With real rapture, I think of these origins of mine."[26] For Arendt, who begins her book with this quote, Rahel's words that allude to the depth of Jewish history signify her return to Jewishness at the end of her life. Tewarson has a strong case, however, in objecting to Arendt's conclusion. As she and others have observed, Arendt omitted the continuation of this sentence, in which Rahel calls Jesus her brother, empathizes with Mary, and affirms the solace she derives from these thoughts. Disagreeing with Arendt, Tewarson concludes that Rahel's "life must have appeared to herself as a small token of historical progress."[27] Possibly, however, it is more fruitful to view her final sentences not in terms of a progressive supersession—whether by Christianity or the Enlightenment—but in terms of the simultaneity of the nonsimultaneous. This coexistence of realities from different times and registers and her oscillation between melancholy and affirmation about the uncertainties manifest in the concreteness of her existence make her a paradigmatic figure of Early Jewish Modernity and a worthy forebear of twentieth-century Jewish critical modernists.

# 2 Tradition and the Hidden: Arendt Reading Scholem

HANNAH ARENDT'S PORTRAYAL of Rahel Varnhagen, in which she simultaneously praises her heroine for preserving and honoring traces of the Jewish tradition and denigrates the world in which this tradition is still alive as a "dark stage
set of poverty, misery and ignorance"[1] points to the duality inherent not only
in Rahel's but also in Arendt's own thinking. Her dual allegiance to the Jewish
tradition on the one hand and to European modernity on the other becomes
strikingly evident in her reflections on the Kabbalah in her review of Gershom
Scholem's *Major Trends in Jewish Mysticism*.[2]

Although Arendt is rightfully considered the least theologically minded of
all the German-Jewish thinkers discussed in this book,[3] her engagement with
Scholem's work goes beyond a secular appreciation of a scholarly study. Arendt
and Scholem's conflicting views on the meaning and importance of belonging
and loyalty to the Jewish people constitute a defining aspect of their encounter.
A close reading of Arendt's comments on Scholem's work regarding Jewish
mysticism—in her essay on Walter Benjamin and especially in her earlier essay,
"Jewish History, Revised,"[4]—provide an insight into the specific dynamics of
Arendt's approach not only to mysticism but also to the Jewish tradition as a whole.

Stéphane Mosès considers Hannah Arendt as the thinker who most radically
epitomizes Jewish critical modernity. She is, according to him, "diametrically
opposed to Rosenzweig or Levinas."[5] In contrast to the latter thinkers, Arendt
"defines modernity as a time when tradition can no longer reach us" because "the
process of transmission has irrevocably been interrupted" ("Le Fil," 107). Any
attempt to deny this break is, for Arendt, a sign of philosophical and ethical blindness. Mosès quotes Arendt's approving view of Kafka and Benjamin, whom she
regards as paradigmatic witnesses of this rupture in the tradition. He contrasts
such approval with her seeming puzzlement about Scholem's "strange decision
to approach Judaism via the Cabala" ("Le Fil," 107).[6] Mosès states that "Arendt
was shocked about Scholem's attitude, not so much because of his choice of the
Kabbalah as an object of study but rather because for her the Jewish mystical
tradition was absolutely incapable of guiding modern man in his concrete ethical, and above all political choices" ("Le Fil," 107). One can understand Mosès's
characterization by considering Arendt's conviction that man's moral vocation is

essentially political and expresses itself in the concrete judgments informing his actions, but it does not tell the whole story.

Moses mistakenly views Arendt's brief reflections in her essay on Scholem's Kabbalah studies and their political impact as a disparaging dismissal. More important, Moses seems to ignore Arendt's significant interest in Scholem's *Major Trends in Jewish Mysticism*. As we shall see, in her essay on this very topic, entitled "Jewish History, Revised," in which she hails Scholem's exploration of the essential role of mysticism in Jewish history, Arendt regards the Kabbalah as one of the most valuable and politically relevant relics of the Jewish tradition.

Moses illustrates his claim that Arendt was dismissive of Scholem's work on Jewish mysticism by citing her description of the Jewish tradition in her Benjamin essay as "exotic matters . . . that don't commit to anything" ("Le Fil," 107) and seem relevant only because of their exoticism. Moses paraphrases Arendt's approving description of Benjamin's ideas thus: "The past spoke directly only through things that could not be transmitted" ("Le Fil," 107). The context of Arendt's essay, an enthusiastic parallel between Benjamin and Scholem, reveals a very different tonality in her reflections on Scholem's work on Jewish mysticism. Arendt particularly values both authors' handling of topics that have not been handed down and that, therefore, have not become part of an established tradition that claims authority for itself. She thus compares Scholem's research on Kabbalah with Benjamin's work on similarly marginal and forgotten topics in European literature and culture. In assessing Scholem's study of the Kabbalah most positively and acknowledging its rebellious and subversive power, Arendt describes his interest in the Jewish mystical tradition as the "exact counterpart of Benjamin's choice of the German Baroque Age as a topic for his *Habilitation* thesis" (WB, 195). What Benjamin's and Scholem's topics have in common is that the mainstream traditions of Benjamin's and Scholem's respective fields of interest—in the one case, European culture, in the other the Jewish canon—similarly regarded the scholars' topics as "downright disreputable" (WB, 195). A valorization of these topics, therefore, constituted a "'return' neither to the German, nor to the European, nor to the Jewish tradition" (WB, 195, translation modified).

Arendt thus did not regard the fact that their topics of choice were "untransmitted and untransmissible" (WB, 195) as a sign of their failure, as Moses surmises; nor did she consider their exotic character a superficial and fashionable attraction. Instead, these qualities were precisely the evidence of such topics' liberating potential, grounded in the awareness of the rupture of tradition in modernity. For Arendt, the potential inherent in Benjamin's and Scholem's topics stemmed simultaneously from their invocation of the tradition and their position outside its continuous, transmitted, and established manifestation. Arendt valued Benjamin's and Scholem's awareness that tradition in its accepted form had lost its validity and their shared resistance to "all claims to a binding authority" (WB, 195) and a canonized "obligatory truth" (WB, 195).

Arendt's earlier essay, "Jewish History, Revised"—an essay ignored by Mosès and rarely discussed in the literature on Arendt—prefigures by more than two decades her appraisal of Scholem's Kabbalah research in the Benjamin article. In many ways, it confirms Mosès's characterization of Arendt as a thinker of critical modernity because it, indeed, converts selected elements of the Jewish religious tradition into secular terms. This essay also shows, however, that Arendt, at least in her early writings, regarded certain of these ancient religious views and practices as valuable precursors of modern ideas and did not fully adhere to an interpretation that envisaged a complete rupture between them and enlightened modernity.

In a letter dated April 25, 1942, Arendt requested that Scholem send her what she calls "a copy of your Kabbalah," his *Major Trends in Jewish Mysticism*.[7] On November 4, 1943, she wrote, "Don't judge me too harshly [for replying so late]. Since I read your book—and I have read it repeatedly in the spring, when I finally got a copy—I have written many 'love' letters' ['Liebes'Briefe)]—to you [in my mind]" (*Briefwechsel*, 37). On May 20, 1944, she wrote, "I thought a lot about you, not only because I spoke with many people about your book but also because it does not leave my mind and accompanies me in all of my own work in ways that are unexpressed—but," she added parenthetically "(certainly not unconscious)" [in einer unausgesprochenen (aber bitte nicht unbewussten) Weise] (*Briefwechsel*, 47). Scholem, in turn, on March 26, 1944, asks the editor of the *Contemporary Jewish Record*, a journal published by the American Jewish Committee, "Do you happen to know Mrs. Hannah Blücher [Arendt's married name] in New York? . . . She is one of the best minds who have come over from Europe and she has sent me one of the two intelligent criticisms of my book" (*Briefwechsel*, 51).

Among the many unwritten "love letters" to Scholem that Arendt claims to have written in her mind, the one that materialized and that her addressee accepted so graciously was her essay "Jewish History, Revised." Originally published in 1948 in the newspaper *The Jewish Frontier*, but written as early as 1944, this short text can be read as a review of Scholem's book but also as a blueprint of Arendt's own later political and philosophical writings. Scholem responded enthusiastically, but he may not have realized at the time that Arendt's review was not an unmitigated love letter. The subsequent notorious quarreling between Scholem and Arendt over her critique of Zionism, which erupted soon after this epistolary exchange, and their later more vehement dispute over her book on the Eichmann trial[8] is prefigured between the lines of her reading of Scholem's book. Arendt's essay, *pace* Mosès, shows that she did endow the Kabbalah with the capacity to guide "modern man in his concrete, ethical and, above all, political choices" ("Le Fil," 107).

Seemingly, both Arendt's interest in Scholem's book and Scholem's approval of her response derived from a common aversion to Jewish assimilation; both sought to establish a Jewish history *sui generis* rather than one motivated primarily by reference to external forces and consisting essentially of a perennial "monotonous chronicle of persecutions and pogroms" ("Jewish History, Revised," 303). Scholem and Arendt, in her favorable review of his book, focus on an inner Jewish dynamic that would—not surprising in the period during and after the Holocaust—restore the dignity and unity of the Jews as a people. Arendt insists that Scholem's reconstruction of Jewish mysticism culminating in the glory and downfall of the Sabbatean movement radically revises previous versions of Jewish history that depicted the Jews as mere passive victims. Simultaneously, this revised Jewish history sought to counteract apologetic attempts (presumably by the members of the *Wissenschaft des Judentums* whom Scholem attacked) to deny the Jewish people's specificity and particularism. Arendt's characterization of mysticism and her description of the impact of mystical practice capture the gist of Scholem's book, although in a selective way and with ever-so-slight shifts in style and vocabulary that co-opt his basic thoughts and foreshadow important categories in her own thinking. Generally, Arendt's insights are motivated by recognizably secular ideas and, in sometimes barely plausible ways, project modern categories onto Jewish mysticism, with, as I argue here, one notable exception.

In her analysis of "Jewish History, Revised," the political theorist Seyla Benhabib speaks of "a curious dialectic twist" that enabled Arendt to portray Jewish mysticism as the source of revolutionary or, more generally, concerted popular action.[9] One could speak similarly of the ways in which Arendt turns Jewish mysticism into a precursor of modern materialism, empiricism, and Cartesian philosophy. It is, indeed, surprising to see Arendt defend mysticism as a forerunner of these modern movements, but her logic is not, in fact, dialectical. In her response to Scholem's book, she argues mostly genealogically as she describes the characteristics of Jewish mysticism as forerunners of modern values that inform her own burgeoning political thinking.[10]

It is indeed striking to see how Arendt derives humankind's "world-building capacities" from Jewish mysticism.[11] Her praise of the mystics reveals the essential values determining Arendt's political ideals: She celebrates their inclination toward action rather than passivity, their sense of reality informed by experience rather than constructed from exegesis, and their founding of a countertradition that would inaugurate a new era in which the Jews, as a unified people even when scattered in the Diaspora, would play a major role in the emergence of modernity.

## Action, Reality, and Countertradition

Among Arendt's fundamental ideas prefigured in her praise of Scholem's approach to Jewish mysticism is the importance of action over passivity. She equates the latter with political irresponsibility, rather harshly terming it "something essentially inhuman" ("Jewish History, Revised," 304).¹² Arendt opposes rabbinic Judaism and Orthodoxy, which she accuses of merely interpreting the law and encouraging submissiveness. Unlike Scholem, however, she is not so interested in an antinomian, transgressive, and anarchist "redemption through sin"¹³ as in mysticism's stimulus to action. The Sabbatean movement endowed Jewish mysticism with antinomian forces, although until then it had "kept itself within the Law" ("Jewish History, Revised," 309). Arendt, however, perceived the movement's political importance as residing in another of its aspects: Its impetus to collective action impelled the rabbis to turn away from "the mere interpretation of the Law" ("Jewish History, Revised," 309), which for centuries had kept them outside the sphere of history and politics. Furthermore, the new collective political action created a bond that could replace Halakhah, which had formerly been "the only tie of the people in the Diaspora" ("Jewish History, Revised," 309).¹⁴ In her discussion of that antinomian messianic movement, she prioritized not the transgression or deactivation of the Law but the empowerment of man on the "public scene of history" ("Jewish History, Revised," 311).

Mysticism's esoteric side hardly fits in with Arendt's view of politics as establishing a public sphere—a crucial element of her later political thinking. She circumvents the problem by indicating that mysticism appealed to all those who were "actually excluded from action" and felt that "they were helpless victims of incomprehensible forces" ("Jewish History, Revised," 306). It made them feel that they were part of a larger whole and participated in influencing it. A crucial quotation from Scholem seemingly resonates with her own imperative of human empowerment. Through a mystical understanding of the *mitzvot*, Scholem writes, "The religious Jew became a protagonist in the drama of the world; he manipulated the strings behind the scene" ("Jewish History, Revised," 304). Arendt, however, translates Scholem's description of the mystic's approach to Halakhah into modern terms and superimposes it onto her own understanding of man as a *zoon politicon*. Indeed, she singles out the aspect of intervention in the world suggested by Scholem's view of the Kabbalah. For her, the confidence that mystical practice could partake "in the power that rules the world" liberated the mystics and the masses who were attracted to the mystics' views from being mere passive victims, and it made them discover "a working knowledge of reality" ("Jewish History, Revised," 306–7).

Arendt portrays the mystics' approach to reality as an early form of modern empiricism. In her description of mystical practice, Arendt emphasizes the difference between Jewish kabbalists—whose "main mystical organon of cognition is experience and never reason or faith in revelation"—and rabbinic Judaism, which relied on "interpretation and logic" ("Jewish History, Revised," 307). The Kabbalistic approach, Arendt writes, "comes very close to the modern notion of an experiment" that "could be repeated and tested" ("Jewish History, Revised,"

307), as in modern science; when applied to one's inner self, such a method could provide reliable insights into human psychology. Arendt links this idea of mysticism as a precursor of modernity to Descartes's *Cogito*, where the inner experience becomes the foundation of reality. In contrast to Christian mysticism's focus on the autobiography of saints and mystics, Arendt relates this idea to the mystic's impersonal foundation of the real. At this stage, Arendt approved of the Jewish disregard for autobiography: "for Jewish mystics, man's own self was not subject to salvation and therefore became interesting only as an instrument of supreme action" ("Jewish History, Revised," 308).[15] And unlike their Christian counterparts who were concerned with the individual soul, Jewish mystics turned their mystical practice into "instruments for active participation in the destiny of mankind" ("Jewish History, Revised," 308). In the immediate cataclysm of the war and the Jewish catastrophe, Arendt endows Jews—those formerly "excluded from action" ("Jewish History, Revised," 306)—with a power both to act and to "participate in the formation of modern man" ("Jewish History, Revised," 304).

Arendt hints at her later political thought through her understanding of the mystics' creation of an alternative Jewish tradition. Unlike Christianity, which, because of its concern with autobiography, individual salvation, and inwardness "hardly had a continuous tradition of its own" ("Jewish History, Revised," 308), Jewish mystics, who used impersonal and "repeatable instruments" to apprehend reality, "founded a genuine tradition running parallel to the official Orthodox tradition" ("Jewish History, Revised," 308). In insisting on the distinction between Orthodoxy and mysticism, Arendt diverges from the primary opposition that concerns Scholem—between mysticism as a crucial antirationalist force in Jewish history and the prevailing ideas of the rationalists, "both medieval and modern," such as Maimonides and Hermann Cohen (*Major Trends*, 38). Arendt thereby secularizes Scholem's appreciation of mysticism,[16] which he viewed as a force still very close to the Jewish religious tradition. Furthermore, this countertradition, linked to what Arendt refers to as "the Myth of Exile"—the idea that the Diaspora was a punishment (cf. "Jewish History, Revised," 309)—could now encompass "the whole Jewish people." It would include the Jews living outside Palestine because of the Lurianic Kabbalah's idea of a mission to "uplift the fallen sparks from all their various locations" and of the "enormous force of action" released by messianic mysticism's interpretation of "exile as action instead of suffering" ("Jewish History, Revised," 309). In this way, Arendt projects onto mysticism, with its "tension towards action and realization" ("Jewish History, Revised," 310), the possibility of gathering together the entirety of the Jewish people, from Hasidism to Reform Judaism and the "proponents of an apocalyptic revolution" ("Jewish History, Revised," 311) on the basis of a common historical origin and a common, active contribution to modernity.

Arendt seems indebted to the secularism of the Enlightenment in her evaluation of mysticism as a countertradition undermining Orthodoxy—an empowerment to action, an experimental approach and, above all, an insistence on political participation. One element, however, does not quite seem to fit: She repeatedly affirms in her text an aspect of mysticism that runs counter to the Enlightenment idea of transparency and the openness of the public sphere. On almost every page of her text, the word "hidden" appears in an affirmative sense at least once: She writes of the "hidden God" ("Jewish History, Revised," 304), of the mysticism that goes hand-in-hand with the idea of the "hidden path" ("Jewish History, Revised," 305), of emanation as a limitation of self-determination ("Jewish History, Revised," 305), of the "hidden experiments of the Jewish mystics" and the "secrecy of their speculations" resembling the "discovery of the philosopher's stone" that is kept "hidden" ("Jewish History, Revised," 306), of the mystic's "efforts to attain a higher reality that was hidden rather than revealed in the tangible world of everyday life," of the "'laws' which, too, work hidden from the eyes of ordinary men" ("Jewish History, Revised," 305–6), and of the hiddenness of the mystic's belief in an "impersonal force as opposed to the God of revelation," a force that is "concealed rather than revealed in the revelation of the Bible" ("Jewish History, Revised," 305).

Arendt undoubtedly deviates here from Scholem's description of the mystics' idea of the hidden God of Gnosticism, which presumes a clear-cut separation between God as creator and God as revealer. Arendt transforms the Gnostic concept into the concept of an impersonal God, a God as force rather than as "personality." Her quasi-Spinozan view of emanation offers a key example of her secularization of the writings of Scholem, who had remarked explicitly that the Jewish mystics' understanding of "creation out of nothing" simply means "creation out of God." According to Scholem, their understanding of emanation, therefore, "stands farthest removed" from what the term stands for "in the history of philosophy and theology" (*Major Trends*, 25).

More striking than Arendt's rereading of Scholem is her own emphasis on a notion of the hidden that understands revelation itself as a form of concealment. How can one reconcile such an emphasis with her later political critique of secrecy "as a basic mode of operation in totalitarian regimes"?[17] In the context of her analysis of totalitarianism, concealment serves to "diminish the very sense of reality" and "obliterates the possibility of distinguishing between truth and falsity altogether."[18] In her political writings, hiddenness aims at precluding "our capacity to share points of view, to form communal and public experiences and understandings."[19]

In view of Arendt's critique of the hidden, one may question the meaning of her enthusiastic insistence, voiced in her "love letter" to Scholem, that his book exerts an "unexpressed" influence on her work. Can one read it, as I have suggested, as an influence on her later work, including her essay on Benjamin? Could the hiddenness that Arendt addresses in her comments on Scholem's book form this subliminal trace of Scholem's impact on her work? Concealed in her affirmation of hiddenness may be more than just an acknowledgment of Scholem's insights into Jewish mysticism.

Possibly, another earlier addressee of her "love letters" is the German philosopher Martin Heidegger, for whom concealment is the precondition of one of his most important ideas, the notion of truth as *a-letheia*. As early as 1924, in his lectures published in English under the title *Plato's Sophist*,[20] Heidegger propounded the idea that truth originates from the hidden and requires *Entbergung*—a bringing forth that occurs in a continuous temporality of becoming—and is inextricably linked to *Verborgenheit*, concealment or hiddenness. Arendt must have heard these ideas while studying with the one she called the "hidden king who reigned in the realm of thinking."[21] Throughout Heidegger's work, his conception of truth relies on the privileged role of the hidden. Heidegger, defining truth as *a-letheia*—literally "unconcealedness"—insists on its hyphenated spelling as "unconcealedness," which points to the necessary condition of hiddenness for truth to emerge: "The uncoveredness of the world," Heidegger writes in *Plato's Sophist*, "must be wrested," and "is initially and for the most part unavailable. The world is primarily, if not completely, concealed."[22] More explicitly, Heidegger concludes his introduction to *Parmenides*, written in 1942, thus: "Indeed it appears that unconcealedness is involved with concealedness in a 'conflict,' the essence of which remains in dispute."[23] The conflict to which Heidegger alludes may be covertly at play in Arendt's reading of Scholem's *Major Trends* and in her confrontation with the Jewish tradition.[24] Possibly—though this must remain speculation—the role of the hidden in Scholem's description of Jewish mysticism evoked echoes of Arendt's earlier writings. At the time she wrote her review of Scholem's book in 1944, this linkage allowed her to reconcile, or else to transpose into a Jewish context, truths she could then—given Heidegger's past political choices—confront only in conflict and dispute, and possibly in concealment.

Notably, more than two decades later, in her essay on Walter Benjamin, Arendt indirectly reconnects Scholem and Heidegger in praising the hidden. Immediately after her comparison between Benjamin's choice of the baroque as a topic of his scholarly pursuits and Scholem's "strange decision" [*merkwürdigem Entschluss*] (WB, 195) to work on a topic as "exotic" as the Kabbalah, she speaks of Benjamin's idea of truth as "concerning a secret" (WB, 196). Quoting Benjamin that truth is not "an unveiling that destroys the secret but the revelation that does it justice" (WB, 196), she brackets two seemingly incompatible modes of this revelation: Truth gains a similar "consistency" when it "comes into the world at the appropriate moment in history—be it as the Greek *a-letheia*, visually perceptible to the eyes of the mind and comprehended by us as 'unconcealment' [*Unverborgenheit*—Heidegger], or as the (audible) word of God as we know it from the European religions of revelation" (WB, 195–96). In this sentence, Arendt, literally in one breath—between two dashes—associates revelation both with Heidegger's *a-letheia* and with the Sinaitic event, the two dimensions almost imperceptibly linked in her essay on Scholem's book. Together, though in opposite directions, Arendt's reference to both Greek and Jewish notions of revelation blurs the boundaries between an affirmation of continuity with Enlightenment secularism and an affirmation of traditional Judaism. Ultimately, however, and in this respect, Mosès's assessment is accurate after all; the former ultimately has the upper hand.

The unresolved tension between Arendt's attraction to Scholem's mysticism and her insistent adherence to the secularism of the Enlightenment emerges in a final, obscure fragment of writing. Missing not only from the English edition of Arendt's *Jewish Writings* but also from the initial version of her article published in 1948 in *Jewish Frontier* are the essay's last three pages. Until their publication in 2010 in the correspondence between Arendt and Scholem,[25] they existed only as unprinted notes in Scholem's library in Jerusalem. In the very last lines of those notes, after reiterating her agreement with Scholem on the operative powers of mysticism, she ends with a major objection that points ahead to the core of her political thought: What the "enlightened professors of history in the nineteenth century [presumably those associated with the *Wissenschaft des Judentums*] didn't know," Arendt writes, "was that mysticism can actually work." Yet she immediately adds a caveat that begins with "however"; this "however" is crucial, particularly in view of her earlier, unlikely appreciation of emanation theory as a predecessor of modern beliefs in the hidden hand pulling the strings behind the scenes. "However," she continues, "no matter how fascinated we may be that mystical thought has fueled our will to action and to the political realization of our own history, we may not forget that it is ultimately up to man to determine his own political destiny, and not the 'invisible stream,' the catastrophic course of which Scholem has revealed to us" (*Briefwechsel*, 483). That these lines remained hidden from public view for such a long time is one of the many paradoxes in this surprising tale. For, with these words, Arendt refutes the legitimacy of the hidden as the nexus that allowed her to connect Heidegger with Scholem, the German with the Jewish past, and importantly, modernity with religious tradition. Although this ending may appear to confirm the characterization of Arendt as the most secular thinker of "critical modernity," nevertheless, the essay as a whole testifies to her interest in reinventing the special role that can be played by the Jewish tradition, in particular the Kabbalah, in building the modern world.

Arendt's attachment to vestiges of the Jewish tradition becomes more visible in a juxtaposition of her thinking with the work of the contemporary Italian philosopher Giorgio Agamben, for whom Heidegger played a major role and whose other important influence was another figure close to Arendt, Walter Benjamin.

# 3  Transmitting the Gap in Time: Arendt and Agamben

"Our inheritance was left to us by no testament."[1] Hannah Arendt's opening words in *Between Past and Future*—a quotation from the poet and resistance fighter René Char—introduce her reflections on the fate of tradition in modernity. Arendt, too, did not provide a testament authorizing her legacy; we thus can evaluate its afterlife by assessing the contentions of those who allude to her in their work. This applies particularly to those who, like Giorgio Agamben, touch upon Arendt's legacy precisely at the point where she herself—like Kafka in "An Imperial Message"—reflects on the implications of the rupture of tradition in modernity and of an inheritance without a testament.

In a letter to Arendt, Agamben writes, "I am a young writer and essayist for whom discovering your books last year has represented a decisive experience. May I express here my gratitude to you, and that of those who, along with me, in the gap between past and future, feel all the urgency of working in the direction you pointed out?"[2] The letter, dated 1970, in which Agamben, who was then twenty-six years old, emphatically assures Arendt of his intention to continue working in the direction she has shown and situates himself and those who think like him in a "gap between past and future"—a distinct reference to the original title of Arendt's work *Between Past and Future*. That title, "The Gap between Past and Future," demarcates the intellectual space to be occupied in the following "Exercises in Political Thinking"—the book's subtitle. In the foreword, Arendt describes the conditions of bestowing an inheritance at a time when transmissibility itself has become problematic. Arendt's "gap in time" designates a break in the linear chronological flow as an intermediate period, an interval, "which is altogether determined by things that are no longer and by things that are not yet," and which, Arendt continues, has repeatedly been shown to contain "the moment of truth" ("Gap," 9). Agamben's written comments at this time on the transmission of a legacy in a period when tradition has been ruptured can, perhaps, illuminate "the moment of truth" about his attitude toward Arendt's thinking.

Agamben wrote the above-mentioned letter to Arendt in the same year that he published an essay in the periodical *Nuovi argomenti* entitled "L'Angelo malinconico." Appearing also as the conclusion to the book *L'Uomo senza contenuto*, the essay was published in English in 1999 under the title "The Melancholy Angel."[3] This essay, like Arendt's foreword, focuses on the proper approach to tradition at a time when experiences, concepts, and cultural and artistic procedures can no longer unproblematically be transmitted to the future. Although Agamben's essay, unlike Arendt's foreword to her political essays, deals primarily with aesthetics and does not refer to her foreword, the latter clearly provided a stimulus for Agamben's thinking. Arendt's description of the "interval in time" is the structural entity within which Agamben inscribes his reflections on the task of art in modernity. The near identity of many turns of phrase is unmistakable. Arendt describes the "gap in time" as a "time-space that is created and limited by the forces of past and future" ("Gap," 12) and in which the sequence of events remains "as it were, in mid-air" ("Gap," 7), as an "interval in time which is altogether determined by things that are no longer and by things that are not yet" ("Gap," 9). Agamben undoubtedly echoes Arendt when he speaks of a "space between past and future" (MA, 110), a state "suspended in the inter-world between old and new" (MA, 114), an "interval between what is no longer and what is not yet" (MA, 112).

Both essays describe the juncture where past and future meet as a crisis point that charges the present with urgency. In both, the interval is a battlefield where the antagonistic forces of past and future clash in the present. Arendt speaks of a "kind of warfare" ("Gap," 8), Agamben of "struggle" and, repeatedly, of a "conflict between old and new, past and future" (MA, 110, 112). The similarity in the wording of Arendt's and Agamben's descriptions of this interval simultaneously reveals significant differences that point to divergent and, occasionally, even contrary views on how to resolve the situation. The main source of these differences is not hard to detect. Numerous references to and citations from Walter Benjamin's writing overlay Agamben's obvious, but only implicit, references to two texts by Arendt: her preface to *Between Past and Future* and her essay on Walter Benjamin,[4] both published in 1968.[5] Agamben's variations and transformations of passages from these texts disclose significant departures from Arendt's thinking at a time when he claims to "feel all the urgency of working in the direction" that she had indicated. These departures arise from their respective views on tradition, on the concept of history, and on the conditions for a new political and cultural beginning. Although neither Arendt nor Agamben explicitly mentioned the Jewish tradition, their respective arguments reveal very different approaches to Jewish concerns.

## Conserving, Destroying, Transmitting

The first pages of Agamben's "Melancholy Angel," which directly refer to Arendt's Benjamin essay, provide an insight into the dynamic of the small but decisive shifts that Agamben makes in the midst of appropriating her text. The opening quotation, the wording, and the order of the initial paragraphs of Agamben's piece repeat almost verbatim the beginning of the third part of Arendt's text, in which she comments on Benjamin's reflections about the function of quotation and the meaning of collecting. As Arendt does, Agamben introduces his essay with a reference to Benjamin's theory of quotation. In the first paragraph, he cites Benjamin's description of the power of quotations, which "arises not from their ability to transmit the past and allow the reader to relive it, but, on the contrary, from their capacity to 'make a clean sweep, to expel from the context, to destroy'" (MA, 104). Arendt quotes the same lines by Benjamin in her essay on him, adding the qualification that the "discoverers and lovers of this destructive power originally were inspired by an entirely different intention, the intention to preserve" (WB, 193). By contrast, Agamben follows the Benjamin quotation in his essay with considerations on the "aggressive force" of quotations, explaining that Benjamin had understood "that the authority invoked by the quotation is founded precisely on the destruction of the authority that is attributed to a certain text by a certain culture" (MA, 104). Whereas in subsequent pages, Arendt stresses Benjamin's "*duality* of wanting to preserve and wanting to destroy" (WB, 196; my italics), Agamben fortifies Benjamin's *dialectic* of a saving destruction. The divergence of their views becomes especially obvious when Arendt acquits Benjamin of the "dialectical subtleties of his Marxist friends" (WB, 200), which in another text she disparages as "a trick where one thing always reverses into its other and produces it" [bei dem immer das Eine in das Andere umschlägt und es erzeugt][6] and instead situates Benjamin in the vicinity of Franz Kafka as a poetical thinker (WB, 205).

Similar discrepancies exist between Arendt and Agamben's comments about Benjamin's reflections on collecting. On the one hand, Arendt writes of the "*ambiguity* of gesture" (WB, 196; my italics) in Benjamin's view of the collector's passion. Agamben, on the other hand, emphasizes the *shattering* of the original order in Benjamin's considerations about the act of collecting. Arendt, therefore, regards not the shattering of the context of tradition as specifically modern in the *gestus* of Benjamin's collector but its recovery marked by the rupture of tradition and in light of the "realities of his time." The figure of the collector, Arendt writes, "could assume such eminently modern features in Benjamin because history itself—that is, the break in tradition which took place at the beginning of this century—had already relieved him of this task of destruction and he only needed to bend down, as it were, to select his precious fragments from the pile of debris" (WB, 200).

Arendt compares the recovery and preservation of these treasures to collecting pearls and corals: This hardly sounds like revolutionary vocabulary, even if these historical fragments are the treasures of revolutions and the moments of freedom. Arendt's emphasis on preservation and appreciation probably does not do justice to the destructive aspect of Benjamin's attitude. Similar doubts, however, arise about Agamben's contrary reading, which addresses exclusively the destructive impulse of Benjamin's understanding of tradition and focuses primarily on the moment of disruption itself. Particularly significant in this context is Agamben's comment on Benjamin's imperative "to shake off the treasures that are piled up on humanity's back . . . so as to get its hands on them."[7] Here,

Agamben comments, "Tradition does not aim to perpetuate and repeat the past but to lead to its decline."[8] Even in Benjamin's image of tearing fragments out of the continuum of the past, however, something remains literally "at hand."

Agamben does concede that Benjamin's relation to the past includes an aspect of "taking possession" of what has been; Agamben considers, however, precisely that "what has *never happened*" and therefore remains an unfulfilled potential is what ought to be cherished of the past.[9] The messianic realm revealed here could not be more alien to Arendt. Agamben calls "what has never happened" "the historical and wholly actual homeland of humanity."[10] This formulation, too, sounds like an echo of Arendt: She, however, calls "the home of mankind on earth"[11] precisely that space of the present in which, in the "constantly flowing, everlasting river" of time, freedom arises out of the struggle against past and future. Its origin is no invocation of "what has never been" but the "intervention of man" [*das Dazwischentreten des Menschen*],[12] for which revolutionary moments of the past can serve as a model.

Arendt's and Agamben's treatment of Benjamin's approach to the past illustrates the differences between their thought processes. Antitheses that Arendt leaves in juxtaposition or in succession consistently transform into one another in Agamben: The view that the new can appear *only* in the destruction of the old, indeed, that it arises from this destruction,[13] contrasts with Arendt's ideas of a new beginning. In the final chapter of *On Revolution*, she thus emphasizes that "the end of the old is not necessarily the beginning of the new" and "freedom is not the automatic result of liberation, no more than the new beginning is the automatic consequence of the end."[14] Only the establishment of a new order can bring about freedom. For Arendt, the interval between the "no longer" and the "not yet," which she calls "the hiatus between old and new orders," interrupts the "omnipotent continuum of time"[15] and opens up the space in which thought, politics, and freedom can develop. For Agamben, there is no space in the interface between old and new: "The continuum of linear time is interrupted but does not create an opening beyond itself" (MA, 113). Where Arendt creates a space, Agamben sees a break; where she opens up a path, he encounters a point of reversal; where she assesses the possibilities of human intervention in history, he performs a turnaround that seems to catapult him out of the time continuum. It is doubtful whether the dimensions of the "gap between past and future" in which Agamben situates himself in his letter to Arendt are adequate to accommodate her legacy.

## On Kafka, Spots, and Spaces

Arendt and Agamben illustrate their views on the interval in time by reference to short Kafka texts that display a strikingly similar topography. Agamben's implicit dialogue with Arendt, in which he disputes many of the key presuppositions of her thinking, thus crystallizes around Kafka. In her foreword, which begins with René Char's statement about the impossibility of carrying forward the experience of the Résistance, this fleeting moment of public and collective freedom, into the postwar period, Arendt quotes Kafka's parable "He" to illustrate the interval.[16] In Kafka's parable, a man risks being crushed between two forces, which Arendt interprets as the past and the future, provoking the man's dream of leaping out of the battle line between them. Struggling against the determination by the past, which pushes man forward in a direction governed by his origins, given conditions, and events, and running up against obstacles that block his way to a future no longer dependent on the past, he dreams of leaping out of the continuum of time, of history altogether. Arendt is critical of what she regards as a desire for a "timeless, spaceless, suprasensuous realm" ("Gap," 11). She outlines a corrective to this dream, proposing to replace the "spot" at which, in Kafka's parable, past and future collide, with a space that she imagines as a "parallelogram of forces." Into this space, which allows for the presence of "the world," Arendt introduces "a third force" constituted by the presence of man as he intervenes in history. Arendt thereby creates a space *within* history that enables human agency.

Agamben, as Arendt does, repeatedly refers to Kafka in his reflections on the place of tradition in modernity, but he is closer to the protagonist of Kafka's parable than to Arendt's alternative. In contrast to Arendt's critique of the dream of "leaping out" of historical continuity, Agamben, driven by his despair about the course of history, goes beyond the dream. Whereas the dream of Kafka's protagonist can be interpreted in light of Kafka's own "perhaps dangerous, perhaps redeeming" activity of writing literature, which, in his diary, he also describes as a "leap out of murderers' row" (D, 406) [*Totschlägerreihe*],[17] Agamben's hope points beyond literature and art, which are still bound to history and the world. He, in contrast, turns to a space outside history altogether.

Agamben's essay traces the genealogy of the contemporary task of art. In doing so, he anticipates a recurring figure in his work—for example, in relation to the state of emergency[18] or to Paul's Letter to the Romans.[19] Something originally undivided has been ruptured; the denial of this break produces a false continuity, but traces of a redeeming remnant are pointing at a true integrality that appears on a messianic horizon. Agamben takes as his starting point the cultural practice of premodern societies, in which the content of tradition and the act of transmission coincide perfectly. In such societies, the absence of a break between past and present ensures that each cultural object can be passed on to the future. In such mythic-traditional systems, culture has no independent value that could be distinguished from tradition. It flows entirely into the practice of the tradition and hence is at no moment stored and "arrested." Only when tradition loses its vitality does that culture assume an independent, autonomous, and intrinsic value. This development, however, also results in a loss: Culture is accumulated, ossifies into a reservoir of cultural goods, and is consigned to a museum archive that can no longer provide any orientation in life. Although the economic value of the accumulated cultural goods increases tremendously, they no longer provide any criteria for thinking and acting in the present. The cultural inheritance, hoarded but now useless, is no more than a burden that crushes and paralyzes. Agamben presents this diagnosis in words that in part unmistakably echo Arendt's "gap between present and future": "Man is deprived of reference points and finds himself wedged between, on the one hand, a past that incessantly accumulates behind him and oppresses him with the multiplicity of its now indecipherable contents, and, on the other hand, a future that he does not yet possess and that does not throw any light on his struggle with the past" (MA, 108).

Whereas Agamben talks of the past explicitly as a burden, Arendt's foreword states: "The first thing to be noticed is that . . . the past is seen as a force, and not, as in nearly all our metaphors, as a burden man has to shoulder and whose dead weight the living can or even must get rid of in their march toward the future" ("Gap," 10). Arendt, therefore, did not view the oppressive weight of the past as the obstacle; instead, she considered that its continuity projected into the future impeded every new beginning. But, Arendt continues, "from the viewpoint of man . . . time is not a continuum, not an uninterrupted succession; it is broken in the middle, where 'he' stands, and his standpoint is . . . a gap in time, which his constant fighting, his making a stand against past and future keeps in existence. Only because man is inserted into time and only to the extent to which he stands his ground" is "the flow of indifferent time" interrupted ("Gap," 11).

For Arendt, man's intervention interrupts the omnipotent continuum of time. For Agamben, no human being stands at the meeting point between past and future; rather, two angels standing back to back occupy this point. Agamben adopted these figures from Benjamin's writings. In the force of the past pressing forward, Agamben sees the storm against which Benjamin's backward-facing angel of history[20] is struggling. In contrast, the angel in Dürer's "Melencholia I," discussed by Benjamin in the *Origins of German Tragedy*,[21] surrounded by now useless objects, gazes forward without moving. Agamben designates as the angel of art the melancholy angel who cannot continue his flight into the future, that is, can no longer transmit anything. Both angels freeze at the intersection of past and future. While the angel of history strives in vain to return to paradise in the face of the storm of progress, the angel of art has, according to Agamben, fallen into a state of "messianic arrest" (MA, 110). The angel of art views the past that the angel of history faces—a past that can no longer be assembled, read, and interpreted—as something that cannot be transmitted. A new truth emerges, however, out of the estranging gaze—the new truth of art. It is the remnant that alone can save man from being trapped between past and future, by making the very impossibility of transmission, of tradition, its content: "By destroying the transmissibility of the past, aesthetics recuperates it negatively and makes intransmissibility a value in itself in the image of aesthetic beauty, in this way opening up for man a space between past and future, in which he can found his action and his knowledge" (MA, 110). In place of Arendt's space of thought that eternally must be regained, Agamben envisions an estrangement through a negative aesthetics that bridges the time interval in which man is wedged between past and future. Arendt's space of thought implies a freedom of movement and entertains the possibility of a new beginning *sui generis*, guaranteed by the fact of being born. For Agamben, who posits only the interface of a rupture, the only possibility of moving remains the dialectic reversal on the spot itself. This reversal is the task of an art that takes its cue from a negative aesthetics and fulfills its contemporary mission: to perceive and register the split. Even this realization of the task, however, is only an interim solution.

Adhering to an apocalyptic outlook, Agamben turns the premodern unity and coherence that has become fake into a longed-for, redemptive absence of differentiation. What is transmitted today can only be inauthentic, a simulacrum, or kitsch because of modernity's break in tradition and the lack of differentiation of transmission. The saving hope lies, however, in the anticipation that even the break with tradition will one day be sundered[22]—the "split itself split," the "division divided"[23]—allowing a new, now positive lack of differentiation, a new messianic unity to emerge. The impossibility of distinguishing, in premodern societies, between transmission and what is to be transmitted, which in modernity has frozen into a radical separation between lost transmissibility and accumulated cultural goods that can be bridged only partially in a negative aesthetics, is supposed one day to turn into a situation in which "past and present, content of transmission and act of transmission are completely wholly identified."[24] This hoped-for state does not mean, however, a return to premodern times; rather, it is directed at something entirely new. One can infer Agamben's vision of this new state from the final section of "The Melancholy Angel." As in Arendt's foreword, Kafka takes the leading role. He is, however, no longer the one inspiring a critique that would open up a free space for human intervention within history but the herald of history's end in redemption. In spite of this seeming allusion to the Jewish messianic tradition, Agamben's apocalyptic and antinomian turn ultimately points in another direction.

## Myth and Law

Arendt and Agamben undoubtedly share common concerns in the political, the social, and particularly the legal realms that support Agamben's claim to be an heir of Arendt: a preoccupation with biopolitical issues; a critique of human rights in relation to the nation-state; special attention to social outcasts—*paria* or *homo sacer*—or the plight and privileges of refugees. The most striking and all-encompassing difference between the two thinkers, however, and certainly the one that touches most closely on the Jewish tradition, is the question of the law. Both Arendt and Agamben consider the authority underpinning the law as a potential source of oppression and constraint. An analysis of their respective searches for an alternative to a strictly legalistic understanding of politics and the oppressive power of the sovereign, however, confirms the divergence in the two thinkers' approach to the law and its relation to Judaism.

An important article by the German critic Eva Geulen on Arendt and Agamben from 2008 concludes, "Neither the problem of violence nor the problem of origins and new beginnings should stand in the center of an imaginary controversy between Agamben and Arendt, but the problem of the law."[25] The following exploration of these two thinkers' conceptualization of the law can substantiate this insight; at the same time, it shows the inextricable connection between their respective approaches to violence, origins, and new beginnings.

Spaces are omnipresent in Arendt's political thought, whether in her description of the public sphere, the sequence constituting the successful revolution, or the condition of thinking itself. By contrast, liminality dominates Agamben's political and philosophical vocabulary. From the *infans* on the threshold between silence and speech to the *muselman* on the border between life and death, from the *enjambement* between poetic verses to the *caesura* interrupting the metric rhythm in Hölderlin's hymns, these instances of division constitute "zones" or "points of indistinction." These thresholds, which in essence lack ground or a foundation, constitute a "pure" and empty interruption that escapes all mediation, preconception, and precondition. Belonging to neither side of the partition, they contain the potential to blur distinctions and counteract division and exclusion—an inevitable consequence of spaces—but they also remain untouched by the concrete particulars of the phenomenal world.

Undoubtedly, the spaces bear a certain similarity to Arendt's conception of a new beginning as an absolute that cannot be constructed or derived and that escapes will and intention: "Not only is it not bound into a reliable chain of cause and effect," but "the beginning has, as it were, nothing whatsoever to hold on to; it is as though it came out of nowhere in either time or space."[26] Her *incipits*, however, are not political in themselves. Arendt's insistence on spaces constitutes her attempt to make room for the impact and elaboration of these ineffable phenomena, to introduce and preserve them in a concrete, historical realm and make their potential available to man's intervention. By contrast, Agamben's political critique rests on a thinking that contemplates cuts, thresholds, and empty spots that escape manipulation, avoid new foundations, and, instead, perform the theoretical enthronement of discontinuity as such.

Arendt's space permits a freedom of movement that hands the enigma of new beginnings over to human agency. The terms "political space," "public space," "social space," and metaphorical spaces of thought are omnipresent in her work. They all designate a conceptual location of human action and intervention.[27] Arendt sees the break in the omnipotent continuum of time as the place of human agency and will. Agamben considers that there is no longer any ground to stand on and certainly none for the concerted action of many—a key concept in Arendt's political thinking. Instead of conceiving a free space within history, where Arendt envisioned building a "stable worldly structure" and deploying man's "world-building capacities,"[28] Agamben collapses end and beginning into a single, spaceless spot and becomes a herald of history's end.

The distinction between Arendt's space and Agamben's spot or line of division clearly entails more than differences in their views on time and history. It explicitly determines the imaginary topography of their respective approaches to the law in its secular and religious meaning, questioning the distinction between those meanings themselves. Agamben, indeed, adopts Carl Schmitt's contention that "all the concepts of modern theory are secularized theological concepts,"[29] particularly the political concepts of decision, exception, and sovereignty. Schmitt—and, in some crucial ways, Agamben—consider the sovereign a "mundane factor that has taken the place of God."[30] The power of the sovereign, who, according to Schmitt, is the one who proclaims the state of exception, turns the radical reversal of this state into messianic redemption. If the state of exception is determined by a ubiquitous law and its reversal is correlated with the demise of the law, then the law clearly conflates religious and secular law. In searching for a law divested of sovereignty, Arendt questions precisely this conflation.

In *The Human Condition*, Arendt, again marking the distinction between space and boundary, evokes the concept of the law in the Greek polis:

> The law originally was identified with [a] boundary line, which in ancient times was still actually a space. . . . The law of the *polis*, to be sure, transcended this ancient understanding from which, however, it retained its original spatial significance. The law of the city-state was neither the content of political action . . . nor was it a catalogue of prohibitions, resting, as all modern laws still do, upon the Thou Shalt Nots of the Decalogue. It was quite literally a wall without which . . . there could not be a political community. This wall-like law was sacred but only the enclosure was political.[31]

In her attempt to protect the political space from legislation, Arendt does not fully embrace the Greek model because it retains the act of an external sovereign legislator.[32] She affirms, however, the Greeks' distinction between the law as the enclosure of a space and this space itself, whereby the space alone is political and the law a mere fence surrounding and protecting it. She thereby divests the enclosure, and with it the political itself, of the dimension of the sacred and its association with sovereignty, which only the walls retain. This divestiture stands in contradistinction to Agamben's concern with the law, the division, and the wall itself. For him, the very wall constitutes the "zone of indistinction," which is responsible for the "inclusive exclusion" of what has to remain outside. The exclusion, nevertheless, keeps the excluded person in thrall to the excluding power, but the zone of indistinction is also the place where redemption occurs. Defining the law as the very principle of division, the "division of the division" that occurs in the very "zone of indistinction," suspends the law, which is, for Agamben, the political gesture per se. For Arendt, the new beginning becomes political within the political space created and sheltered by the wall-like law. For Agamben, the new arises by transgressing this wall—a boundary that retains its sacred, theological dimension. Contrary to Arendt's distinction between the wall and the enclosure—the division and the space, the sacred and the political—Agamben's conflation of these realms underlies his antinomian idea of a reversal of the state of exception in which we live. In making the wall and the enclosure indistinguishable and in identifying the Messiah with an inverse sovereign, Agamben remains—be it *ex negativo*—within the logic of sovereignty. In his implicit critique of enclosures—their ongoing and inescapable structure of exclusion and tendency toward immutability—Agamben points to possible strictures on Arendt's ways of conceiving a space of freedom. His own alternative, however, radically reverses her legacy: In eliminating a space for human intervention at the scene of new beginnings, he discards a crucial aspect of Arendt's intervention in the debate about the status of the law and its relation to the political in the modern age.

Agamben's Kafka stares at a vanishing point outside history that Arendt would like to deny him, with the messianic gaze of the angel of art. According to Agamben, Kafka, in Benjamin's words, "sacrificed truth for the sake of transmissibility"[33] (that is, entirely dissolved the content of what is to be handed on into the *task* of handing on and made this task the sole content of tradition) and takes negative aesthetics to its utmost limit, where it no longer remains bound to its positive antithesis. Kafka's art positions man between past and future, not in the negating "destruction" of accumulated cultural goods but in their dissolution into the act of transmission, the writing of subversive stories, itself.

The differences between this place and Arendt's perceived interval in time are most evident in the closing section of Agamben's essay. With concluding Kafka quotations, no doubt drawn from Benjamin, Agamben—without even mentioning Arendt—opposes essential aspects of her idea of a productive "gap in time." Arendt conceives the dream of Kafka's "He" as the possibility of becoming an umpire judging past and future while located in a present inserted *in* history.

Agamben's view is darker: He quotes Kafka's aphorism of a divine Last Judgment, which "is actually martial law"—*un stato d'assiedo*—and which calls upon everyone present to account for himself or herself (MA, 113). He measures this accounting, however, against neither the past nor the future but against the messianic potential that would bring history to an end. Arendt may view the gap in time as offering the possibility of clearing "anew and undauntedly" a "narrow path of non-time," which "the activity of thinking opens up in the time-space of mortal me" ("Gap," 13). Agamben, in contrast, quotes Kafka: "There is a goal, but no way. What we call way is hesitation" (MA, 113). Far from affirming this hesitation, Agamben asserts the responsibility to terminate it—and every path (which is always also a new continuum). Arendt sees the path that thinking can stake out as marked in moments of the past in which—as in Char's experience of the Résistance—freedom could appear. Countering this idea, Agamben quotes Kafka: "Hence the revolutionary spiritual movements, which declare everything past to be null and void, are in the right, because as yet nothing has happened" (MA, 113). Agamben introduces the closing section of his essay with a lengthy quotation from Kafka's diaries that bears a patent resemblance to the Kafka text that forms the crux of Arendt's foreword. At the same time, these quotations sum up the tendency in Agamben's selections to point in the opposite direction from Arendt's "gap between past and future."

To illustrate humankind's inability to find a place between past and future, Agamben cites an image from Kafka's diary entry on October 20, 1917, in which travelers are on a train that had an accident in a tunnel. "And this at a place where the light of the beginning can no longer be seen and the light of the end is so very small a glimmer that the gaze must continually search for it and is always losing it again, and furthermore, it is not even certain whether it is the beginning or the end of the tunnel" (MA, 112).

The similarity between Kafka's diary text and Arendt's foreword is striking. Both passages depict a crisis at a place between past and future. The travelers at the scene of the accident in the diary text are stuck just like the man in Arendt's quote from Kafka in her foreword. In both cases, a search ensues for a way out of a predicament. Whereas the man in Kafka's "He" dreams of jumping out of the time continuum, in the passage quoted by Agamben, the travelers involved in the accident long for an exit from the tunnel. In both texts, the way out remains hypothetical—a nighttime dream in "He" and impenetrable darkness in the image of the tunnel. Just as striking as these parallels, however, are the differences, which, together with the accompanying commentaries, offer an insight into the significance of the choice of each of the quoted texts and establish an implicit dialogue between them.

In Arendt's Kafka quotation, as she stresses in her comments, the forces of past and future are unlimited: "the one [because it is] coming from an infinite past, the other from an infinite future" ("Gap," 12). Agamben's Kafka quote is quite different: It is concerned not with "furnishing" a space between infinities, but with discerning the light at the beginning and end of a tunnel, although, ultimately, it no longer is possible to distinguish between the two extremes. Whereas in Arendt's interpretation of Kafka's "He," the predicament lies in the struggle against determinations and obstacles, for Agamben, it consists of being lost in the darkness. Instead of seeking a free space of thought and action within the continuum, he is pursuing an exit strategy that concludes in an apocalyptic collapse of beginning and end into each other.

Arendt and Agamben sum up their respective visions of Kafka's art in poignant images that reveal in a most compact form the differences between their thinking. In her introduction to Kafka's "He," Arendt describes Kafka's parables as "rays of light, which, however, do not illuminate [an] outward appearance but possess the power of X-rays to lay bare its inner structure" ("Gap," 7). Agamben concludes the final section of his "Melancholy Angel," where he describes the present task of art and finds its most consistent fulfillment in Kafka's work: "According to the principle by which it is only in the burning house that the fundamental architectural problem becomes visible for the first time, art"—the art practiced in exemplary fashion by Kafka—"at the furthest point of its destiny, makes visible its original project" (MA, 115). The comparison between the analytic force of X-rays, which make visible the various layers and finally the frame itself, and the dialectic turn of the burning house that reveals its original blueprint in the process of destruction, speaks for itself.

Ultimately, Agamben, in contrast to Arendt, is concerned neither with creating a space in history, nor in leaping out of it, but with the possibility and necessity of conceiving its end. This goal, according to Agamben, is attainable in every "interval in time," that is, in every "now-time" [*Jetztzeit*], as a gate, one might add, "through which the Messiah can enter at any moment."[34] Because no path, no relationship, and no human intervention lead to this goal, only "the late stubbornness of a messenger" whose sole task is to bear this message can impart to man a space of action and of knowledge.[35]

With the message of a "pure transmissibility" that has no content except its own task, Kafka, in Agamben's interpretation, comes closest to fulfilling this aim and thus performs the "assault on the last earthly frontier" (MA, 114). To Agamben, the true goal lies only beyond this border: "At the limit of its aesthetic itinerary, art abolishes the gap between the thing to be transmitted and the act of transmission and again comes closer to the mythical-traditional system, in which a perfect identity existed between the two terms" (MA, 114). Yet, Agamben continues, art alone cannot cross this boundary. It can, as in Kafka's case, rehearse the assault, but it is not able to transcend it. In a significant variation on Benjamin's dictum that history in its totality will become readable only to redeemed mankind, Agamben liberates man from his distressing situation. The result, however, would probably make not only Arendt but also Benjamin shudder: "When [*sic*] man could appropriate his historical condition . . . , he could exit his paradoxical situation [and] would at the same time gain access to the total knowledge capable of giving life to a new cosmogony and turning history into myth" (MA, 114). Agamben thus not only outbids Kafka's "He," whom Arendt would like to prevent from leaping back into metaphysics, but he also calls for a transformation of history into myth, the very antithesis of those elements of the Jewish tradition that inspired Arendt.

PART II

# LAW AND NARRATION

# 4  "As if Not": Agamben as Reader of Kafka

IF IT BECAME apparent that the circus rider in Kafka's "Up in the Gallery"[1] was really an ailing artist teetering on a horse before an insatiable audience, that she was driven mercilessly in a circle by a cruel director, and that this performance would continue interminably into the grayest of futures; if the world were to show itself in its total and absolute despondency, then the young spectator up in the gallery would unhesitatingly rush down into the ring and shout, "Stop!" He would not call merely for a respite or request a pause, but he would demand the definitive halt that would end the ongoing torment and save the suffering creature. Because the world's misery is veiled by illusions and its dejection is fully exposed only in a state of exception, a revelation is required to disclose the naked truth that the seemingly stately rider is, in reality, consumptive, the devoted director is a tyrant, and the audience's ovations are muting steam hammers preventing the would-be savior from correctly assessing the situation and putting an end to its intolerable infinity.

No one more radically than Giorgio Agamben currently proclaims that the state of exception is ubiquitous and that sovereign tyranny holds the world in the thrall of an all-pervasive domination. Unmasking the illusions of modernity, Agamben exposes the lurking doom inherent in the oppressive structures of modern society, and, in his prophecies, allows the wretchedness of the present to swell before our eyes to the point where only a messiah could save us, where only an all-redeeming halt could rescue our planet, interrupt its merciless cycle and suspend its laws, transforming the concentrationary universe we live in into a space of freedom for happy infants—a circus, a feast.

In Kafka's story, salvation does not occur. The "fanfares of the ever changing orchestra" obstruct the perception of the world's need for redemption.[2] The illusions of beauty, order, and justice, kept in Kafka's text in a misleading indicative mode, triumph over the naked truth of suffering and evil, which is repressed into the unlikelihood of the subjunctive form. The false appearances lull the spectator up in the gallery. Instead of saving the victim, he slips off into a deep dream, in which only an indestructible, unconscious remnant of the world's true condition remains in his unconscious, causing him to weep. The redeeming "stop!" does not occur; the "decisive moment of humanity" is still "ongoing," as the end of one of Kafka's late aphorism suggests: "Nothing has happened yet."[3]

Indeed, nothing has happened, unless we read Kafka's story as Agamben would. We would then view the beginning of salvation in the remnants, in the mere revelation of the state of exception. This revelation would then transform the deceptive indicative mode of our consciousness into a different, "true" subjunctive one that would no longer indicate a repressed condition or a missed opportunity but rather the potentiality of redemption. We would see the ailing circus artist as though she were not suffering, the audience's ovations as not affirming the cruel show, the director as not exploiting the miserable creature, and the gallery spectator as though he were not weeping. This hypothetical exegesis *à la manière d'*Agamben unmistakably pays tribute to Paul's First Letter to the Corinthians: "I mean, loving brothers, the appointed time has grown short; from now on let . . . those who weep be as if they were not weeping, and those who rejoice as if they were not rejoicing . . . and those who deal with the world as if they had no dealings with it. For the present form of the world is passing away."[4]

## The Messianic Inversion

In *The Time That Remains*,[5] Agamben's reading of the Letter to the Romans, which was inspired by Jakob Taubes,[6] Agamben calls Paul's *hos me*, this "as if not," "the most rigorous definition of messianic life" (Time, 23). It contains an about-face that is not directed at a specific other state of being, but one that, out of an inner tension, negates the status quo without either turning it into its opposite or reversing it to a former state; instead, it indicates—and thereby performs—the potentiality of change itself. In Agamben's words, Paul's *hos me* produces "a division of the division," a suspension of distinctions that undoes the very differentiation between opposites and exposes a remnant that made the inversion possible in the first place. This remnant undoes the division, which Agamben calls "the very principle of the law" and simultaneously transforms the oppressive "state of indistinction" that could ensue, a condition in which the law itself oversteps its bounds and becomes indistinguishable from life, into a redemptive state in which the law's oppressive power is undone. An image of the world's disappearance in its present state and a belief in the eventual elimination of all distinctions underlie Agamben's entire structure of the messianic and his theory of the "'state of emergency' in which we live."[7]

In recasting age-old antinomian conceptions situated in the interstices between Christian eschatology and Jewish messianism and applying them to his bleak vision of a subjugated world, Agamben partakes of the tradition of radical politico-theological thinkers of the twentieth century. He conceives the messianic task of our times as an interruption of chronological continuity, counteracting either misleading calls for a perpetual state of waiting inspired by the Jewish tradition or Christian concepts of the now as the afterlife of an event that has already occurred. Agamben opposes all forms of Christianity that stipulate new commandments after the old Law has been rescinded. In his writings, he distances himself even more starkly from the messianic theories elaborated by modern Jewish thinkers from Gershom Scholem to Jacques Derrida. To thwart the perpetuation of both the world's dismal state and the "bad infinity" he considers at work in these theories, Agamben proposes a figure of thought (cf. Benjamin's notion of *Denkbild*) that would interrupt the eternal deferral of the end and the unbounded reign of the Law. He invokes Paul and Walter Benjamin as his allies, and, in a Jewish reading of Paul[8] and a Pauline reading of Benjamin,[9] conflates their visions.

"From a political-juridical perspective," Agamben writes in *Homo Sacer,* "messianism is therefore a theory of the state of exception—except for the fact that in messianism, there is no authority in force to proclaim the state of exception; instead, there is the Messiah to subvert its power."[10] In keeping with the antinomies of messianic precepts, Agamben equates the conditions of redemption with the structures governing the decline: Both rely on the self-suspension of the Law. Whereas the negative state of exception proclaimed by the sovereign spills over into every aspect of life and puts the entire planet under the ban of an oppressive Law, the genuine, messianic state of exception—a notion Agamben borrows from Benjamin[11]—suspends the validity of the Law and releases bare life from its ban into a new freedom. Only when life has absorbed the Law to the point of suspending it, instead of letting it rule over life, will the ban be abolished and humanity redeemed. Despite the seemingly logical structure of his arguments and diagrams, Agamben himself calls the path to redemption—the way this about-face at the extreme "point of indistinction" is to occur—"a Gordian knot, not so much the solution of a logical or mathematical problem" but "an enigma" (*Homo Sacer,* 48). For this reason, it is appropriate to seek an answer in Agamben's readings of literary texts rather than in his theoretical writings. His repeated recourse to Kafka's tales and parables illuminates both the assumptions and the parameters of his messianic design, exposing it to specific scrutiny.

In his letter to Gershom Scholem dated September 15, 1934, Walter Benjamin calls his writings about Kafka "the crossroads of the roads of my thinking."[12] The same can be said about Kafka's place in Agamben's work; in his case, however, "crossroads" would signify not only the point where roads leading in divergent directions intersect but also, literally, the final road taken by the redeemer on his way to the cross. In his interpretations of Kafka's stories, Agamben sets himself apart from—and often explicitly argues against—Scholem's, Adorno's, and Derrida's readings and, at least in his own opinion, largely adopts Benjamin's exegeses of the Prague author. Agamben's reinterpretation of Benjamin's position and his transforming of him and Kafka into Paulines in the process certainly ranks among the more dubious feats in Agamben's oeuvre. In *State of*

*Exception*,[13] Agamben delineates the two aspects of Kafka's work that he deems the most important in terms that resemble Benjamin's assessment of Kafka: a critical diagnosis of the bleak state of the world, on the one hand, and the hidden sparks of a coming reversal of these conditions, on the other. In his letter to Scholem of June 12, 1938, Benjamin writes that the "negative characterizations of the situation" in Kafka's work are certainly more portentous than the positive possibilities.[14] Similarly, Agamben finds in Kafka's work "the most precise account of life in the state of exception" in the ban of an oppressive law; simultaneously, he derives the significance of "Kafka's figures in their respective strategies of studying," of "playing with," and of "deactivating the spectral figure of the law in the state of exception."[15] In his interpretations of Kafka's parable "Before the Law" and "In the Penal Colony" and in numerous other references to Kafka's stories, such as "Prometheus," "The Silence of the Sirens," "The New Lawyer," "About Parables," Agamben illustrates his idea of the oppressive state of exception and its reversal through a suspension of the Law. With often violent, truly mortifying means, he tears away some of Kafka's texts and figures from prevailing interpretations and inscribes these stories into his own messianic project. An analysis of some of Agamben's interpretations of Kafka's writings can thus yield the blueprint—the *dynamis* and *telos*—of Agamben's messianism.

In *Homo Sacer*, Agamben identifies a "peculiar characteristic" in the endings of Kafka's parables: "At their very end, they offer the possibility of an about-face that completely upsets their meaning" (*Homo Sacer*, 58). Agamben's readings focus on these unsettling endings. They are, in his view, the place where Kafka's messianic structure of inversion from an oppressive to a saving state of exception occurs, where the "division of the division," the suspension of the Law, succeeds in undoing the power of the ban. According to Agamben, Kafka's tales correspond to the circumstances of life in a state of exception that has become the rule. In this dismal condition, the Law has overstepped its bounds, making it impossible to distinguish between the workings of the Law and life itself. For Agamben, as for Benjamin, this "negative indistinction" is paradigmatically exemplified in "the kind of life lived in the village at the foot of the hill" (*Homo Sacer*, 55) described in Kafka's novel *The Castle*. Redemption is the symmetrical reversal of this state. Referring to the interpretive differences that mark Scholem's and Benjamin's approaches to this condition, Agamben writes, "On the one hand, there is the view of Scholem, who sees in this life the maintenance of the pure form of law beyond its own content—a 'being in force without significance' [*Geltung ohne Bedeutung*]—and, on the other hand, that of Benjamin, for whom the state of exception that has become the rule signals the fulfillment of the law. . . . By becoming indistinguishable from the life over which it ought to rule, it has entered the messianic process of consuming itself" (*Homo Sacer*, 55). In Agamben's view, Scholem remains in the thrall of the sovereign ban, whereas

Benjamin perceives its redemptive reversal. Aside from Kafka's parable "Before the Law," discussed in the following chapter, "In the Penal Colony" is the most compelling example of such an about-face from the negative state of exception, in which life is subjected to the Law, to a real, messianic state of exception, in which the force of the Law is rescinded.

## In the Penal Colony

Agamben draws a close parallel between the structure of the Law and the structure of language: Like the Law, language subjects man to an inescapable, preset code, and, like the Law, language exercises a ban: it always proves inadequate and prejudiced in its claim to capture reality, yet one cannot step outside language in order to fathom what cannot be said in it. Agamben thus contends: "Our age does, indeed, stand in front of language just as the man from the country in the parable stands in front of the door of the Law" (*Homo Sacer*, 54) in a state of ban, which only the "division of the division," the abolition of the differences that elicit meaning, the revocation of the signifying structure of language can resolve. In Kafka's "In the Penal Colony," which features an instrument of execution that operates by means of an inscription of sentences on the body of the condemned, the link between language and the Law is obvious. However, in positing an absolute homology between Law and language, Agamben's exegesis in "The Idea of Language II," one of his short essays in *Idea of Prose*,[16] goes one step further than previous interpretations of the story. He writes, "A singular light is thrown on Kafka's tale of the Penal Colony when one realizes that the machine of torture . . . is in fact language" (Prose, 115). The assertion that "the machine is primarily an instrument of justice and punishment" and that "on earth and for men, language is also such an instrument" (Prose, 115) evokes Walter Benjamin's theory of language, which is itself adopted from kabbalistic sources. According to Benjamin's theory, the arbitrariness of the signs, that is, the loss of an Adamic language of names, is a result of man's fall into sin. It continues into bourgeois modernity, representing today the invisible symptom of humankind's generalized state of despondency. In this view, only the Messiah can save humankind and, at the same time, rescue language, returning it to its former immediacy. Agamben accordingly interprets the destruction of the torture machine at the end of Kafka's "In the Penal Colony" as a simultaneous redemption from both language and Law.

In his theoretical elaborations on the state of exception, Agamben conflates the lifting of the ban with a rescinding of language. In correlation with the negative "state of exception we live in," language appears in Agamben's interpretation of "In the Penal Colony" as the written word and, therefore, in a condition that most clearly reveals its proximity to the Law. In the true, messianic state of exception, the Law, formerly placed in opposition to life, will be inverted and become entirely subservient to life. Language will then undergo a similar inversion, as Agamben states in citing and commenting on Benjamin: "The impenetrability of a writing," which, in the negative state of exception, has become undecipherable and "appears to be life itself," contrasts with language in its messianic state and "the absolute intelligibility of a life wholly resolved into writing" (*Homo Sacer*, 66). In this vein, Agamben reads the punishment of the condemned in Kafka's "In the Penal Colony" as both murderous Law and unfathomable written language, which inscribe the convicts' guilt into their flesh until, in the sixth hour of their torture, an epiphanic inversion occurs, transforming the previous darkness besetting the tortured prisoner into the "perfect clarity" of his now integrally legible life.

Agamben's messianic dissolution of the written word corresponds to Paul's abrogation of the written Law, which Agamben describes in *The Time That Remains*: The Pauline message "cannot be something like a written text containing new and diverse precepts. . . . In other words, it is not a text, but the very life of the messianic community, not a *writing*, but a *form of life*" (Time, 122). For Agamben, who quotes kabbalistic sources, this form of life resembles the Torah reduced to mere letters, a condition of pure potentiality, in which the difference between what has happened and what has not is resolved into a *restitutio in integrum* of sheer potentiality. This potentialization has far-reaching consequences and risks negating concrete historical events of the past. For example, at the beginning of his interpretation of "In the Penal Colony," Agamben cites "a contemporary figure from a novel": "I'll let you into a terrible secret: language is the punishment. All things must enter it and perish there according to the scale of their sin" (Prose, 115). Agamben borrows these sentences from the novel *Malina* by Ingeborg Bachmann, to whom he also dedicates his text. Although Agamben treats the sin within a purely ontological realm, he seems to neglect historical facticity because in Bachmann's novel, the sin takes on a specific, historical horizon. In the context of the novel, the passage refers to Austria in the postwar era: "One has long since returned to business as usual in the new world. . . . [From this vantage point,] . . . one must tolerate the past completely . . . the true untimely ones sitting in their countries *are the speechless who reign at all times*. I will tell you a terrible secret."[17] These sentences are then followed by the passage Agamben quotes. Bachmann is obviously concerned with the unacknowledged sins of the Nazi past. The "speechless ones" are not, as for Agamben, those who are freed from the thrall of an imperfect language, but those who fail to face and speak of their past crimes. Using language to formulate and express the perpetrators' crimes would reveal them: language here is clearly a medium of justice.

For Agamben, justice does not come about in and through language as it does for Bachmann, but, on the contrary, in the redemption offered by its destruction. The redemptive about-face occurs in the destruction of the language machine. Here, Agamben writes, "justice triumphs over justice, language over language" (Prose, 117). Instead of punishing, the machine now kills: at the point at which the Law is abrogated, its murderous essence is revealed as the distinction between punishment and murder disappears. Far from rendering justice impossible, however, in the absence of law, all punishment now reveals its murderous nature. At this extreme point of nondistinction, redemption lies in the revelation of the homicidal essence of the Law. Agamben interprets the end of Kafka's story accordingly, offering a new reading of the figure of the officer who was in charge of the executions. Kafka's story ends with the officer surrendering himself to the machine, which, at this point, self-destructs, without, however, bestowing the officer with the epiphany experienced by the other convicts in the sixth hour of their torture.

Agamben's interpretation alludes to but supersedes other readings that view the officer, in his capacity as a judge, as paying for his previous injustice, while the machine suffers its demise as his partner in crime. Agamben's reading homes in on the redemption that occurs as a result of the machine's destruction. He thus emphasizes that the precept "be just" inscribed onto the officer's skin does not refer to the decree the officer has broken; rather it must be read as the officer's instruction to shatter the machine. Justice demands the revocation and destruction of the written law and ultimately of language itself. The Pauline origin of Agamben's reading is evident.

Agamben emphasizes that the officer inserted "the instruction into the machine in the intention of destroying it" (Prose, 117). This reading turns the officer into a Christ figure. The image of the dying man with his "calm and convinced" look, "who bears through his forehead the point of the great iron spike" (Prose, 117), could not be more suggestive of the suffering redeemer's crown of thorns. The officer fails to experience revelation in the sixth hour—the biblical hour of Christ's death—as do the others who preceded him, and the failure reveals itself as a salient element of this interpretation. Agamben reasons that "at this point, there is nothing left in language for the officer to understand" (Prose, 117). This, indeed, makes sense if the officer is Christ: He who has come to abrogate the law knew about the true sense of language all along. He experiences no illumination because he already knew that language in its messianic state signifies nothing and is no longer subject to exegesis. He does not require any revelation of the "sixth hour." And if the officer's facial expression is the same in life and death, it is because he, like Christ, does not really die. In the officer's death, the ultimate reversal from the negative to the positive indistinction occurs: The dying officer personifies the suspension of the most extreme of all differences—the one between life and death. In yet another text invoking Kafka, Agamben explicitly proclaims a redemptive halt to the sheer endlessness of exegesis and ultimately of the written word itself.

## The Inexplicable

"Kafka Defended against His Interpreters," the last text in *Idea of Prose*, deals with the "eventual end of all exegesis."[18] Here, too, language exerts an oppressive ban; here, too, a sudden reversal at the "point of indistinction" brings about redemption on the "day of glory." The first sentence contains an allusion to Kafka: "The most diverse legends circulate about the inexplicable" (Prose, 137). This line echoes Kafka's short text "Prometheus," which lists four legends about the mythical Greek figure and, more generally, contemplates the explanatory power of legends: "[The] legend attempts to explain the inexplicable; because it arises from a ground of truth, it must end again in the inexplicable."[19] Kafka's parable reflects on the thwarted human drive to explain the inexplicable, on the increasing distance of these explanations from the "ground of truth" [*Wahrheitsgrund*] through the centuries, and on the ultimate persistence of the inexplicable. In "Kafka Defended against His Interpreters," Agamben rehearses his own version of the origin and failure of explanations.

As the title suggests, Agamben is less concerned with Kafka than with his interpreters. "Kafka Defended against His Interpreters" is a poetic polemic against those hermeneutic theories that view the infinite possibility of exegesis of texts as the best way to preserve their unattainable core. The forefathers of today's exegetes already thought that "the only way to explain that there is nothing to explain is to give explanations" (Prose, 137). Their successors, whom Agamben calls "the present guardians of the Temple," go one step further in their belief that the inexplicable remains unscathed only in explanation (Prose, 137). The advocates of the dogma of the infinity of interpretations are, to Agamben, the new high priests, from whom we—and of course Kafka—have to be defended and protected. Or, perhaps, even redeemed? These Temple guardians before the inexplicable today proclaim a ban that arises from their self-decreed commandment to produce endless explanations in order to preserve the inexplicable. The analogy with Agamben's account of the state of exception is evident: As with the Law and with language, it is impossible to avoid violating this commandment, because every position one adopts with respect to the inexplicable, every relationship that one establishes with it becomes "meaningful." Congealing immediately into an explanation, it inevitably fails to measure up to the inexplicable. As in the faulty state of exception, so, too, in the theories Agamben disparages, explanation and what is to be explained become indistinguishable. In a daring reversal of this situation, Agamben posits an about-face into a redemptive indistinction that would correspond to the "real" messianic "state of exception."

In "Kafka Defended against His Interpreters," Agamben refers back to "our illustrious fathers—the patriarchs" (Prose, 137), who added "an inseparable *post-script* to this doctrine"—just as the Apostle Paul literally added a text to the (Jewish) statutes. "The present keepers of the Temple"—that is to say, Derrida and other adepts of deconstructive readings[20]—removed this Pauline postscript, which said, Agamben continues, that "explanations would not last eternally, and [that] on a certain day, which they [the patriarchs] called the 'day of Glory,' explanations would end their dance around the inexplicable" (Prose, 138). Agamben firmly rejects the recent dogma of the indeterminacy of meaning and the ensuing infinity of interpretations, which he categorizes as idolatry of the endlessly invoked golden calf of the inexplicable. To him, in the no longer anticipatory but messianic time in which we live, "the task of explanations is exhausted" (Prose, 138). They have lost their significance and now exert merely a paralyzing effect. As with Paul's *hos me*, as with Agamben's interpretations of "Before the Law," to be discussed in the next chapter, and "In the Penal Colony," the ban disappears only with the deactivation of the exegetic commandment "Explain!"—the Talmudic practice of infinite commentary. Instead, he calls for a messianic "point of indistinction" between primary text and commentary: "Only the explanations were, in truth, inexplicable, and the legend was invented to explain them. What was not to be explained is perfectly contained in what no longer explains anything" (Prose, 137). Under the sign of the messianic reversal of a hopeless indistinction into a redemptive one, Agamben again revokes the faulty infinity of eternally deferred references and mediations and—as a new Apostle Paul—proclaims the glorious, messianic day on which the compulsion to interpret is suspended and the inexplicable is no longer explained. On that day, language will coincide with the inexplicable and signify nothing but itself.

Although in Kafka's "Prometheus," too, nothing ultimately remains but the "inexplicable mass of rock," the function of the legend differs in Kafka's text and in that of Agamben. For Agamben, "the legend was invented in order to explain the explanations"; it is, therefore, one mediating degree further removed from the inexplicable than the explanations. For Kafka, the legend—and literature along with it—represents, in the shape of Prometheus, man's betrayal of the gods. Telling legends and writing literature robs the gods of the inexplicable and delivers it to man. Agamben's messianic rejection of explanations and legends, on the other hand, returns the inexplicable to the gods. Whereas in Kafka's "Prometheus" the legend itself is the booty stolen from the gods that hands the inexplicable to humankind, for Agamben it becomes, like language and its ban, the punishment for this theft. In line with this thinking, in his very last sentence, he turns to a messianic hope and leaves the legend—and all storytelling—behind.

In Kafka, too, the legend ends with the inexplicable, but precisely the failure to conquer it leaves it open to further possibilities of interpretations—even for that of Agamben himself. Like the officer in the penal colony, Agamben emulates the Pauline removal of the commandment to interpret the Word, which he sees as a liberation from the keepers of the Temple.

## The Students

In "Idea of Study," an additional text from *Idea of Prose* (Prose, 63–65), Agamben's messianic hope for an end to all explanations and liberation from the keepers of the Temple coincides with an implicit invocation of an end to studying altogether. In his introduction to "The Idea of Study," Agamben recalls how, after the destruction of the Holy Temple in Jerusalem, the study of the scriptures became, in the Jewish tradition, a surrogate for the sacrificial rituals. In contradistinction to rabbinic commentators such as Maimonides who envision messianic times in terms of a reconstruction of the Temple and a reinvigoration of the Torah and its commands, Agamben echoes kabbalistic speculations about the eventual end of all commentaries, and he conflates the deposing of today's hermeneutic temple keepers with a messianic anticipation of an end to all study.

In the course of his argument, Agamben takes up, but radicalizes and slightly shifts, Benjamin's reflections about the messianic mission carried out by the scribes and students in Kafka's stories and novels. These reflections, which constitute the last pages of Benjamin's Kafka essay, develop the thought that "the law which is studied and not practiced any longer is the gate to justice."[21] In keeping with Benjamin's interpretation, Agamben considers the study of the law a beneficial substitute for its practice and a subversive assault on the power of the priests, but in Agamben's messianic design, study itself is only an intermediary stage leading eventually to a renunciation of a messianic reconstruction of the Temple and, ultimately, to its vanishing from human memory.

Benjamin, on the other hand, views Kafka's students as the forebears of the Messiah because they are the ones who assure that "the best" [thing] is not forgotten, "for it involves the possibility of redemption."[22] Studying, for Benjamin, becomes tantamount to a redeeming resistance against the progression of time and forgetting of the past. Benjamin describes the messianic task of Kafka's students as a journey backward, a flight toward the past. Citing Kafka's aphoristic text "The Wish to Be an Indian," Benjamin illustrates the ecstatic vision of such a ride. He likens the equestrian flight "over the smoothly mown heath, with the horse's neck and head already gone" to the fulfillment of the "fantasy about the blessed rider," who gallops toward the past in an "untrammeled, happy journey," in order to redeem what has been forgotten.[23] In the penultimate paragraph of his essay, Benjamin once again takes up the comparison between studying and the "fantasy about the blessed rider." Benjamin's assessment of this rapturous ride changes, however, after his remark that Kafka's students are "pupils who are no longer in possession of the Holy Writ." "Now," Benjamin writes, "there is nothing to support them on their 'untrammeled, happy journey.'"[24] This ecstatic flight without "the horse's neck and head," without weight, without law and reality, might be happy, but, Benjamin seems to be saying, it is also as empty and imaginary as a "pure potentiality," a mere fantasy. Accordingly, Benjamin, indeed, distinguishes Kafka's path from the one taken by the students who have lost the scriptures. Unlike them, Benjamin writes, Kafka "has found the law of his own journey."[25] Benjamin finds Kafka's "law" most powerfully expressed in the short story "The Truth of Sancho Panza."[26] Benjamin calls this story, which he quotes in its entirety at the end of his essay, Kafka's "most perfect creation, not only because it is an interpretation."[27] Could Kafka be, after all, about a *law*, and, at his best, produce *interpretations*?

According to Agamben, the messianic task of Kafka's students no longer lies in practicing or observing the law, but in studying it in order to deactivate it and ultimately drive it into oblivion. Benjamin's reflections omit this last step. He, too, considers that Kafka's writings, as in the case of the Aggadah, the transmission of the Law in stories, do not simply lie at the feet of the law—the Halakhah—but instead raise "a mighty paw" against it. Benjamin, however, does not go so far as Agamben, who portrayed Kafka as setting out on an empty, happy journey devoid of the Law and the written word. Benjamin's recasting of Cervantes' tale pays tribute to an older text in reinterpreting it. Kafka reconfigures Cervantes' idealistic knight Don Quixote into the product of Sancho Panza's imagination, his pragmatic and responsible companion:

> Without ever boasting of it, Sancho Panza succeeded in the course of years, by supplying a lot of romances of chivalry and adventure for the evening and night hours, in so diverting from him his demon, whom he later called Don Quixote, that this demon thereupon freely performed the maddest exploits, which, however, for the lack of a preordained object, which Sancho Panza himself was supposed to have been, did no one any harm. A free man, Sancho Panza philosophically followed Don Quixote on his crusades, perhaps out of a sense of responsibility, and thus enjoyed a great and profitable entertainment to the end of his days.[28]

Losing all sense of reality in his desire to save the world, Don Quixote is seconded by Sancho Panza, who has decided to trail the crusading knight. Fearing the knight's destructive fantasies and follies, he follows him everywhere and watches over his actions. He thus provides himself—and we might add us as well—with a "great and edifying entertainment." In a letter to Gershom Scholem from August 11, 1934, Benjamin underscores his deep appreciation for Kafka's Sancho Panza: "Sancho Panza's existence is exemplary because it consists in Kafka's rereading of his own foolish and donquixotic" side.[29] Kafka's "law" and the perfection of his writing, which Benjamin discovers in "Sancho Panza," does not lie in the fantasy world of Don Quixote's riding off into the void, but in his servant's self-reflecting, vigilant wisdom. In Kafka's exegesis of Cervantes' characters, Sancho Panza reins in his own destructive devil and lightens the world's burden by providing it with wondrous stories about knights and their adventures. The law that Benjamin unearths in Kafka's story is indeed of a very different nature from anything related to sovereignty or power: The wisdom of Sancho Panza's "great and profitable entertainment" uncannily resembles the circus of literature.

## Coda

"What," Agamben asks at the end of the closing text of *Profanations*,[30] one of his most compelling volumes of essays, "should we do with our fantasies?" The text bears the title *The Six Most Beautiful Minutes in the History of Film* and invites a comment similar to Benjamin's assessment of Kafka's "Truth of Sancho Panza": It could very well be a "rereading of his own most foolish and donquixotic side," not least because it is a self-interpretation, his most perfect creation. Agamben's one-page text describes a scene in the Orson Welles film *Don Quixote* that gives the impression of a montage of scenes taken from Kafka. The scene is set in the cinema of a small provincial town; Sancho Panza enters the cinema, looking for Don Quixote.

> He finds him sitting apart, staring at the screen. The auditorium is almost full and the upper tier—a kind of gallery—is packed with screaming children. After a few futile attempts to reach Don Quixote, Sancho sits down in the orchestra, next to a little girl (Dulcinea?) who offers him a lollipop. The show has begun, it is a costume movie, armed knights traverse the screen, and suddenly a woman appears who is in danger. Don Quixote jumps up, draws his sword out of the scabbard, rushes down, lunges at the screen, and his blows begin to rupture its fabric. The woman and the riders can still be seen, but the black tear made by Don Quixote's sword is getting wider and wider, inexorably destroying the images. In the end, there is nothing left of the screen, and all that remains is the wooden structure to which it was attached. The audience leaves the hall, dismayed, but the children up in the gallery do not stop screaming encouragements at Don Quixote. Only the little girl in the orchestra looks at him reprovingly.[31]

Joining fragments from "The Truth about Sancho Panza" and "Up in the Gallery," Agamben spins Kafka's gloss on Cervantes' tale further and weaves himself into its fabric. Unlike Kafka's young man "up in the gallery," who fails to rush down and cry "stop" to rescue the oppressed performer in the circus ring, Don Quixote does rush down to save the endangered Dulcinea. This salvation, however, is tantamount to the destruction of all illusion. Although his revolutionary admirers up in the gallery continue to support the savior, the alter ego of the historical Dulcinea, possibly a young and affluent Dulcinea enjoying a lollypop and lounging in the orchestra seat, is sulking because she is now deprived of her entertainment. Agamben closes this cinema scenario, and his book, with enigmatic thoughts that are undeniably self-reflexive: "What shall we do with our fantasies? Love them, believe them—to the point where we have to deface, to destroy them (that is perhaps the meaning of the films of Orson Welles). But when they prove in the end to be empty and unfulfilled, when they show the nothingness from which they are made, then it is time to pay the price for their truth, to understand that Dulcinea—whom we saved—cannot love us."[32]

In a remnant of self-irony, Agamben lets us in on the doubts besetting the savior in the aftermath of his act of bravery. With humorous self-doubt, Agamben offers us his own Sancho Panza, who, in the guise of Don Quixote, sends forth his demon—his wild fantasies of redemption—but meanwhile follows him everywhere, carefully watching over him. Obsessed by his own impulse to cry "stop!" to dispel the mirages of our times and expose the naked truth, he teasingly paints himself as a Don Quixote rescuing Dulcinea and saving the ailing planet. Just as Don Quixote in the cinema, he, too, had to destroy the screen of illusions and reveal the bare scaffold that upholds it. With a premonition of his critics' rebukes, he identifies with Cervantes' mad Knight of the Sad Countenance, knowing full well that, just as Dulcinea repulsed her savior, the world will not love him. Instead, it will crucify him for revealing the bare, unveiled truth, the wooden structure behind the shining screen. It would not be surprising if the wooden structure bore the shape of a cross.

In the end, the new Messiah smiles wistfully at himself, transforming the sixth hour, the hour in which Christ, unrecognized and despised, died on the cross, into the six most beautiful minutes in the history of film. In this self-reflective miniature, Agamben reveals his awareness that he himself may be driven not only by the radical fantasies of a late metaphysician, but also by the poetic imagination of the man of letters. Literature reveals the scaffolding behind the dreams of salvation. It also unmasks the pose of the savior. Possibly, in his own variation on Cervantes, Agamben, a free man, possesses the serenity and healthy sense of responsibility that enables him philosophically to accompany his Don Quixote and warily observe his redemptive adventures. He has thereby offered us "a great and profitable entertainment."[33] Whether it relieves the world of its burden remains a point of contention.

# 5   Kafka, Narrative, and the Law

If it is a world you want, then strict justice is impossible. And if it is strict justice you want, then a world is impossible.

   Bereshit Rabba 49: 20[1]

The crows maintain that a single crow could destroy the heavens. Doubtless, that is so, but it proves nothing against the heavens, for the heavens signify simply: the impossibility of crows.[2]

   Franz Kafka


"Before the law stands a doorkeeper. To this doorkeeper comes a man."[3] These first words of Franz Kafka's most famous parable, "Before the Law" [*Vor dem Gesetz*], evoke an archetypal narrative situation: The juxtaposition of the verb "stands" with the verb "comes" sets up a confrontation between something static and stable with the onset of an event, a potential encounter. This narrative situation occurs in the context of the law, which is generally regarded as in conflict with narrative. Commentators question, however, whether this encounter between law and man ever takes place in Kafka's parable. This question implies an understanding of the relationship between the law, presented as an abstraction, and the man whose life is a narrative. What happens when this particular man appears—the point at which narrative confronts the law?

Kafka's parable, one of the most widely read and interpreted texts of the past century, describes a scene in which a man seeking access to the law is denied entry. He waits at the door until the end of his life, when the doorkeeper tells the man, who has just seen a shimmer of light emanating from the door, that this entrance to the law was meant for him alone and the doorkeeper will now close it. The parable consists mainly of a description of the man's negotiations with the doorkeeper as he strives to gain access to the law. The narrative, however, does not specify the nature of this law. Initially, the only certainty is that it designates an immutable entity in contrast to the man, who has an origin, a history, and a destiny. We ascertain that the man left his "homeland" [*Heimat*] and set out on a journey, that he has a purpose—access to the law—and arrives at its gate, where he will wait, search and reflect, discuss and negotiate, desire and curse before growing old and dying, presumably without having attained his goal.

Whereas the law in Kafka's parable is abstract, timeless, and integral, the man is concrete and specific: He lives in a time of waiting and a state of wanting. The doorkeeper characterizes him as "insatiable" [*unersättlich*] as he asks about the access to the law, and he dies unfulfilled. The law, which, the man from the country contends "ought to be accessible to everyone at all times" but remains unattainable for him, is confronted with the singularity, temporality, and situatedness of lived life in all its creaturely contingency. Emphasizing the creaturely aspect is the fact that "the man from the country," as many have noted, is literally a translation of the Hebrew word *am haaretz*, which means not only "a man from the land," but also a person who is ignorant of the law. Beyond suggesting that the *am haaretz* is outside the law because of his ignorance of it, the author implicitly opposes him to a *talmid hakham*, a student of the law. It is, however, doubtful whether the *am haaretz* would have fulfilled his desire to enter through the door had he turned into a true student of the law. The doorkeeper, both mediator and barrier to the encounter, is described as the lowest-ranking representative of the law. He is some legal or rabbinic authority who marks the separation but also the link between the law, which is said to be immutably there, and the man who has a story—a minimal one, but a story.

## "Before the Law"

In Kafka's parable, the law remains not only unattainable for the man from the country but also eludes readers' attempts to pin down its meaning and effects. Interpretations of Kafka's law-related texts abound—particularly of "Before the Law," but also of his novel *The Trial*, of which the parable is a part, and, to a somewhat lesser extent, of *The Castle* and stories such as "In the Penal Colony," "The New Advocate," and "The Question of Our Laws." It remains uncertain, nevertheless, whether the law in his work is to be understood in primarily legal, social, and political terms or in metaphysical, theological, and religious ones. This ambiguity has elicited numerous, sometimes contradictory, interpretations and has inspired often opposing notions of justice and of the dichotomy between narrative and the law. I shall explore how certain major thinkers interpreted Kafka in the context of concepts of justice that intertwine the religious and the secular realms. My focus will lie on the role these interpretations assign to the relationship between the law as an authoritative, normative ordering system and narrative as an expression of creaturely life.

Most interpretations of Kafka's stories involving the law identify law with the juridical apparatus of the modern state, on the one hand, or the Jewish tradition, on the other. Adherents of the first approach, who consider Kafka solely in secular terms, as is the common practice in recent readings by "Law and Literature" scholars, depict him either as a critic of the juridical systems of his time[4] or as an author who prefigures the present situation and can provide insights into the shortcomings of contemporary jurisprudential procedures.[5] In contrast, readings of Kafka's legal narratives that invoke the Jewish tradition generally equate the law with divine judgment and its inaccessibility, that is, with the Jewish concept of God as man's all-powerful but remote "Other." Both approaches often disregard the possibility of ambiguity—that Kafka deliberately left open the question of whether to understand the law in secular or religious terms. Occasionally, the two realms come together, sometimes to the point of identity, as in Carl Schmitt's idea that all juridical and political instances are transpositions of religious ones.[6] In such cases, the common denominator underlying both state law and Jewish law is the idea of an all-powerful, almighty sovereign who rules oppressively. Kafka's narratives depict a terrifying law-ruled world and embody the potential of literature to reveal the impossibility of attaining justice through the law and to condemn the inaccessible sovereign power ruling over man.

Walter Benjamin succinctly writes that it is debatable whether Kafka's work "is devoted to elevating the law or to burying it." He contends that, "Kafka has no answer to these questions."[7] It is, indeed, difficult to ascertain whether, in Kafka's world, the obstacle to justice is that the law is omnipresent or that it is distorted [*entstellt*], compromised, and crippled to a point that makes it indistinguishable from lawlessness. Determining a possible alternative to the dismal state of the world depicted in Kafka's stories is even more challenging. Kafka's parable "Before the Law" and his other writings dealing primarily with the law, indeed, depict a world in which the law is both inaccessible and omnipresent, boundless, pervading all levels of human existence, but, at the same time, paradoxically, failing to perform its primary function, the marking of distinctions and divisions that would instate a moral and just social order in the world.

Kafka's world order blurs all borders and limits. In his novel *The Castle*, the law is everywhere and nowhere; everyone belongs to the mysterious network of the rulers, yet everyone is also terrorized by it. The magistrates receive their plaintiffs in bars and bedrooms, and the protagonist K. becomes entangled in an inscrutable network spun by the rulers of this world that exhausts him to death. Similarly, in *The Trial*, the law is inscrutable: The actual court cannot be found or is located in dark attics, the law books turn out to be pornographic booklets; the judges and lawyers are either invisible or fake; yet the effect of their authority is lethal.

In the world of Kafka's narratives, the law is unquestionably "out of joint," but critics interpret the consequences of this situation in different and often contradictory ways. I shall contrast two important interpretations of Kafka's relation to the law, one by the contemporary Italian philosopher Giorgio Agamben in dialogue with the French philosopher Jacques Derrida, and the other by the German-Jewish thinker Walter Benjamin in dialogue with his friend, the historian of Kabbalah Gershom Scholem. Both Agamben and Benjamin consider the law in Kafka's writings in religious as well as in secular terms, but they reach radically different conclusions about Kafka, the law, and Judaism. Agamben combines a political perspective with a theological one; Benjamin, in contrast, focuses on the political dimension, rejecting transcendental theological interpretations in favor of the Jewish *juridical* tradition. Agamben equates state law and Jewish law, whereas Benjamin distinguishes between them.

## Agamben on "Before the Law"

Agamben advances his Pauline reading of Jewish law most forcefully in his interpretation of Kafka's parable "Before the Law." He perceives Kafka's parable as perfectly representing the structure of the sovereign action of an oppressive, omnipresent law. For Agamben, the situation in which the doorkeeper prevents the man from the country from entering through the door of the law illustrates the essence of the law's tyrannical power that has "lost its significance but continues to be in force" (*Homo Sacer*, 55). In his reading of Kafka's story, the open door that cannot be entered points to the world in a state of exception. No decree forbids the man's access to the law, but he is literally held in a ban that simultaneously includes and excludes him: he neither attains access to the law nor can he turn away from it. Whereas traditional interpretations see the situation of the man from the country as a failure because he waits in vain before the door of the law until the doorkeeper pronounces that he will close it, Agamben views the shutting of the door positively, contending that the country man's "entire behavior" is nothing but a "complicated and patient strategy to have the door closed in order to interrupt the law's being in force" (*Potentialities*, 174).

Agamben's surprising reading of Kafka's parable explicitly counters Derrida's interpretation of the parable as an endless but positive waiting and an ongoing negotiation with the representatives of the law. Agamben rejects this vision, which he ascribes to the Jewish tradition of a "life lived in deferral and delay" (*Potentialities*, 166). In Derrida's interpretation, the confrontation between narrative and the law leads to an intermingling that creates an undecidability concerning each one's status. The man from the country waiting before the entrance to the law embodies the inability to decide; in Derrida's words, the man "decides to put off deciding."[8] The constitutive inability to reach closure, which stands at the core of Derrida's reading, for Agamben, epitomizes our prevailing condition "of a petrified or paralyzed messianism" (*Potentialities*, 171). Derrida's stance contrasts with the provocation of Agamben's man from the country that leads to the closing of the door: Agamben sees Kafka's man from the country as a Christ figure who, as the gospels say, fulfills the law in the *pleroma*, fullness, thereby ending its oppressive effects and inverting the negative state of exception into a state of freedom.

Agamben explicitly attributes a strategy—a calculated goal—to the man from the country, a strategy aimed at closing the door and suspending the law. Agamben's statements of allegiance to Benjamin notwithstanding, positing such a calculated design diverges from the latter's idea of eliciting a positive reversal of the world's present state. Benjamin's most explicitly messianic text, the "Theologico-Political Fragment," in which he depicts "messianic intensity" [*messianische Intensität*] and the "dynamics of the profane" [*Dynamis des Profanen*] in the form of two parallel arrows pointing in opposite directions while propelling one another forward, does not envision such a directed deactivation of the law. The divine kingdom cannot be established by a transgressing abrogation of the law but through the earthly pursuit of human happiness and justice. Agamben, in contrast, emphasizes the destructive impulse, approving of the heretical messiah Shabbetai Zvi, for whom "overstepping the Torah [is] its fulfillment" and "fulfilling the Torah [is] its banishment from memory" (*Potentialities*, 167–68). Turning Kafka's narrative into a modern gospel and reducing the narrative aspect of Kafka's parable to the mere function of illustrating a theological-political doctrine, Agamben conflates state law with Jewish law and Paul's proclamation of the demise of the Jewish law with his own anarchist therapeutic prescription for our planet.

The question remains: how did the man from the country succeed in getting the doorkeeper to shut the door to the law? We cannot ascertain what—or whether anything—has occurred "before the law." Agamben provides a possible answer in the final sentence of his essay, when he claims that in Kafka's parable, "something has really happened in seeming not to happen" (*Potentialities*, 174). He thus directly and explicitly contradicts Derrida's conclusion that Kafka's parable is "an event that succeeds in not happening . . . an event that happens not to happen."[9] For Derrida, the "success" constitutes the man's remaining before the law, not actually entering it. For him, entering the law rather than, for example, commenting on it or studying it from a distance, would imply that an actual fulfillment of the law is possible. Indeed, Agamben's notion of the messianic task of fulfilling the law by abrogating it assumes the potential—and mission—carried out by Jesus, who allegedly enacted the ultimate *fulfillment* of the law, a notion that is omnipresent in Christian theology and absent from the Jewish idea of justice. Furthermore, in contradistinction to the Jewish concept of messianic times as entailing a publicly visible change, Agamben seemingly views Paul's gesture of revelation as something that has already happened but is not yet visible. Finally, Agamben excludes from his analysis the faint glimmer of light that in Kafka's story shines through the door of the law before the man's death and has repeatedly been interpreted as the rays of the *shehinah*, the divine glory emanating from the Torah; it does not form part of his reading. Benjamin conceives of Jews and Justice very differently when he interprets the relationship of Kafka's narrative to the law.

## The Fulfillment of the Law

Reading Kafka's parable "Before the Law" in terms of a Pauline rescinding of the law, Agamben, in his introductory words, claims to interpret it "from the perspective of Walter Benjamin's conception of messianic law."[10] Benjamin himself does not offer an elaborate interpretation of the parable, merely alluding to "the cloudy spot" [*wolkige Stelle*] at its core that lends itself to infinite reflections.[11] In his notes for a letter to Scholem, Benjamin calls the law the "blind spot" [*toter Punkt*] in Kafka's oeuvre.[12] However, Benjamin's elaborations on Kafka in his important essay "Franz Kafka. For the Tenth Anniversary of his Death" and in his exchange about the Prague author in his correspondence with Scholem deal extensively with questions of the law. In these writings, Benjamin's views on the law differ significantly from Agamben's Pauline reading. Agamben and Benjamin's perspectives on the secular legal system, however, reveal clear similarities. Similarly to Agamben, Benjamin regards state laws inherently as instruments of abusive sovereignty. In his essay "Critique of Violence,"[13] he points out their mythical nature, and in his writings on Kafka, he shows how the legal system wantonly exerts its violent power everywhere, infiltrating the most personal and intimate realms of existence to the point of making it "indistinguishable from life itself." Agamben shares Benjamin's's perspective on *The Trial*, and even more so on *The Castle*, as poignant illustrations of a world where obscure legal instances inflict arbitrary, opaque, and repressive regulations on individuals who remain ignorant of the laws that govern them. Benjamin viewed the dismal world of Kafka's novels as one of unregulated "unbounded promiscuity,"[14] the lowest stage of human existence. Benjamin calls this world a prehistoric swamp world [*Sumpfwelt*] in which everyone is guilty and everyone is also a victim of the law; it is, above all, as Rodolphe Gasché remarks, "a world that renders impossible any discriminating between right and wrong."[15] The world depicted by Kafka is instead constituted "by the very impossibility of a clear decision," an "impossibility that perpetuates the order of wrong [*Unrecht*], thus also excluding the very possibility of justice."[16]

Benjamin's Kafka essay points out the paradoxical simultaneity in Kafka's novels of an omnipresent law and absolute lawlessness. In contrast to Agamben, Benjamin considers this lawlessness equally if not more responsible for the terror of Kafka's world than the tyranny of the law. In fact, Benjamin describes life in the village in *The Castle* in terms of utter lawlessness: "Even the people in power are so lawless that they appear on the same level as those at the bottom of the pile; without any distinctions [*Scheidewände*], creatures of all realms teem together [*wimmeln durcheinander*] indiscriminately and the one and only bond that secretly unites them is a feeling of utter anxiety."[17]

In his outline for an essay that he never wrote, "Versuch eines Schemas zu Kafka," Benjamin elaborates most explicitly on the development of this lawlessness. The one-page outline sketches a miniature theory of history and civilization. Benjamin writes that Kafka, in his books, contrasts the "swamp world" with "the lawful one of Judaism. . . . Its purity and dietary laws display the defense mechanisms against this [swamp] world. . . . In other words, only the Halakhah still [ex negativo] contains traces of this [prehistoric] mode of existence of mankind that is long past."[18]

"Kafka's books," Benjamin continues, "contain the missing Aggadah [the narrative component of the Talmud] to this Halakhah [its legal aspect]. . . . Intertwined with this Aggadic text is the prophetic dimension in his books."[19] The world as it appears in *The Trial* and in *The Castle*, this world without distinctions and divisions, without boundaries and order, thus both is a prehistoric *Vorwelt* and prophetically announces the return of this oppressive lawlessness in the present. Benjamin writes: "Kafka's novels take place in a swamp world. But then, this world is also our world, because we have not overcome it, only repressed and forgotten it."[20] The lawless world of prehistory depicted by Kafka is, for Benjamin, also the measure of his own present: Writing as a Jew in the 1930s, Benjamin describes the legal system of his own times through a characterization of Kafka's swamp world in which the laws have become identical with the ultimate lawlessness reigning in an oppressive state of exception. Thus far, this description of state law does not vary much from Agamben's view. In a significant difference, however, Benjamin contrasts both the prehistoric and contemporary situation, in which the law is "bastardized" with lawlessness and all boundaries disappear, with Judaism; Agamben, in contrast, implicitly identifies the Jewish legal system as oppressive.

Considering that revealed law instituted the possibility of justice, Benjamin expressed the view that only "justice serves as the point of departure for Kafka's critique of myth."[21] According to Benjamin, the defense against a world without boundaries, separations, and distinctions would thus be Jewish law itself, which not only differs from an oppressive state law based on sheer power but also is—or rather would be—its antidote. In a letter to Scholem on August 11, 1934, Benjamin writes, "Indeed, if we follow Kafka's presentation, the work of the Torah has been thwarted" [Das Werk der Thora nämlich ist—wenn wir uns an Kafkas Darstellung halten—vereitelt worden].[22] In his drafts for this letter, Benjamin added, "And everything that Moses once accomplished would have to be recovered in our world epoch" [Und alles, was einst von Moses geleistet wurde, wäre in unserm Weltzeitalter nachzuholen].[23] Benjamin differs from Agamben in this surprising defense of Jewish law. He carefully distinguishes, however, between his reflections on Kafka's halakhic dimension and Jewish *theological* readings. In his outline for the unwritten essay, he states, "[Kafka's] prophecy for his immediate future"—which is the state of the world in Benjamin's time itself—"is much more important for Kafka than the Jewish *Theologumena*, which one only wanted to find in his work. The punishment [the return of the swamp world] is more important than the one who punishes. The prophecy is more important than God."[24] Undoubtedly, Benjamin had Max Brod in mind, whom he elsewhere criticized severely with respect to his Jewish theological reading of Kafka. This comment may, however, also be addressed to Gershom Scholem, his main interlocutor on Kafka, although Scholem's theology, based on the Kabbalah, is fundamentally different from Brod's.[25]

Between 1925 and 1938, Benjamin and Scholem exchanged a stream of letters that count among the most profound interpretations of Kafka's work.[26] In the course of their correspondence, important dissonances emerged between the two friends.[27] The dissonances concern the role of theology in interpreting Kafka, the importance and nature of the law in Kafka's work, and the understanding of Halakhah and Aggadah in such a context. Underlying these dissonances is a dissimilar outlook on justice and the Jewish tradition. It is surprising that Scholem, who is generally considered the more "Jewish" thinker of the two, is further removed than Benjamin from certain core aspects of the Jewish tradition. Less surprising is that Benjamin shows more interest than Scholem in aspects of this tradition that relate to the worldly, more precisely the political, rather than the divine realm.[28]

Benjamin and Scholem disagree on the justification of a theological reading of Kafka. In his reply to Benjamin's account of Kafka's world as a swamp world that has its counterpart in the Torah, Scholem writes: "The existence of the secret [kabbalistic rather than halakhic] law destroys your interpretation: in the pre-historical world there hardly is this chimerical muddle and certainly not one of the kind that announces its [persistent] existence. *There* you went much too far with your elimination of theology and threw the baby out with the bathwater."[29] Scholem, indeed, regards the "possibility of divine judgment" [*die Möglichkeit des Gottesurteils*] as the sole concern of Kafka's writings. Kafka's work, and in particular "Before the Law," is for him the perfect illustration of what Stéphane Mosès called the "other side of a lost transcendence."[30] Scholem invokes Kafka as the ultimate witness of a negative theology, in which, in Mosès' words, "all we can assert of God is the very fact of his absence."[31] Kafka, in Scholem's view, still represents an instance—borderline to be sure—in the history of revelation. It is—and here Kafka, in Scholem's estimation, rejoins the heretic Kabbalists—"the nothingness of revelation" [*das Nichts der Offenbarung*].[32] Whereas Scholem views Kafka's references to the law in theological categories, Benjamin, although acknowledging a certain "shadowy" [*beschattet*][33] theological dimension in his own writings, is less interested in *Gott*. He focuses more on the ways the Jewish Talmudic tradition, in particular the interaction between Halakhah and Aggadah, provides insights—and a possible alternative—to the dismal realm of Kafka's fiction that seemed visible in the world of Benjamin's time. Instead of Scholem's idea of a kabbalistic "nothingness of revelation," Benjamin regards the "distortion of existence" [*Entstellung des Daseins*] of the "upcoming [political] legal system"[34] as Kafka's "fixation" and "one and only concern."[35] Benjamin nevertheless reintroduces the Jewish dimension that he deems necessary for a reading of Kafka by defining this distortion precisely in terms of "a world in which the Torah has been thwarted."[36]

Benjamin and Scholem also have a different understanding of the Halakhah.[37] On the one hand, Benjamin sees it as an antidote to the chaotic medley of the prehistoric—and present—swamp world. Scholem, on the other hand, in line with his own views of Kafka as a heretical, antinomian Kabbalist in the tradition of Shabbetai Zvi,[38] is skeptical of the Halakhah. Scholem writes to Benjamin, "Not, dear Walter, the *absence* [of the revealed law] in a pre-animistic world is the problem, but instead the *impossibility of fulfilling it*."[39] Scholem comes close to Agamben's Pauline view in regarding the Halakhah as the "absolutely concrete, which is the unfulfillable as such" [das absolut Konkrete als das Unvollziehbare schlechthin].[40] This correlates with Scholem's view of Kafka as one who "ceaselessly compares the concrete reality of human existence with the ideal of absolute justice, an ideal that the Jewish tradition, for its part, symbolizes in the image of divine judgment."[41] Judaism, however, does not assume that the ideal of absolute justice or fulfilment of the law can be attained in this world. In assuming the possibility of fulfilling the law, Scholem echoes, however faintly, the argument developed in Paul's letter to the Romans that the Jewish law must be abrogated because it can never be fully implemented.[42] Paul regards Jewish law as the very source of sinfulness.[43] For him, the coming of Christ and his death on the cross fulfilled the law once and for all; therefore, the "works"—that is, the *mitzvot*, the observance of the commandments—must be suspended and replaced by the interiority of divine grace and love. Scholem's reading of Kafka points in this direction but does not go as far. In his exchange with Benjamin, and elsewhere, Scholem's anarchist impulses remain within the boundaries of Jewish antinomian Kabbalah, and he categorizes Kafka as a late representative of this tradition.[44]

Benjamin and Scholem also disagree on the meaning and function of the Aggadah. This is not evident, at first, in the most precise parallel—and distinction—that Benjamin draws between the Aggadah and Kafka's stories: "Kafka's writings," Benjamin notes in a letter to Scholem,[45] "do not modestly lie at the feet of the doctrine as the Aggadah lies at the feet of the Halakhah. Though apparently reduced to submission, they unexpectedly raise a mighty paw against it" [Kafkas Dichtungen sind von Hause aus Gleichnisse. Aber sie legen sich der

Lehre nicht schlicht zu Füssen wie sich die Haggada der Halacha zu Füssen legt. Wenn sie sich gekuscht haben, heben sie unversehens eine gewichtige Pranke gegen sie].[46] Scholem regards this passage as a confirmation of his own view of Kafka's antinomian attitude.

Benjamin's image could, indeed, be read this way, but Scholem's interpretation misses the nuances of the gesture described by Benjamin. Scholem validly objects to Benjamin: "The antinomian nature of the Aggadic that you mention is not a characteristic of Kafka's Aggadah alone; it is inherent in the nature of the Aggadic as such."[47] He is, however, only partly correct: While Scholem rightly points out that the narrative component of the Talmud is less subservient to the Halakhah than Benjamin suggests, Scholem misreads the contrast Benjamin draws between the Talmudic Aggadot and Kafka's. Not only is Benjamin's image of the raised paw—as I shall show—not truly antinomian, but also not all Aggadot relate to the Halakhah in this way, as Scholem believes. Moshe Halbertal distinguishes between three paradigms for the relationship between Aggadah and Halakhah: "The first and simplest," he writes, "is when the narrative provides a basis for the law"; the second "emphasizes the way in which the story permits a transition to a different sort of legal knowledge" and "allows us to see how the law must be followed [as] we move from 'knowing that' to 'knowing how.'" Only the third paradigm, which Halbertal calls "the most delicate," corresponds to Benjamin's description of the relation between the Aggadic aspect of Kafka's stories and the law. In this third paradigm, Halbertal writes, "the story actually has a subversive role, pointing out the law's substantive limitations."[48] This last paradigm is certainly the one that applies to Benjamin's statement about Kafka's Aggadic dimension, but it is crucial to distinguish this idea of subversion from an antinomian approach to the Halakhah.

A closer look at Benjamin's distinction between Kafka's stories and the Aggadah reveals that Benjamin's view is far from antinomian. What does Benjamin's strange image of the "mighty paw" raised against the Halakhah imply? It evokes the manifestation of a creaturely presence, a gesture of threat that comes to a halt, and a motion of keeping at a distance. The implications of this image become clearer by referring to Benjamin's essay "Franz Kafka: Building the Wall of China," in which he elaborates on the analogy between Kafka's writings and the Aggadah. In a passage immediately following his diagnosis of "Kafka's fixation on the sole topic of his work—namely the distortion of existence," Benjamin explains that Kafka's prose resembles the Aggadah in what may "appear to the reader as obsessiveness," a mode of writing that goes beyond any morality that could be drawn from it. Speaking of Kafka, Benjamin writes, "We may remind ourselves here of the form of the Aggadah, the name Jews have given to the rabbinical stories and anecdotes that serve to explicate and confirm the teachings—the Halakhah. Like the Aggadic, the narrative parts of the Talmud, [Kafka's] books, too, are stories; they are an Aggadah that constantly pauses, luxuriating in the most detailed descriptions, in the simultaneous *hope and fear* that it might encounter the Halakhic order, the doctrine itself, en route."[49]

Benjamin calls this hesitation, the ambivalence between hope and fear of encountering the law, "deferral" or "postponement" [*Verzögerung*],[50] a term that, with a slight shift, could perfectly fit the waiting of the man at the door of the law. As in the Talmudic Aggadot, Benjamin continues, Kafka's parables "show the true workings of grace" [das eigentliche Walten der Gnade] in that [in them], "the law never finds expression as such—this and nothing else is the gracious dispensation of the fragment."[51] The Aggadah avoids turning into a Halakhah, as in Kafka's parables—or, rather, antiparables that do not yield a doctrine or a moral. In this passage, Benjamin no longer contrasts but identifies the Talmudic Aggadot with Kafka's writings. The Aggadah is here more similar to Kafka's writings than the earlier image of its lying modestly at the feet of the Halakhah would suggest. In stopping short of encountering the law, it also circumscribes the law by keeping it from overstepping the boundaries that are set by creaturely lived life itself. It is crucial that the "mighty paw" that Benjamin associates with Kafka's parables does not crush the Halakhah. Not to be confounded with antinomian transgression or abolishment of the law, Kafka's gesture thus corresponds more closely than it seems at first sight to the structure of dynamic interaction between Halakhah and Aggadah, between narrative and the law inherent in the Jewish concept of justice.

## What Happens "Before the Law?"

What, then, is happening "before the law"? Agamben views it as something that has already happened but is not yet visible—a fulfillment of the law that, however, must still await a second coming before all can see it. Derrida considers it something "that succeeds in not happening"[52]—an infinite deferral that is analogous to the unbounded openness of human expectation. For Scholem it is the "nothing of revelation"—the doxa of a negative theology. Finally, for Benjamin, it is the coming of the man of the country to the law, just as the Aggadah comes to the Halakhah. For him, as, I believe, for Kafka, this arrival of narrative both halts the law and stops short of reaching what happens, and remains *before* the law.

Indeed, only an *am haaretz* wants actually to access the law, unaware that one does not "enter" it or that negotiating with its representatives, the rabbinic authorities, is in the Talmudic tradition, the very encounter with the law itself. Were he a *talmid hakham*, he would know the Talmudic saying "*Tzedek, tzedek tirdof*" [justice, justice, thou shalt pursue]. One can strive for justice but it cannot be attained or realized in this life. The man from the country in Kafka's parable—and we, its readers—realize that the door to the law is open but it is not about entering, about fulfilling it. It takes an *am haaretz* such as the man from the country, however, to *approach* the law, to bring the human, creaturely element of the Aggadah to the Halakhah, in order to point at its limits and subvert it: not by suspending or abrogating it but by marking the necessary complementarity of law and narrative, which is itself the notion of justice upheld by Judaism. Kafka himself brings the Aggadah of his stories to the Halakhah, the experiential human dimension to the immutable law. Only in their confrontational togetherness may the law be designated for this single man alone. When the man from the country, the singular existence, dies, the door to the law also closes. Full justice can be attained only after death, by divine justice in the kingdom of heaven or after the coming of the Messiah. As it is said in the Midrash Bereshit Rabba: "If it is a world you want, then strict justice is impossible. And if it is strict justice you want, then a world is impossible." The law has to be limited by the man from the country, by Aggadah and narrative, because they provide the necessary human dimension that enables the law to reckon with lived life. It is in this sense that Kafka writes in his diaries: "Aus dem Talmud: Geht ein Gelehrter auf Brautschau, so soll er sich einen *amhorez* mitnehmen, da er zu sehr in seine Gelehrsamkeit versenkt das Notwendige nicht merken würde" [When a scholar sets out to look for a bride, he should take with him an *amhorez*—(the Yiddish expression for *am haaretz*), because, too engulfed in his studiousness, he would not see what is necessary].[53] As with the Aggadah joined with the Halakhah, the man from the country is the necessary companion of the *talmid hakham*. He alone can see "*das Notwendige*," that which is necessary for life.

## Coda

My initial epigraphs taken from the Talmud, Bereshit Rabba, and from Kafka's notes seem unrelated: How do Bereshit Rabba's comments on strict justice relate to crows? "The crows maintain that a single crow could destroy the heavens. Doubtless that is so, but it proves nothing against the heavens, for the heavens signify simply: the impossibility of crows." Crow is an almost literal translation of the word Kafka, which in Czech means "jackdaw," a crowlike bird. Kafka and the other crows are storytellers who believe that narration and its correlative, the singularity of the crows' creaturely existence, could undo the heavenly truth and the absolute authority of the law. In truth, narration and the singular life threaten the law, but, ultimately, this threat of destruction remains ineffective. The heavenly absolute is capable of warding off the crows and remaining untouched by their messy affairs; in that case, however, it would no longer be a world for crows, for storytellers, or for humans.

# 6    Kafka's Other Job: From Susman to Žižek

ALTHOUGH KAFKA NEVER mentions Job by name, critics often read Kafka's works in the light of this biblical figure who challenges the claim of divine justice in the face of human suffering. In recent decades, scholars have noted fairly convincing, specific, and detailed similarities between Kafka's work and the Book of Job. Most notably, Northrop Frye, in *The Great Code* (1982), regarded the writings of Kafka "as a series of commentaries on the Book of Job" and termed Kafka's most famous novel, *The Trial*, "a kind of *Midrash*" on the biblical book.[1] Other critics consider Kafka's novel "a conscious parallel of the Book of Job,"[2] if not its "true" and even "indispensable translation."[3] Some argue, "Kafka pushes the perceptual dilemma of Job's story to its unrelenting and catastrophic limit"[4] and state that "the court in *The Trial* affirms the same set of moral values found in the Book of Job."[5] Indeed, Harold Fisch, who views Kafka's writings as "a profound and sustained attempt to render Job for modern man," noted that "the analogy with Job" has become "a commonplace of Kafka criticism."[6]

A group of German-Jewish thinkers in the late 1920s and 1930s who drew on the Jewish textual tradition in their reflections on the fundamental predicaments of modern existence postulated the most radical and daring, but also most contentious, parallels between Job and Kafka. These figures engaged and contested each other's work, often echoing one other. Margarete Susman, in her 1929 essay "The Job Problem in Franz Kafka," contended that no other modern oeuvre embodies "as purely and deeply the traits of the age-old confrontation of Job with his God."[7] Likewise, Max Brod, both in his 1931 essay "Franz Kafkas Grunderlebnis" and in his biography of Kafka (published in 1937), suggested that "the old question of Job"[8] lies at the core of Kafka's life and work. In a letter dated August 1, 1931 to Walter Benjamin, Gershom Scholem wrote, "I advise you to begin any inquiry into Kafka with the Book of Job."[9] Martin Buber wrote, "Kafka's work is the most important Jobean commentary of our time."[10] In 1934, Günther Anders asserted—albeit without presenting concrete evidence—that the Book of Job accompanied Kafka throughout his life.[11]

These German-Jewish thinkers, among Kafka's earliest and most prominent interpreters, considered him the author who incomparably captures the human condition in modern times. They analyzed Kafka in the course of their respective endeavors to conceptualize modernity in light of Jewish scriptures, rethink the foundations of Judaism in the face of the rupture with tradition, and, more generally, reflect on the possibilities of a divine order after the "death of God." In doing so, each invoked central features of the Book of Job. In the figure of Job, a character who wrangles with God, they recognized not only a human voice addressing God against all odds, but also a precursor of modern man's doubts about divine justice. The Book of Job's multiperspective mode, narrative inconsistencies, and blatant plot incongruities lent themselves particularly well to these thinkers' desire to reconcile the Jewish biblical tradition with the modern world rendered so keenly in Kafka's modernist prose.

The Book of Job's hermeneutic difficulties and, above all, its deeply paradoxical nature contribute to making it an illuminating companion to Kafka's work. As in Kafka's writings, the Book of Job yields no clear moral or message. Moreover, its paradoxes and incongruities are manifold. Most important, the "Job question," in itself, can be regarded as a paradox: If there is no justice in the world—in that the righteous and the sinners suffer alike—how can one claim that God is almighty? Moreover, there are other, more specific inherent paradoxes. Unlike Job's friends and supposed comforters who justify the ways of God and interpret the existence of evil as punishment, didactic ordeal, or trial, Job rebels against God and accuses him of injustice, indifference, and inaccessibility. Job does so, however, in a most direct and intimate address that confirms God's closeness. God's surprising response presents a related paradox: Despite Job's rebelliousness, God praises his attitude and rejects the friends' words as empty flattery. Finally, the resolution of the dialogue between God and Job remains puzzling. In his speech from the whirlwind, God delivers a most indirect, if not unsatisfactory, reply to Job's accusations; Job nevertheless eventually submits to God "in dust and ashes" (Job 42:6).

One can, indeed, read the similar paradoxes and unsolvable hermeneutic puzzles forming the very texture of Kafka's work in light of motifs from the Book of Job. Kafka almost literally echoes Job's central question about the justice of God who "destroyeth the perfect and the wicked" (Job 9:22) alike. A diary entry from 1915 notes, in reference to the respective heroes of *America* and *The Trial*, that "the innocent and the guilty [are] both executed without distinction in the end."[12] Many of Kafka's texts also display the paradox of enacting closeness while claiming inapproachability. Among them are "Letter to the Father" and "Before the Law" and certain lesser-known stories, such as "A Little Woman" and "Community," where the narrators display proximity, even intimacy, with an adversary. Similarly, the paradox of Job's treacherously virtuous friends who seek to return Job to the true path can be compared to Kafka's "Little Fable." Opening with the lamentation "ach," this brief text then relates the story of a mouse who, upon following a cat's advice literally to "turn around," is promptly eaten by her.[13] The paradox of Job's submitting himself to God after witnessing a display of God's might can be compared to the perplexing ending of Kafka's *The Judgment*, in which the son submits himself to his father's demonstration of power and, following the father's verdict, drowns himself in the river.

These and other parallels between Kafka's work and the Book of Job are not, however, unique to Kafka and do not capture the specific formal features of his prose, most notably a recurrent stylistic element manifested in his seemingly infinite "buts," "yets," and "howevers." This particular quality—variously termed "infinite regress,"[14] "chiastic recourse,"[15] "oscillating negation,"[16] or "rotating dialectic"[17]—entails rescinding every statement just made, only immediately to take it up again with a barely perceptible shift, and then, often, to retract it yet again within the same sentence. Readings that fail to account for this dearth of resolution, one of the most singular aspects of Kafka's work, tend to resolve the writings' undecidability and become misreadings, revealing more about the interpreters than about Kafka's work.

The early German-Jewish thinkers who alluded to the Book of Job in analyzing Kafka's work all addressed paradoxes that they perceived in an author for whom modernity is a godless world, but for whom, in Günther Anders's words, this experience is a "religious fact."[18] These commentators invariably interpret the Book of Job selectively in ways that resolve its paradoxes and project the resulting "solutions" onto Kafka's work. They thus divest the book of Job and Kafka's writings of their resistance to closure—arguably their most singular and potentially disturbing feature—and become illustrations of larger theological constructs. This feature is particularly striking in Susman's and Brod's portrayals of Kafka and, in a more complex way, of Scholem's presentation. All of these critics refer to the Book of Job in their respective analyses of Kafka, yet they derive from the parallels between the biblical figure and his modern counterpart radically different visions of Kafka and, more generally, of the relationship between God and man in modernity.

## Saving Suffering: Margarete Susman's Judeo-Christian Theodicy

Susman's essay "The Job Problem in Kafka," published in 1929, is among the earliest German studies of Kafka.[19] It offers a philosophical portrait of the Prague author within an interpretation of Job and a Jobean understanding of the fate and mission of the Jewish people. Susman regards Kafka as the ultimate representative of the Jobean experience in modernity. Modern man, moreover, more acutely experienced Job's plight—his suffering, his desperate hope to be heard by God, his search for divine justice. Any understanding of the connection between guilt and suffering, starkly problematized in the Book of Job, now lay entirely beyond human grasp. Life had lost any direction, weight, or meaning. Kafka succeeded artistically, in Susman's words, in finding "the form of this nothing itself" (Hiob, 192). And yet, Susman believes, Kafka's work intimates that a hidden, omnipotent law permeates every aspect of life, even if this law has become absolutely unattainable and indiscernible, leaving us with nothing but chaos and confusion. In short, "Kafka's work envisions a world that is truly abandoned by God—and yet—and this is its great mystery (*Mysterium*)—although He has forsaken it, everything in it is His revelation" (Hiob, 201).

Susman bases her argument upon a dialectic reversal of opposites that resolves the incongruities and contradictions arising both from her readings of the Book of Job and of Kafka and from her comparison of the two. In this essay, her mode of argumentation relies on a pronounced literary device, namely, the striking reiteration of "buts" and "howevers" throughout her text. These conjunctive words introduce logical reversals, and—at least in their appearance and frequency—seem to resemble Kafka's own recurrent use of this stylistic feature. The two authors, in fact, utilize this rhetorical form for an opposite function and effect. In Kafka, it indicates an infinite oscillation between different possibilities, a wavering that never reaches a conclusion. Susman, however, uses this construction uniformly to transform the negativity that she diagnoses in Kafka's vision into a positive affirmation, rendering it a suitable tool for an accomplished theodicy.

In fact, Susman explicitly intended to resolve the paradoxes of the Book of Job and the complexities of Kafka's work into a theodicy. For her, the Book of Job and the writings in its tradition—primarily those of the Jews in exile, and foremost among them Kafka's work—are a justification of the divine order. Susman perceives Jewish thought as a result of the Jews' predicament as victims: "The very fact that [the Jews] suffer, and suffer for reasons unknown . . . imposes on them again and again the attempt to justify God and to explain suffering and guilt and their connection. There is not one great achievement of Judaism that at the bottom is not a theodicy" (Hiob, 188). In this context, via a paradigmatic dialectic reversal, she explains away the Book of Job's central paradox, the suffering of the innocent. Furthermore, she renders Job as the one who, although he "continuously searches for his own guilt" (Hiob, 185), is incapable of finding it because he does not understand, until the end, that this guilt lies not with him personally but in human sinfulness. Susman considers that precisely because of his innocence, Job's suffering gains meaning and becomes a revelation of God's radical Otherness: The suffering of the guilty would be a mere causality and thus could be integrated into human measures. Similarly, even more emphatically, she views Kafka as a representative and spokesman for the poor and suffering. Indeed, her Kafka is more righteous than Job because, unlike Job, Kafka "does not plead for himself but for his world" (Hiob, 195). For Susman, the abysmal suffering of such figures as Kafka's ailing hungry artist, the sickly circus rider, and the failing acrobat effect a reversal, the revelation of the hidden divine power to which we ought to subject our lives.

Through this dialectic reconciliation of opposites, Susman's interpretation of Kafka likewise amplifies and resolves the other central paradoxes present in the Book of Job. Hence, Job's intimate lament to a distant God becomes Kafka's extended monologue addressed solely to Him who, in modern times, has withdrawn completely. Similarly, the paradox of God's acceptance of Job, the blasphemous accuser, and His rejection of Job's friends who had sought to justify the divine order, become, in Susman's essay, a vision of Kafka as the ultimate representative of the Jews, elected by God in spite of—or rather precisely because of—his rendering of a world from which justice has vanished. For Susman, the paradox of Job's submission to God after His inadequate response from the whirlwind—His demonstration of the grandeur of His creation, which in no way answers Job's questioning of God's claim to justice—constitutes the very epiphany of Job's experience of divine revelation. Precisely God's distancing Himself from human understanding turns Job's submission into a full expression of faith. Not Job the rebel but Job the martyr thus becomes the emblematic figure of the Jewish people and the model for Susman's *homo religiosus*.

Susman starkly underscores this point by noting Kafka's abstention from protest in the face of a God who remains inscrutably silent: "*Kafka klagt nicht*," she observes (Hiob, 200). He does not even lament or protest, she explains, because in his world, the distance to God has become so great. So absolute is His withdrawal that there is no longer anyone to listen, let alone answer. That Kafka does not lament is, for Susman, an expression of pure piety. In the most radical reversal of opposites, she hails the reaction of the victim (whom Susman labels "*der Gerichtete*," or the one who is judged), when, like Job, and even more like Kafka, he accepts his fate. "Totally unquestioning submission," she writes, "appears as the only force that at least temporarily shows a way out of total doom" (Hiob, 199). Kafka, like Job, and, by extension, the Jewish people, in taking the suffering of humanity upon himself, paradoxically become(s) a kind of Christ figure, suffering for—and thereby saving—the whole of humanity.

Susman bolsters her interpretation with a mix of Jewish and Christian theologumena. She links Job's questioning of divine justice and his daring accusations against God directly to the legal aspect of Judaism. In her view, the Jews, more than any other people, believe in—and are entitled to expect—divine justice. Susman's idea of Judaism, however, has unmistakable Christian undertones. In contrast to the Talmudic view that the Jews' chosenness depends upon their acceptance of the Torah and its laws, Susman views Jewish election from a Christian viewpoint as a direct correlate of suffering: Their election becomes manifest through their subjection to the sufferings inflicted upon them.

In this view of the Jews' redemptive suffering, Susman envisions their dismal fate as divine retribution for their wrongdoings. Her vision of the Jew in modernity thus echoes the speeches of Job's friends, who justify his suffering as punishment for his sins. In disregarding the fact that God, in his final address from the whirlwind, rejects the friends' false comforting, Susman echoes their attitude, for she considers the greater distance from God that has emerged in modern times to be a punishment for the modern Jews' godlessness and assimilation to modernity. Indeed, as with Job, this punishment is precisely the sign of Jewish election. Taking this analysis a step further in her book from 1946, *Job and the Jewish People*,[20] Susman argues (though referring only sporadically to Kafka) that the Jews' suffering is not only a manifestation of the privilege God has bestowed upon his people but also their very mission in the world. Indeed, any alleviation of their condition as an exilic, homeless people and scapegoat of the world's nations would run counter to this mission. Written in the immediate aftermath of the Holocaust, this work not only displays various problematic implications discernible in Susman's earlier Jobean interpretation of Kafka, but also comes close to a disconcerting justification of the ultimate Jewish suffering in history.

## Bridging the Gap: Max Brod's Positive Jewish Theology

Susman's writings on Kafka and Job circulated widely among her contemporaries, including Felix Weltsch, Hans-Joachim Schoeps, Gershom Scholem, and Max Brod, all of whom referred to her work on the subject. Although Brod did not overtly direct his writings on Kafka against Susman, they nonetheless amount to an attack on her readings of the author. Brod repeatedly invokes the "Job question" and, in his biography of Kafka, quotes extended passages from Job's laments and protests, some of which partially overlap with Susman's citations. Brod, however, implicitly negates the salient parallels Susman posits in her reading of Kafka. He rejects the idea of representative suffering and regards human sinfulness as mere accidental weakness. In this context, doubts about God emerge from a misunderstanding of divine justice. In his only explicit reference to Susman's reading of the relationship between Kafka and Job, Brod contests her historical explanation of the differences between the two. For Brod, these differences derive not from the growing abyss between God and man in modernity; rather, they lie in Job's arrogant certainty about his own integrity and innocence. Kafka, unlike Job, recognized himself as flawed. Susman considers this humility as submission to God's glory. Brod, however, analyzed it merely as a weakness resulting from Kafka's situation, which, in contrast to Susman's glorification of exile, he diagnoses in Zionist terms: "As a member of a people without a land, one lacks the strength to live rightly."[21]

Brod does not attempt to resolve paradoxes through dialectic reversals of extremes; he rather harmonizes such oppositions by allowing them to exist side by side. Brod, like Susman, follows each reference to Job with "but." These are, in fact, "but alsos" and merely introduce the contiguity of seemingly incompatible positions. This occurs paradigmatically in one of Brod's key sentences aligning Job's suffering with the despair pervading Kafka's world: "The majority of Kafka's sentences that disempower man certainly overwhelm the reader. But freedom and hope are *also there!*" (FK, 181; emphasis Brod's). Brod sees Kafka's fiction, as in the Book of Job, as portraying a cruel, immoral God; this seems true, however, only when viewed from the human perspective presented in each work and does not preclude Kafka's belief in a benevolent divine power. In Brod's reading, Kafka asks "*die alte Hiobsfrage*" (FK, 181). Unlike Susman, Brod does not resolve the paradox that Job submits to God despite not having received an adequate answer. Instead, Brod affirms Job's—and more so Kafka's—respective rebellions, *simultaneously* leaving God's justice intact by introducing evil powers that intervene between God and man: Not God but "intermediary figures full of guile and poison" [Zwischeninstanzen voll Tücke und Gift] (FK, 195) are responsible for the world's injustice and cruelty. Moreover, he explains that for Kafka, God is infinitely good, despite any image of him that may emerge through the confusion. The infinity that Brod assigns here to the goodness of Kafka's God may, however, be misplaced; for although Kafka's writings present an idea of infinity, it is of an altogether different sort. It manifests itself with its infinity of "buts" and "yets" as an endlessness of hesitation that never becomes a final judgment. Although he does not deny Kafka's skepticism, Brod specifically repudiates any possibility of its extending to infinity: "An infinite doubt? No." Brod avers, "There was a limit, a very distant limit" (FK, 184).

In alluding to the Book of Job, Brod addresses the same problem that Susman does: namely, the incommensurability of the human and the divine realms. Their approach to this issue, however, reveals a fundamental difference. Susman regards the impossibility of reconciling the human and divine spheres in both the Book of Job and Kafka as the very locus of divine revelation; Brod disputes not only her identification of Job and Kafka but also her understanding of Kafka's theological beliefs. Although Brod, indeed, considers that the Book of Job illustrates the unbridgeable gap between God and man, he sees in Kafka the affirmation of a common ground between them. He finds in Kafka a mere "lack of clarity" [*Undeutlichkeit*] (FK, 183) about the relationship between the two spheres; moreover, he reconciles Kafka's views with the traditional Jewish belief that ethical commandments function as the area of encounter between God and man. According to Brod, Kafka directly expressed in his letters, aphorisms, and diaries his belief that the "mysterious bond between man and the transcendental kingdom of God" (FK, 186) is the very foundation of human existence. In contrast, the pessimism in Kafka's fictional writings is an expression of the punishment suffered by those who have lost their trust in unity with the divine. Indeed, Brod, even more than Susman, echoes Job's friends, who cling to their belief in the causal link between suffering and guilt. With this, he seals his modern theodicy.

### Revealing Nothing: Gershom Scholem's Negative Theology

Explicitly rebuffing all attempts at a theodicy, Gershom Scholem rejects the premises both of Susman's Christological reading and of Brod's positive Jewish theology. He, too, however, is not always immune to the temptations of closure. Scholem referred to Job at various points in his life, most notably around 1918 in his work on Jewish laments and dirges and, during the 1930s, in his epistolary exchange with Benjamin (BK, 63–93). The differences in Scholem's approach to the story of Job at these two stages in his thinking are striking. His later references, which occur primarily in relation to Kafka, rest on the biblical book's content and yield a fixed, determined meaning. His earlier commentary on Job, however, preceded his reading of Kafka and dealt with Job in terms of lament as a genre. It is surprising that these earlier reflections bear greater affinity to Kafka's own "infinite" mode of writing.

Scholem makes fewer but more enigmatic associations between Kafka and the Book of Job than either Susman or Brod; nevertheless, he, too, develops a theological interpretation of Kafka in which references to Job play a significant role. These readings, however, serve primarily to support Scholem's own views of a God who has withdrawn, leaving man in a state of inconsolable despair. In his correspondence with Benjamin, Scholem (BK, 64)[22] advises him to begin with the Book of Job in order better to understand Kafka's work. This, Scholem explained, would enable him to perceive "the possibility to deal in a poetic work with the question of divine judgment," which Scholem regards as "the only topic of Kafka's output" (BK, 64). In a letter to Benjamin written in 1931, Scholem describes Kafka's writings as an attempt at "a paraphrase of divine judgment [*Gottesurteil*] *in [human] language*" (BK, 65; emphasis mine). Scholem's idea of divine judgment, however, differs radically from both Susman's and Brod's. He implicitly discards Susman's dialectic of suffering and election and explicitly rejects Brod's idea of a flawed human perception of divine justice as an illusory theodicy. Scholem similarly rejects Susman's apocalyptic messianism and Brod's more straightforward note of hope; moreover, in his references to the link between Job and Kafka, he develops a melancholic vision that carries traits of a negative theology with a Gnostic bent. This tendency manifests itself in accusations against a God who is absent yet is also the source of the world's injustice and suffering.

In a certain sense, Scholem extends Susman's dialectical logic of opposites even further, but never resolves it into a positive synthesis. Instead, he opens up a perspective onto an infinite and desperate quest that remains unfulfilled. In a letter to Benjamin from 1931, Scholem notes, "Kafka's world is the world of revelation, but of revelation seen from the perspective in which it is returned to its own nothingness" (BK, 74). Whereas this may initially seem to echo Susman's idea of Kafka's world as the "nothing" that permeates modernity, it is, in fact, a far more pessimistic vision, which stops short of Susman's dialectical reversal into salvation. Scholem saw no indications of such a possibility in the present state of the world. In his view, Kafka depicts a world in which "redemption cannot be anticipated." Scholem maintains that one must view Kafka's world in a theological light, albeit one permeated by darkness. "So mercilessly," Scholem writes, "the light of revelation never burnt before" (BK, 65). In an interpretation that seems compatible with Brod's "Jewish" reading, Scholem states, "Kafka incessantly compares human existence with the ideal of absolute justice, which the Jewish tradition symbolizes in the image of divine judgment."[23] Unlike Brod, however, Scholem believes that this comparison precludes both a possible common ground and an encounter between God and man in revealed law.

Apart from his advice to Benjamin, which inaugurated an intense discussion about Kafka marked by various disagreements between the two, Scholem refers most explicitly to the relationship between Job and Kafka in a poem he sent to Benjamin. Titled "With a copy of Kafka's *The Trial*," the poem is a melancholic meditation inspired by Scholem's reading of Kafka's novel. Its fourteen stanzas lament the fate of revelation in a period when God has withdrawn completely and "the great deceit of the world / is now consummated" (*Angel*, 153). The sixth stanza reads:

> Our position has been measured
> On Job's scales with great precision.
> We are known through and through
> As despairing as on the youngest day. (*Angel*, 153)

Scholem's reference to "Job's scales" alludes to a metaphor that occurs twice in the Book of Job. The first image occurs in Job's reply to Eliphaz, when he wishes that his "anguish but be weighed, / and my disaster on the scales be borne. / For now it would be heavier than the sand of the sea. / Thus my words are choked back" (Job 6:3). Job refers to the scales as a metaphor of justice that has become disjointed and buried under the weight of his misery. The metaphor reappears toward the end of the book, when Job asks God to judge him fairly, to be "weighed on fair scales" (Job 31:6). In Scholem's poem, this request remains unanswered, and his reference to the scales draws a parallel between Job's suffering and the weight of desolation he finds in Kafka. The metaphor also suggests the reign of a divine power responsible for this hopeless state. The precision and passive form of the subsequent verses indeed indicate that a higher power is performing the measuring and weighing, but that it is neither within human grasp nor is it just.

This "absent presence" and its finality are confirmed by the transparency suggested in the verse "We are known through and through" (*Angel*, 153): Man has become fully exposed to God's omniscience, yet what ensues is sheer despair. More important, the very form of Scholem's poem repeats and radicalizes the central gestures of the Book of Job, namely, Job's lament about the state of a godforsaken world, his protest against the lack of justice, and his explicit declaration of God's silence, each of which takes the form of a direct address to God. Scholem sustains this paradox throughout the poem, which climaxes in an explicit antitheodicy:

> Your trial began on earth.
> Does it end before your throne?
> You cannot be defended,
> As no illusion holds true here. (*Angel*, 154)

The question posed in the first verses of this stanza could refer both to Job's trial that followed God's wager with Satan and to the inversion of this trial in Job's subsequent accusations against God. Scholem's response to these questions clearly rejects any defense or justification of the divine order. He also formulates this point in another stanza:

> From the center of destruction
> A ray breaks through at times
> But none shows the direction
> The Law ordered us to take. (*Angel*, 154)

This central complaint acknowledges a momentary revelation amid the darkness—undoubtedly a reference to the radiance that shines through the door shielding the law in Kafka's "Before the Law." In pointing to the essence of Jewish teachings [*Lehre*], he suggests, however, that the law it has brought us provides neither sense nor orientation. Scholem, commenting on Kafka in another letter to Benjamin, calls revealed law the "absolutely concrete, which is absolutely impracticable" (BK, 66). This law has burdened man with orders that he cannot possibly fulfill. In a lucid interpretation of Scholem's enigmatic expression, Stéphane Mosès emphasizes the connection between this characterization of the law and Scholem's view of Kafka's mode of writing: "Jewish law, which is defined by its extreme concreteness, the minute precision with which it codifies the slightest aspects of daily conduct . . . reminded Scholem of the endless deliberations of Kafka's characters, their hesitations at the slightest concrete decision" (*Angel*, 159). In this poem, Scholem views the "great precision" of the scales upon which God weighs man's deeds on Judgment Day in the context of a legal system that has retained its oppressive force even as it has lost its function as an existential compass.

In the Book of Job, the most merciless aspect of God's judgment is that He conceals His verdict and leaves Job's questions without resolution. Nevertheless, for Scholem, this openness—in contrast to his earlier references to Job and to Kafka's understanding of his own "endless" writing—terminates in the bleakness of divine judgment, which, in Scholem's poem, has the final word: "Oh, we must live all the same / Until your court will judge us" (*Angel*, 154). The finality suggested in Scholem's poem fails, however, to capture key formal features of Kafka's prose; foremost among them is the impossibility of arriving at any conclusion. Scholem—at least in his interpretation of Kafka—does not account for this absence of resolution, one of the most singular aspects of Kafka's writings. Indeed, Scholem tends to resolve Kafka's irresoluteness in a way that says more about Scholem's concerns at the time he wrote the poem—in particular his wariness about the rise of Fascism in Europe and his disappointment with Zionism— than about Kafka's writings.

In his magisterial essays[24] on Kafka, Walter Benjamin offers a different explanation for the infinite recurrences and the nonclosure that characterize so many of Kafka's texts. Benjamin also refers to Jewish scriptures but not to the Book of Job. In a letter responding to Scholem's poem, he writes that he can fully agree with all the stanzas starting with the seventh; this is the stanza after the verses referring to Job (BK, 76). One can surmise that Benjamin disagreed with Scholem's association of Kafka with the bleak despair Scholem derived from his Jobean references. In response to Scholem's verse "Only your nothingness is the experience / [this time] is entitled to have of you" (BK, 77), Benjamin formulates cautious messianic hopes: "I may relate my interpretive effort to precisely this passage with the following remarks: I endeavored to show how Kafka sought—on the nether side of that 'nothingness,' in its inside lining, so to speak, to feel his way to redemption (BK, 77).[25]

Benjamin finds this concealed spark of hope in Kafka's writings in its affinity with the "Aggadic parts of the Talmud"[26] and their resistance to submit to doctrine or the law, as discussed in the previous chapter. Benjamin differentiates between his own understanding of this postponement and Brod's interpretation of Kafka's "strange, and so often strikingly meticulous, attentiveness to detail" as "a search for perfection" and "the right path" (BK, 77). Indeed, Benjamin considers this form of writing as simultaneously a redeeming gesture of hope and an expression of Kafka's "fear of the end."[27] Whether this end implies death, a verdict, or the conflation of the two is not made explicit. This last possibility is the most plausible: Kafka's *The Trial* ends with Josef K. being brutally executed by two anonymous men who, as the novel's penultimate sentence notes, observe "*die Entscheidung*," the decision: They are watching the man they just killed. Deciding is thus identified with murder, with death. Deferring the end entails postponement of the execution, both in the literal sense suggested in this scene and in a

more general sense of a verdict, the implementation of a judgment, the completion of a procedure or, in an even wider sense, the arrival at a conclusive message
or meaning altogether.

## Another Scholem: The Language of Lament

In his reflections on Job and Kafka, Scholem formulates a vision of modernity
that is as bleak as it is definitive: It is a world in which "the great deceit" has now
been "consummated" (*Angel*, 153). He formulates his description of a godforsaken
world, his protest against the lack of justice, and his explicit assertion of God's
silence as a direct address to God. Permeated with unanswered and unanswerable
questions, and, in contrast to its conclusive, and conclusively negative, content,
this address shows traces of what Scholem, in his earlier writings, had described
as the idea and nature of lament. These traces are found in the poem's daunting
string of questions, which, in the final verse—"Can such a question be raised?"
(*Angel*, 154)—culminates in the *mise en abîme* of questioning the act of questioning. This single yet highly significant sentence in this particular exchange with
Benjamin hints at texts written in Scholem's youth, albeit without mentioning
lament as such. These earlier reflections on Job and lament not only prefigure
Benjamin's thinking about Kafka; they are also closer to Kafka's actual prose than
are Scholem's later writings. His subsequent theological interpretation of Kafka
insists on a negativity that becomes a kind of closure; these early texts, however, deal with a language of deferral that shares key characteristics with Kafka's
prose: It not only postpones accomplishment, resists change and progression, and
thwarts any message or conclusion, but also, ultimately, refuses meaning altogether, even as it correlates its deferral with a logic of ethics, care, and justice.

Immediately after his advice that Benjamin should take Job as a point of
departure in reading Kafka, Scholem mentions "the thoughts [that] I formulated
many years ago in my theses on justice that you know and which, in their relation
to language, would be the leading thread of my reflections on Kafka" (BK, 64).
Scholem is referring here to his "Twelve Theses on the Order of Justice," a text he
wrote in 1918, more than two decades before he composed his commentaries on
Kafka.[28] The theses are derived directly from, and sometimes quote, Scholem's
"On Jonah and the Concept of Justice," written earlier the same year. In the latter
text, he compares the biblical prophet Jonah with Job and argues that Job, unlike
Jonah, has "an inner relation to lament" (*Tagebücher*, 525) because Job asks questions man is not entitled to pose, primarily the question of divine justice. These
questions are not only unanswerable but also subvert the established order and
the very language subtending the system of communication.

In a similar context, Job also figures prominently in several of Scholem's diary
entries from the same period, a time when he was exchanging lengthy letters with

Benjamin about his work on Hebrew scriptures.[29] In one entry, Scholem sketches an argument that he apparently intended to use in a later, more thorough analysis of the Book of Job (*Tagebücher*, 376–78). For Scholem, the book contains an ironic, inverted message that is not stated explicitly; instead, it is conveyed *ex negativo*, for it concerns the legitimacy of questioning divine justice. Job initially seems guilty of asking this question, but, as his question proves neither answerable nor refutable, he is shown to be in the right ("*Hiob ist im Recht*" [*Tagebücher*, 377]). The very form of the book—its endlessly circular dialogues—suggests that the search for divine justice is not a legitimate concern: Instead of replying to Job's ethical question, God shows him the magnificence of His creation. By refusing to answer, God invalidates Job's question (and questioning) and extricates himself from the human idea of justice. What remains for man to do in the face of this withdrawal is to lament; indeed, it is his only appropriate response. "And so [Job] legitimately laments," Scholem writes, "and this lament is infinite in all its dimensions, it is of a higher infinity than life itself" (*Tagebücher*, 378). His conclusion comes strikingly close to one of Kafka's central themes, especially when Scholem compares the Book of Job to a "court in front of which an accusation is continuously being repeated . . . without the judge ever appearing" (*Tagebücher*, 378).

Scholem's references to Job in his early writings culminate in a short text appended to his translation of the third chapter of the Book of Job. This text, probably written in late 1918, is part of a series of comments on his German translations of Hebrew laments and dirges and his more general, theoretical text "On Lament and Dirges" (*Tagebücher*, 544–47). In the Job texts and the appended one on Lament, Scholem reflects on the nature and language of lament, pointing to Job's monologues as a paradigmatic instance of the genre. In the comment to his translation of Job's monologue in which Job curses the day he was born, Scholem distinguishes lament from accusation: Accusation always targets a particular addressee, whereas lament "accuses language itself" as a carrier of meaning, as a goal-oriented mode of communication that transports a message (*Tagebücher*, 545). Scholem defines the characteristic of lament, and Job's lamentation in particular, as "an infinite and cyclical annihilation" (*Tagebücher*, 546) that occurs not as the result of an outside factor (as a meaning bestowed upon its construction), but, rather, from within the language of lament. What occurs in this language, Scholem writes, "is an extraordinary internal liquefaction of the poem, inextricably interconnected with the law of recurrence, which shows this to be the lamentation. In the proper meaning of the poem, the question 'why does He give light to the sufferer?' is not given in order to receive a response. . . . Rather, there is no response to this infinite, plaintively recurring question. Everything in this song recurs" (*Tagebücher*, 546). The recurrence, in fact, is endless.

This ongoing questioning—that expects no answer and is intrinsically infinite—can, as Scholem notes about Job's lament, "never turn into a final verdict" (*Tagebücher*, 546) nor even into a conclusive indictment of God, as his later Kafka poem suggests. Its essence, situated at the limits between language and silence, is deferral itself. In a brief note, Scholem writes, "Deferral in the word, the linguistic principle of lament" [Verstummen: Aufschub im Worte, das sprachliche Prinzip der Klage] (*Tagebücher*, 365). Precisely because lament is an endless and infinite expression, or rather a gesture [*eine Gebärde*], it annihilates its object in a monotonous repetition (as Scholem notes, "all monotonous things are related to lament" [*Tagebücher*, 148]) and it absorbs impending destruction into language itself. In referring to the question of suicide, which Job's wife raises in the Book of Job, Scholem writes, "Lamenting over one's birth signifies the desire for death, but not the act of bringing it about. Judaism, however, does not acknowledge more than the lament about being born. If it recognized more, suicide would have a legitimate place in it. In lament, however, suicide is eliminated through a medium [*Mittleres*], the suicide of language can be reached (and may even be a source of reconciliation?)" (*Tagebücher*, 564).

Lament defers not just suicide. As Scholem notes in his "Twelve Theses on the Order of Justice": "Acting in deferral saves from death" [Im Aufschub handeln errettet vom Tod] (*Tagebücher*, 534). Scholem's idea that lament postpones the execution of suicide and defers death parallels his more general idea about justice. He calls lament, rather enigmatically, "the language that is just in its very principle" (*Tagebücher*, 362). This statement becomes more transparent when considered in the context of the relationship he establishes between justice and deferral. Scholem's "Twelve Theses" contains his most succinct statement about justice: "Justice means: that one may judge, but the executive power must remain radically independent of it. . . . The actual legal order [*Rechtsordnung*] is sublated in the deferral of the executive" (*Tagebücher*, 533). Scholem illustrates this definition of justice with a verse from the Book of Jonah: "And he reflected upon the judgment that he announced he would execute upon them, and executed it not" (Jon 3:10). Scholem's very definition of justice in action (*Tagebücher*, 528), to which he adds the Hebrew *tsedek* [justice], lies in the gesture of deferral: "Deferral turned into deed is justice in action" [Der zur Handlung gewordene Aufschub ist Gerechtigkeit als Tat]. Because this deferral occurs in language, a language of endless recurrence, it cannot be transformed or translated into another language. It is precisely the language of lament that achieves this deferral of the end (*Tagebücher*, 128).

Nothing could be closer to Kafka's "*stehender Sturmlauf*," this intense movement that does not progress, stays itself and leaves everything unchanged, than Scholem's description of the language of lament that, "as far as it is lament, remains always the same" (*Tagebücher*, 129). Indeed, in Scholem's understanding of the language of lament, rather than in his interpretation of Kafka, one finds his greatest affinity to Kafka's writing and to Benjamin's idea of deferral [*Aufschub*]. Unlike Scholem's interpretation of Kafka that dates from the 1930s, in which the infinity of unanswered questions resonates with a negative theology, his early comments on Job prefigure Benjamin's interpretation of Kafka's "infinite" writing as an avoidance of closure. One can illustrate and specify the aptness of Benjamin's insight into Kafka and Scholem's comments on Job's lament through a reading of a particular short text by Kafka that allows the reader to imagine how Kafka would have read the Book of Job.

## Imagining Kafka's Job

A text included in Kafka's letter to Robert Klopstock from June 1921 opens with the statement "I can imagine another Abraham."[30] Kafka's text is an implicit response to his reading of Kierkegaard's reflections in *Fear and Trembling*, on Abraham and the binding of Isaac. Kierkegaard praises Abraham's obedience to God's call as an "infinite resignation that is the last stage before faith"[31] and, in a similar spirit, terms Job a "knight of faith," hailing his surrender to God after His speech from the whirlwind. Kafka never mentions Job, but his conjecture of "another Abraham" may be the closest one can come to imagining how he would have read Job.

Kafka imagines another Abraham, one who would not go to Mount Moriah to sacrifice his beloved son. This Abraham, Kafka writes, "to be sure, would not make it all the way to patriarch, not even to old-clothes dealer" (*Letters*, 285). Like the biblical patriarch, Kafka's "other Abraham" is "a pious man and would be ready to execute the command for his son's sacrifice with the promptness of a waiter" (*Letters*, 285); in contrast to the biblical Abraham, however, Kafka's Abraham, when the time came to carry it out, "would still never be able to perform the sacrifice" (*Letters*, 285). Kafka then describes two distinct scenes that enact different reasons for preventing Abraham from fulfilling the divine order. In the first, Abraham, in an imaginary reply to God, argues that "he cannot get away from home, he is indispensable; the household needs him, there is always something that must be attended to, the house isn't finished" (*Letters*, 285). Later, Kafka continues this phantasmagoria and elaborates on Abraham's excuses for procrastinating rather than obeying God's order. His "other Abraham" now stands in the plural, for he has become a type, embodying an existential attitude. The "other Abrahams: They stand on their building sites and suddenly had to go up on Mount Moriah" (*Letters*, 285). These Abrahams, as imagined by Kafka, are called by God while they are attending to their daily lives: The divine injunction reaches them when they are in the midst of their home, their house, their world building, and they are thereupon ordered to abandon all this in order to serve God. As much as Kafka's "other Abrahams" would otherwise have been willing to oblige, they are too immersed in the care of their "building site" [*Bauplatz*] and will not heed God's call.

Two years after writing this letter, Kafka wrote the story "Der Bau,"[32] the ultimate "infinite" narrative. It consists of a long monologue by a molelike

animal obsessively attending to his burrow. The animal constantly makes obser-
vations and decisions and confirms facts, only to instantly dismiss these with a
"but" or a "however" and turn to a variety of alternatives that quickly suffer the
same fate. The incessant reflections and calculations give expression to an excessive attention to detail and a continuous frustration about never grasping the
whole, suggesting an endless task. The burrow, which can be neither repaired nor
completed, yet also neither abandoned nor truly inhabited, is the perfect image
and embodiment of Kafka's writing, which likewise continuously cancels itself,
thus becoming an infinite process beyond any purpose and result. On the final
pages of the story, the animal, both fearing and hoping for an interruption, hears
a noise and imagines that "someone may be calling it to itself" with an "invitation [it] will not be able to resist."[33] The animal conjectures that the noise he hears
in the burrow stems not from many little animals, but "from one single, large
one."[34] The creature continues to go about its business, however, and the story,
after sixteen closely written manuscript pages and yet another "but," breaks off
in midsentence, suggesting that it could go on forever.

The final sentence of Kafka's first scene in his imagining of an "other Abraham" provides an explanation for this endlessness, an endlessness that prefigures
Benjamin's idea of procrastination precisely in the face of a possible call from a
unique and ominous "someone." Referring to his "other Abrahams," who resist
the invitation of the call to sacrifice because they must attend to their house,
Kafka speculates: "All we can do is suspect that these men *deliberately are not finishing their houses* . . . so as not to have to lift their eyes and see the mountain that
stands in the distance" (*Letters*, 285; emphasis mine). The mountain is Mount
Moriah, where Abraham's sacrifice of his son was to take place; it could, however,
also be Mount Sinai, where the voice of God called out and the Law was revealed.

If one were to imagine Kafka's "other Job" in the likeness of his "other Abraham," it would certainly not be the Job who, after God's speech from the whirlwind, takes on his suffering and submits himself to God in "dust and ashes" (Job
42:6). Nor would it be Job the accuser, who indicts God. Instead, this "other Job,"
like Kafka's "other Abraham," would know of this mountain in the distance; yet
he would not lift his eyes to see it. He would rather turn his lament—an insistent
mourning that is the last possible way of tending to his house—into the very
means of keeping the mountain at a distance. This Job would expect no answer
from God; moreover, he would transform his lament into the poetry that, in fact,
exists in the Book of Job—an ongoing, unanswerable utterance, in what Scholem,
in his reflections on lament, would call a language wrested from silence. Job's
lament points in this direction when he speaks of his misery that is "heavier than
the sand of the sea. / Thus my words are choked back" (Job 6:3). These words
express their own impossibility and are as infinite as the silence from which they
emerge. They would constitute the ongoing lament of Kafka's "other Job," just as
their endlessness would avert the verdict and closure. Likewise, because there

is always one more thing "that must be attended to" (*Letters*, 285), because the infinite details of any situation cannot be exhausted, any final judgment would amount to injustice;[35] in short, the need to attend to worldly cares requires the relinquishing of any claim to finality. Yet Kafka does not end there.

"But take another Abraham" (*Letters*, 285). These first words of Kafka's second Abraham scene—a classroom with a teacher who punishes and rewards—introduce yet another argument for an Abraham inclined to refuse, or resist, the divine call. This Abraham, too, is a pious man, "who certainly wants to carry out the sacrifice properly and, in general, correctly senses what the whole thing is about, but cannot imagine that he was the designated one. . . . He does not lack the true faith, for he has this faith; he wants to sacrifice in the proper manner, if only he could believe he was the designated one" (*Letters*, 285). This Abraham, uncertain that he is indeed the elect, the one who has been called, fears making himself ridiculous; he envisages "the world would laugh itself sick over him. . . . An Abraham who comes unsummoned! . . . It is as if at the end of the year, when the best student was solemnly about to receive a prize, the worst student rose in the expectant stillness and came forward from his dirty back bench because he has misheard, and the whole class burst out laughing" (*Letters*, 286). Just as Kafka's "other Abraham" hides in the last row of the class, his "other Job" would forego the privilege: In the biblical book, Job asks God to avert his attention from him: "Am I the Sea, or the Dragon, that you set a watch over me?" (Job 7:12), and "Will You not look away from me for a while?" (Job, 7:19). No longer being singled out by God, no longer being the elect would save him from sacrifice and suffering. Kafka's Job would be the "other" of Susman's: namely, the Job, the Kafka, the Jewish people elected in and through suffering. Indeed, Kafka imagines even this possibility. In the final lines of his Abraham text, a commenting narrator, perhaps Kafka himself, focuses on the teacher who distributes rewards and assigns punishments. The narrator's words raise the possibility that Abraham has made no mistake: "he has not heard wrong; for his name was actually spoken, because the teacher intended to accompany the reward of the best by the punishment for the worst" (*Letters*, 286). This prospect brings even Kafka's ongoing ruminations to a chilling halt: He offers only one, final comment about this authority who designates suffering—bearing the punishment of sinful humanity—as a reward for the elect: "Terrible things—enough" (*Letters*, 286).

## Slavoj Žižek on Job and Kafka

Kafka's horrified rejection of a theodicy based on an essentially Christian sacrificial logic of representative and redemptive suffering[36] does not imply the rejection of divine power per se. Nor does the Abraham imagined by Kafka negate God's existence, but, like his biblical namesake, and not so differently from Job, he argues with Him. Similarly, Kafka does not present his Abraham's ultimate resistance to complying with the divine commandment as heresy or transgression; Abraham merely "politely" apologizes as he diverts his attention away from his divine interlocutor to his worldly tasks.

Unlike Kafka, who shudders as he envisions the possibility of justifying suffering as a mark of election, some recent Marxist thinkers who adhere to a Christian political theology rehabilitate Christ as the elected redeemer and present his suffering for mankind as a revolutionary event. Among the most prominent of these intellectuals is Slavoj Žižek, a Slovenian philosopher and cultural critic associated with the "new Paulines." Although Žižek does not link Kafka and Job directly, he assigns these two figures an aligned role in his grand design of a renewed, revolutionary Christianity. In this scheme, Judaism retains a major role: by upholding the (illusion of a) supreme sovereign, it makes it possible to overthrow him.

Echoing old supersessionist beliefs with a decidedly new twist, Žižek asserts that the true core of Christianity is revolutionary in that Christ's death on the cross reveals God's powerlessness and thereby dismantles His sovereignty. Judaism, by contrast, stubbornly holds on to its old, legalistic beliefs and legitimizes divine sovereignty against all odds, including its own awareness of God's impotence. Žižek, indeed, contends that Judaism, as the Book of Job demonstrates, was always aware of God's powerlessness, but concealed this insight in order to ensure the survival of its faith. Christ's death on the cross brings the secret of God's impotence out into the open. This is, Žižek writes, "why Christianity can occur only after Judaism: it reveals the horror [of God's impotence] first confronted by the Jews."[37] This revelation is, for Žižek, "the Christian breakthrough itself" and Christianity, therefore, is "the true religion of revelation."[38] His interpretation of the monotheistic tradition also informs his reading of the Book of Job and his cursory interpretation of Kafka's *The Trial*.

"The key to Christ," Žižek writes, "is provided by the figure of Job, whose suffering prefigures that of Christ."[39] For Žižek, "the almost unbearable impact of the Book of Job resides not so much in its narrative frame," which indeed supports a theodicy, "but in its final outcome,"[40] which ensues because of God's speech from the whirlwind. Žižek describes it as "empty boasting," and, in typically irreverent fashion that invokes contemporary popular culture, as a "kind of cheap Hollywood horror show with lots of special effects,"[41] in which God acts like one whose limitations have become manifest and who pathetically but ineffectively tries to save face. The Book of Job, Žižek writes in an insightful remark, "provides what is perhaps the first exemplary case of the critique of ideology in human history, laying bare the basic discursive strategies of legitimizing suffering: Job's properly ethical dignity resides in the way he persistently rejects the notion that his suffering can have any meaning."[42] In linking Job's refusal of theodicy to Christ, Žižek's reading of the Book of Job performs a questionable reversal of the relationship between Judaism and Christianity: It is now Judaism that holds on to a theodicy, whereas Christianity discloses it as a lie. Christianity, for Žižek, is no longer an affirmation of Christ's (and, according to Susman, by extension, of Jewish) "representative suffering" that justifies God in the face of human misery, but resembles the child who reveals that the emperor has no clothes. Like Job, Christ on the cross laments that God does not come to his rescue. Because Christ, however, is ultimately an intrinsic part of God himself, his suffering along with his cry "Why hast Thou forsaken me?" is a transgressive, revolutionary act signifying the demise of divine sovereignty. In a strange way, however, this inversion represents another theodicy: Suffering remains a mark of election that is justified as a means of liberating humankind from the supreme authority: it results in deicide, albeit one initiated by God himself.

If Job is, for Žižek, a precursor of Christ, and the Book of Job a radical unmasking of divine authority, Kafka is one of his successors and his writings a reenactment of the Christian deicide—the demise of the (Jewish) division between man and God as the absolute Other. In one of his characteristic radical paradoxes inspired by Jacques Lacan's theory of desire, Žižek contends that Kafka's greatness lies in his "trespassing of the frontier that separates the vital domain from the judicial domain."[43] As in the "cheap Hollywood horror show" in the Book of Job, the judges' law books that turn out to be pornographic booklets in Kafka's *The Trial* unmask the dignity of authority equated with the ultimate law-giving authority, the Jewish God. Kafka's transgressive gesture is, for Žižek, like Job's, like Christ's lament, a revelation of God's "ungodliness" and a revolutionary, liberating act: It frees one from the oppressive authority of the law conceived in Lacanian terms as the Law of the Father. Precisely because of his Jewish background, however, Kafka performs this transgression in a unique way that "depends," Žižek writes,

> upon his Judaism: the Jewish religion marks the moment of the most radical separation of these domains [of sexuality and sacredness]. In all previous religions, we encounter a place, a domain of sacred enjoyment (in the form of ritual orgies, for example), whereas in Judaism the sacred domain is evacuated of all traces of vitality and the living substance is subordinated to the dead letter of the Father's law. Kafka trespasses the divisions of his inherited religion, flooding the judicial domain, once again, with enjoyment.[44]

Seemingly, the only instances in which it is possible to save the Jewish tradition is where it lets itself be reduced to what is to be overcome. The Book of Job and Kafka's writings can, in turn, be saved for modernity insofar as they are collaborators in this operation. The Jewish "critical modernity" imagined by Kafka in his letter to Robert Klopstock, however, does not consist of overcoming, transgressing, or trespassing. Kafka's Abrahams may, indeed, avert their eyes from the "sacred domain"—the mountain in the distance—but they seem to find sufficient "vitality and living substance" in building their forever unfinished dwelling, of which the judicial domain conceived as an endless striving for a just order may be a part.

# PART III

# MESSIANIC LANGUAGE

# 7  Pure Languages: Benjamin and Blanchot on Translation

WALTER BENJAMIN AND Maurice Blanchot are considered two of the most important and idiosyncratic theorists and literary critics of the twentieth century. Although their writings address many similar topics and concerns, their affinity is far from obvious and has remained largely unexamined. On the one hand, there is Benjamin, the German-Jewish thinker, who was persecuted by the Nazis and committed suicide in 1940; his work, first marked by Jewish theology, then by an idiosyncratic Marxism, is considered the main inspiration for the Critical Theory of the Frankfurt School. On the other hand, there is Blanchot, the writer and thinker from the heartland of France, who, in the 1930s—years when Benjamin prophesized the impending catastrophe of Fascism in Europe—associated with the French nationalist right wing and whose political thinking took a radical turn after the war. He subsequently became a participant in the antiauthoritarian movement of 1968, a staunch critic of antisemitism, an admiring commentator on the Jewish tradition, and a major precursor of deconstruction. A closer look at Blanchot's slim but significant reception of Benjamin's thought sheds light on the precarious afterlife of its Jewish dimension.

Benjamin does not seem to play a major role in Blanchot's oeuvre, but the French thinker evidently read at least some of the work of the man whom he calls "this excellent essayist." He mentions Benjamin explicitly on three occasions. The first is in the short text "A Rupture in Time: Revolution," published in 1968 in his *Political Writings*; the second is in reflections about the aura of the work of art in the chapter "Ars Nova" in *The Infinite Conversation* (1969). The third and by far most detailed and important reference to Benjamin appears in "Translating" (Traduire), which Blanchot wrote during the same period and is included in his collection of essays, *Friendship*, published in 1971. In this text, Blanchot states that Benjamin's important essay from 1921, "The Task of the Translator" [Die Aufgabe des Übersetzers], was the inspiration and source of his own reflections on translation. Blanchot took three pages of notes while reading Benjamin's essay.[1] They consist exclusively of selected passages from this text, which Blanchot translated into French and partially incorporated into his own essay on translation.[2] As translated passages of Benjamin's essay on translation, these notes are particularly revelatory of how Blanchot's practice of translation relates to the theoretical reflections he derived from his reading of Benjamin's essay. Because translation is a topic that encompasses questions of language, history, and politics, these notes and the essay "Translating" are indicative of central similarities and differences between the two thinkers. This applies in particular to the treatment of the Jewish tradition in their respective approaches to translation.

In "The Reception of the Essay on Translation in the French Sphere," Alexis Nouss severely criticizes several authors who have discussed Benjamin's essay—George Steiner, Henri Meschonnic, and others—but he praises Blanchot's article "Translating," insisting on the Frenchman's affinity with the German-Jewish thinker. Nouss writes, "Nothing could signify better the accuracy and elegance with which [Blanchot] was able to render the theses expressed [in Benjamin's essay]. His lines articulate as closely as possible the two aspects [of this essay] that, we have underscored on several occasions, are lacking in the works previously examined: the revelation of differences in the historico-messianic becoming of languages."[3]

Significantly, Nouss notes the alleged accuracy of Blanchot's rendition of Benjamin's theses by emphasizing "the revelation of differences" among languages, a point on which Benjamin and Blanchot indeed agree. Nouss eschews, however, the major issues on which they differ, namely, the implications of what he calls the "historico-messianic" dimension of Benjamin's theory of translation. The messianic aspect of this theory cannot be reduced to a mere "becoming of languages," as Nouss seems to suggest. It is, instead, oriented to redemption that transcends any historical origin and development of languages. In Benjamin's philosophy of language, this redemptive element is manifest in the idea of a "pure language" [reine Sprache], a concept first elaborated in his major essay from 1916, "On Language as Such and the Language of Man" [Über Sprache überhaupt und die Sprache des Menschen]. Read in conjunction with this essay, "The Task of the Translator" reveals Benjamin's view of the task of the translator who, through retrospection and anticipation, can bring about the appearance of this pure language, which is at once a paradisiacal "Ursprache" and the messianic language of a future and accomplished redemption.[4] The degree of proximity to this redeemed state of language[5] provides the measure of the historical becoming of languages, in which translation participates.

From the outset, Blanchot explicitly presents his article "Translating" as a reflection on Benjamin's text: "From one of Walter Benjamin's essays, in which this excellent essayist speaks to us of the task of the translator," writes Blanchot in the first paragraph, "I will draw several remarks on this particular form of our literary activity" ("Translating," 57). Although the introduction prepares the reader for an annotated summary of the main ideas of Benjamin's theory of translation, the essay proves instead to be a significant variation and partly even a rejection of Benjamin's views. Blanchot's distortions and dismissals of Benjamin's text occur precisely in those passages that deal with elements derived from the Jewish tradition. Blanchot's notes reveal the slight shifts that enable him in "Translating" to formulate his own thoughts by interweaving them with those of Benjamin. He then arrives at a position one could consider nearly opposed to the one occupied by his imaginary interlocutor.

Strikingly, the two authors meet, as Alexis Nouss notes accurately, where they envision the effect of a virtually insurmountable difference between languages. As I shall demonstrate, however, their crucial dispute concerns the most important term of their convergence, the key expression present in both texts but envisioned in a fundamentally different manner: that of a pure language made perceptible by what they consider a true translation. Indeed, the two authors similarly contest a standard approach. Blanchot and Benjamin regard the translator's task as consisting of work that resists transmission, reproduction, and the representation of meaning. Both question the usual concept of translation as transferring the content of one language into another in order to make a work accessible to a reader who does not understand the original language. Both consider that the tensions of inter- and intralinguistic difference, not the communicability of languages, constitute the essence and the active realm of translation. One can thus speak of a "same otherness": a common attraction to alterity—and a shared dismissal of the idea that information should be transferred as accurately as possible in order to ensure the communication of a unique and circumscribed meaning. On the other hand, they disagree about the possibility of transcending this difference through a pure language. The two authors conceptualize this notion so differently that one can speak of an "other sameness"—of fundamentally divergent ideas about the nature of a true, unified, indivisible, and absolute language, devoid of the mediation and imprecision that characterize existing languages. Both Benjamin and Blanchot believe that existing languages are imperfect and incomplete—not only in relation to one another but also intrinsically—and that this deficiency is revealed through translation. The two authors differ in the way that they see pure language offering harmonious unification and perfect completion. This "other sameness" and "same otherness" are manifest in their respective approaches to three domains or principal arenas of inquiry: the status of the subject involved in translation, the relation between translation and the literary work, and, above all, the origin and the τέλος [telos] of translation. This last question, which addresses the concept of a "pure language" most directly, opens up the greatest divergence between Benjamin's and Blanchot's views: It concerns the particular intellectual, philosophical, and cultural tradition in which this idea of an originary and ultimate language is embedded. Blanchot's notes introduce all three aspects of their differing approaches.

Let us consider, for example, a key passage in which Benjamin defines the task of the translator and then its translation in Blanchot's notes. In both texts, the translator's task lies in the interval, the gap, the difference between languages.

The two authors' visions of this task coincide where the confrontation with the foreign language entails breaking the boundaries of the translator's own language, but they attribute different roles to the translator. Benjamin does not characterize this role primarily as a concrete act but instead as a particular disposition, as receptivity rather than activity (cf. "Aufgabe," 19). In Blanchot's notes, the translator's task entails not merely fostering the emergence of pure language but also actively crossing the boundaries between languages.

Blanchot's translated note reveals another crucial difference: Whereas pure language, according to Benjamin, is *"gebannt"*—banned, exiled—in the foreign language, it is imprisoned—*"gefangen"*—in the original work. Refraining from presenting the poetic work of art as a prison, Blanchot contracts these two aspects of pure language into a single one and speaks of the "imprisonment in the foreign language." Blanchot also drops the suggestion of messianic redemption that the word used by Benjamin—*"erlösen"* (redeem)—connotes, retaining nothing but the notion of liberation, which in German would be *"Befreiung."* Moreover, Blanchot considers that this liberation has already taken place (he uses the past form *"était"* [was] to translate Benjamin's present *"ist"*), having occurred when pure language passed into the translator's own. Benjamin, however, considers that pure language can only momentarily appear through the process of translation. It cannot be fixed and certainly cannot be transposed into an existing language, as Blanchot suggests; one can only anticipate it messianically, in a fleeting moment in the course of translating. As the ultimate aim in the passage between existing languages, pure language does not happen: It is the ultimate messianic fulfillment that is yet to come. In this paradigmatic passage, one sees the differences that I shall delve into further: Blanchot highlights the action of the translator, whereas Benjamin emphasizes the process of translation. Blanchot omits everything in Benjamin's text that might seem to call the literary work into question. Above all, Blanchot distances himself from the redemptive and messianic finality of pure language toward which the entire Benjaminian theory of language tends.

## Translator or Translation?

Blanchot begins his article "Translating" with the rhetorical question "Do we know all that we owe to translators and, even more, to translation?" (57). It is even more striking, therefore, that, in his notes, he translates the word *Übersetzung* [translation], which designates an intrinsic phenomenon of language in Benjamin, with "translator" in the majority of instances, insisting on the translator's active and creative role. For example, to describe the effect of translation, Benjamin evokes the image of an echo resonating in a forest. In Benjamin, it is translation that makes the echo resonate; in Blanchot, it is the subject aiming at the foreign language, namely, the translator.

Benjamin also emphasizes the distinction between the practical question of finding an adequate translator, which he considers minor, and the fundamental aspect of the potential translatability of a work, which is inherent in it, to the point of being independent of human intervention. In this spirit, Benjamin begins his essay with a well-known paragraph denying that the work of art—and, even more so, its translation—is addressed to an audience, a spectator, or a reader. He discusses concepts of relationship that maintain their "foremost significance . . . if they are not from the outset used exclusively related to man"[6] [besten Sinn . . . wenn sie nicht von vorne herein ausschließlich auf den Menschen bezogen werden] ("Aufgabe," 10). In this passage, which Blanchot omits, Benjamin introduces another sphere, one where a transcendent, namely messianic, task of translation will take place, a domain beyond mankind that prepares the theological aim of his discourse. In Benjamin, this preliminary remark leads to the explicit reference to the "realm in which it [a claim unfulfilled by man] *is* fulfilled: God's remembrance" [ein Gedenken Gottes] (Translator, 254; "Aufgabe," 10). The only time that Blanchot mentions the divinity—a reference that does not appear in his notes—is in the article where he calls the translator, who wants to reach the heavens like the builders of the Tower of Babel, an "enemy of God" ("Translating," 58).

Several times, Benjamin contends that the potential of translation to point to pure language inheres in existing languages, that it is "*verborgen*," hidden in the works ("Aufgabe," 12, 14). The messianic task of translation thus occurs in the passage from one language to the other; the translator acts as a medium rather than one creating out of his consciousness or will. In Blanchot's notes, we read: "La traduction ne tend à exprimer que le rapport le plus intime entre deux langues: elle ne peut révéler cette mystérieuse relation, ni la restituer, se contentant de la représenter en l'actualisant sur un mode inchoatif ou intentionnel." [Translation does not tend to express anything but the most intimate relationship between two languages: it can neither reveal nor restore that mysterious relationship but rather settles for representing it, by actualizing it in an inchoate or intentional mode.]

In his translation, Blanchot substitutes the term "mystérieux" for "verborgen" (hidden) and, at other times, when this word or analogous terms appear in Benjamin's German, he writes "énigmatique" (enigmatic). His choice causes this aspect of pure language—which, as the word "*verborgen*" suggests, resides *in potentia* in the relationship between existing languages and can be revealed through translation—to disappear. Even more important, Blanchot translates "*herstellen*" in Benjamin's remark on the impossibility "dieses verborgene Verhältnis . . . her[zu]stellen" ("Aufgabe," 12) [the impossibility to create this hidden relationship] with "restituer" [to restore]. Whereas Benjamin's verb suggests that the translator cannot create this relationship, Blanchot's implies the impossibility of returning to a prior state. In Benjamin's theory, however, precisely the return to a paradisiacal language orients his messianic anticipation.

In "On Language as Such and on the Language of Man," Benjamin describes Adamic language as a "language of names" (*Namenssprache*) (*Gesammelte Schriften* vol. 2, pt. 1: 146): God gave Adam the ability to name things, but Adam is not a creator; he is above all "*sprachempfangend*" (*Gesammelte Schriften* vol. 2, pt. 1: 150), the recipient of the divine word. For Benjamin, the translator is the medium for the divine word rather than a mediator ("*Mittler*" or "*Vermittler*"). This earlier essay, in particular, which is intimately related to the essay on translation, indicates that these are explicitly negative terms in Benjamin's work. The same negative associations appear in his important article on Goethe's *Wahlverwandtschaften*. In the novel, a go-between called "Mittler" forces compromises and thus eliminates the singularity of opposite viewpoints. Benjamin describes this personage as the devil incarnate. This derogatory aspect of mediation vanishes in Blanchot's translation of the first passage, which he retains in his notes and which is crucial for Benjamin's formulation: "Was 'sagt' denn eine Dichtung? Was *teilt sie mit*? Sehr wenig dem, der sie versteht. Ihr Wesentliches ist nicht *Mitteilung*, nicht Aussage. Dennoch könnte diejenige Übersetzung, welche *vermitteln* will, nichts *vermitteln* als die *Mitteilung*—also Unwesentliches. Das ist denn auch ein Erkennungszeichen der schlechten Übersetzungen" ("Aufgabe," 9, my emphasis).

In these few lines, Benjamin repeats variations on the word "Mittler": "mitteilen," "vermitteln," "Mitteilung." Having omitted "was teilt sie mit" in his notes, Blanchot translates: "Que dit une oeuvre littéraire? Très peu à qui la comprend. Son rôle essentiel n'est ni de communiquer ni d'énoncer. Une traduction qui se veut communication ne communique que la *transmission*, cad l'inessentiel. C'est le trait de la mauvaise traduction." [What does a literary work say? Very little to the one who understands it. Its essential role is neither to communicate nor to express anything. A translation that wishes to be communication communicates nothing but *transmission*, that is to say, the inessential. This is the feature of a bad translation (My emphasis)].

While preserving the essential meaning of Benjamin's sentences, Blanchot not only ignores his emphasis on the negative connotation of words from the same root as "*Vermittlung*," but also uses the word "transmission" as if it were a synonym of "*Mitteilung*." In the course of Blanchot's sentence, this word becomes glossed as "the inessential," whereas the German word for "transmission" has, for Benjamin, positive connotations. Transmission, in the sense of *Tradierung*, occurs through the medium of translation and, in contrast to *Vermittlung*, it resists any voluntary and—especially from the messianic point of view—premature synthesis.

This important difference between Blanchot's emphasis on the translator and Benjamin's emphasis on translation and Blanchot's surprising effacement of

Benjamin's rejection of any voluntary and premature synthesis is starkly evident in the article "Translating." Almost in opposition to Benjamin's text, Blanchot renders the translator a veritable hero, precisely as a result of his "pouvoir unificateur" [unifying power] and his "pur pouvoir d'unifier" [pure power of unifying] ("Traduire," 73). In the first and last paragraphs of his article, Blanchot praises translators as "men who valiantly enter into the enigma that is the task of translating," and as "hidden masters of our culture" ("Translating," 57). Comparing them to "Hercules drawing together the banks of the sea" ("Translating," 59), Blanchot, like Benjamin, though very differently, ends with a description of a particular poet-translator, Hölderlin, who advanced "fearlessly" [*téméraire-ment*] toward the abyss of madness. Benjamin perceives the work of translation as a linguistic event independent of a subject or a deliberate action; Blanchot, by contrast, understands translation as a heroic individual act. The two visions converge, however, in their opposition to the view of the translator as a rational and conscious Kantian subject. For both Benjamin and Blanchot, translation opens the horizon toward what Blanchot explicitly calls "a state that is other" ("Translating," 59), but this state would be messianic for Benjamin and mad according to Blanchot.

## Translator and Poet

Both Benjamin and Blanchot begin with the literary work in thinking through the nature of translation, but the role and the signification they accord it differ fundamentally. In "Translating," Blanchot writes that translation is the "forme originale et si l'on continue de dire à tort ou à raison: il y a ici les poètes, là les romanciers, voire les critiques, tous responsables du sens de la littérature, il faut compter au même titre les traducteurs, écrivains de la sorte la plus rare, et vraiment incomparables" ("Traduire," 69) [original form; and if one continues to say, rightly or wrongly: here are the poets, and there the novelists, indeed the critics, all of whom are responsible for the meaning of literature, then one must take into account in the same way the translators, writers of the rarest sort and truly incomparable ("Translating," 57)].

Benjamin, on the other hand, attaches importance of an entirely different order and magnitude to translation. He accentuates the difference between writer and translator in a metaphysical sense. In a passage that Blanchot does not include in his notes, Benjamin distinguishes between the translator's and the poet's tasks, and he maintains that translation exerts more power on language than the poet does. Whereas translation aims at language as such, in its totality, the poetic work [*Dichtwerk*] concerns itself only with the relations among specific contents. Translation thus has an impact of an order transcending the work of poetry ("Aufgabe," 16), one that is simultaneously historical and messianic.

Benjamin considers that history manifests itself in the survival of works through translation, but what is at stake cannot be reduced to the renewal of the works. Rather, translation aims at pure language, which will, however, arrive only at the messianic end of time, when pure language will correspond to redemption in its totality. Translation, the medium for the process that anticipates this state, is destined to dissolve there after it has accomplished this task. In contrast to the poetic work, translation is oriented, for Benjamin, toward this final stage of language. Omitting the idea of a final and definitive phase, Blanchot translates thus: "Toutefois, ds la traduction l'original connaît une nouvelle croissance, il s'élève jusqu'à une atmosphère plus haute et plus pure." [However, in translation, the original experiences new growth, it rises toward a higher and purer atmosphere.] For Blanchot, too, translation "se vide de sa valeur" [is emptied of its worth], but he regards the survival of the work as more important. Likewise, Benjamin distinguishes the intention of the poet, whom he characterizes as "*naiv, erst, anschaulich,*" [spontaneous, primary, manifest] from that of the translator, who is "*abgeleitet, letzt, ideenhaft*" [derivative, ultimate, ideational] ("Aufgabe," 16). In his translation, Blanchot reverses the order, giving the final word to poetry. By translating "anschaulich," a term that Benjamin subordinates to the ideational, to the very idea of translation, as "nourrie d'intuitions" [nourished by intuition], Blanchot displaces Benjamin's consistent emphasis on the visual. He thus suggests a contrast between cognitive or rational functions and the intuition of the creator, giving priority to the poet.

This difference gains its full significance when Blanchot translates those passages where Benjamin explicitly approaches the messianic aim of translation. Benjamin writes of the work's longing for the completion of language [die große Sehnsucht nach Sprachergänzung] ("Aufgabe," 18). In his translation of this great desire, this hope to witness the way languages complement each other—Benjamin's ultimate messianic aim—Blanchot accentuates the transformative force of the original: "sa grande nostalgie de voir perfetionner [sic] sa propre langue" [its great nostalgia to witness its own language perfected]. The divergence of priorities between Benjamin's messianic hope for the unification of incomplete languages through the medium of translation and Blanchot's articulation of nostalgia for the completion of the translator's *own* language is astounding. It is related directly to the theological dimension of Benjamin's text, from which Blanchot keeps his distance.

## Two "Pure Languages"?

This difference, which one could consider in terms of transcendence and immanence or of theology and poetics, has weighty consequences, which manifest themselves in the ultimate aim of Blanchot's article "Translating." One can already discern them in his notes. Blanchot's mistranslation or outright omission in his notes of certain key passages from Benjamin's essay, especially those that refer to the messianic tradition and to Jewish mysticism, bring out this significance. Benjamin's "pure language" comes principally from the Jewish—biblical and kabbalistic—tradition. References to this notion abound throughout Benjamin's oeuvre, beginning with his interpretation of Genesis in "Über die Sprache überhaupt und über die Sprache des Menschen." In that essay, he describes Adamic language, which is distinguished by an absolute correspondence between the word and what it designates; the dispersion of languages after the destruction of the Tower of Babel; and the fall that leads to the arbitrary nature of the sign.[7]

Benjamin returns to pure language in the last notes that he wrote in 1940 in preparation for his theses on the philosophy of history. In those notes, he speaks about a universal language that can come into being only with the coming of the Messiah. If a paradisiacal state is at stake in his first references to a pure language, these last writings are essentially messianic and directed toward a future. In his article "Translating," Blanchot briefly takes up Benjamin's biblical and messianic allusions of pure language, but the tone is different, and the transformation of this concept in his writing proves radical. In "Translating," he mentions in passing the biblical story of the Tower of Babel—where, let us remember, the translator is identified as the "enemy of God" ("Translating," 58). He distances himself, however, from most of Benjamin's references to the Jewish tradition in his essay, including pure language, which, moreover, Blanchot most frequently terms "language in the pure state." In Blanchot's formulation, it still remains language though in a different "state," whereas for Benjamin, it is a metaphysically different language altogether. In his essay, Blanchot not only radically alters Benjamin's concept of divinely inspired Adamic language that has a messianic goal but he places it in an entirely different, in some contexts even antagonistic, tradition.

"In the past," Blanchot writes somewhat disparagingly, "one believed it possible thus to return to some originary language, the supreme language that it would have sufficed to speak in order to speak truly. Benjamin retains something of this dream" ("Traduire," 70). Blanchot expresses his skepticism—even a certain disdain—toward this belief by paraphrasing Benjamin's theory subsequently in the subjunctive. He concludes dismissingly that it is "visiblement" [clearly] a matter of "un jeu utopique d'idées" [a utopian play of ideas] ("Traduire," 70). Indeed, Blanchot insists that Benjamin is suggesting something else: "Every translator lives by the difference of languages; every translation is founded upon this difference even while pursuing, or so it appears, the perverse design of suppressing it ("Translating," 58).

Benjamin considers that the difference between languages that the translator confronts enables translation to effect the revelation of a messianic potential, but Blanchot inverts the order of things. According to Benjamin, this difference constitutes the prerequisite for the translator's messianic task of exposing the incompleteness of existing languages and, through an inverse dialectic, revealing and anticipating through this lack their future unification in a pure language. The translations of passages from Benjamin's essay in Blanchot's notes already indicate the ways in which Blanchot distances himself from this idea. When Benjamin speaks of the intimate relationship among *all* languages that translation expresses, Blanchot translates thus: "le rapport le plus intime *entre deux* langues" [the most intimate relationship *between two* languages (my emphasis)], thus minimizing the totality and the completeness that, for Benjamin, represents the τέλος of translation. Where Benjamin invokes "das große Motiv einer Integration der vielen Sprachen zur einen wahren" [the great motif of integrating the many languages into one true language] ("Aufgabe," 16), Blanchot translates this vision of an absolute unification of dispersed languages with an integration that is only partial and—introducing a subjunctive form that is absent in Benjamin's essay—conditional. Blanchot renders this passage as: "the grandiose intention to integrate a *plurality of languages into a single language that would be* the real one" (my emphasis).

Blanchot's choice to distance himself from Benjamin's explicit messianism expresses itself most clearly in his translation of Benjamin's formulation "das messianische Ende ihrer Geschichte [der Sprachen]" ("Aufgabe," 14) as "une sorte de terme messianique" [a sort of messianic term]. Recopying a few sentences from Mallarmé, which Benjamin quotes in French in support of his own thesis of pure language, Blanchot replaces an adjectival phrase that further determines the feminine substantive "la [langue] suprême" with the masculine abstract substantive "le suprême." This is, no doubt, an error of haste, but even if unintentional, it transposes Benjamin's citation of Mallarmé's words into an unspecified, absolute "supreme" that no longer refers to the linguistic phenomenon at the heart of Benjamin's messianic thinking.

Blanchot obfuscates the passages where Benjamin refers explicitly to a messianism inspired by Jewish mysticism. He thus omits an important phrase in which Benjamin describes how translation participates in the messianic harmonization of languages into one pure language in terms of the "Scherben eines Gefäßes" [shards of a vessel] ("Aufgabe," 18). This undoubtedly alludes to the kabbalistic notion of the breaking of the vessels that corresponds to the end of the paradisiacal state of man and language and suggests the hope of *tikun olam*, the messianic healing of the world. This image links Benjamin's text inextricably to the tradition of Jewish mysticism. Benjamin associates existing languages with these shards, which, in order "to be glued together must match one another in the smallest details, although they need not be like one another. In the same way a translation, instead of imitating the sense of the original, must lovingly and in detail incorporate the original's way of meaning, thus making both the original and the translation recognizable as fragments of a greater language, just as fragments are part of a vessel" (Translator, 260). Blanchot abridges and translates thus: "Au lieu de s'identifier au sens du texte, la traduction doit, par un mouvement d'amour qui s'étend au détail, incorporer ds sa propre langue le mode de visée qui était celui de l'original." [Instead of identifying with the meaning of the text, translation must, through a movement of love that extends to detail, incorporate in its own language the mode of aiming that belonged to the original.] The reference to the shards of the vessel has disappeared.

More important is what disappears completely both in Blanchot's notes and in his article. Blanchot's last note includes a translation of the passage from Benjamin's essay in which he invokes Hölderlin's translation of Sophocles' *Oedipus* and *Antigone*. Benjamin conceives of these translations, which Hölderlin carried out literally, disregarding German syntax and forfeiting clear comprehensibility, as "prototypes of their form" (Translator, 262) [*Urbilder ihrer Form*] ("Aufgabe," 21). This destruction of intelligible meaning through the "Wörtlichkeit" (literalness) of Hölderlin's translation reveals the inherent difference between languages. The power of translation anticipates their eventual harmonization precisely through their insurmountable difference in the here and now. According to Benjamin, translation barely touches upon comprehensible meaning and in this way approaches most closely the accomplished complementarity he had envisioned in the idea of pure language:

> Confirmation of this . . . is supplied by Hölderlin's translations, particularly those of the two tragedies by Sophocles. In them the harmony of the languages is so profound that sense is touched by language only the way an aeolian harp is touched by the wind. . . . For this very reason, Hölderlin's translations, in particular, are subject to the enormous danger inherent in all translations: the gates of a language thus expanded and modified may slam shut and enclose the translator in silence. Hölderlin's translations from Sophocles were his last works; in them meaning plunges from abyss to abyss until it threatens to become lost in the bottomless depths of language (Translator, 262).[8]

In his notes, Blanchot translates:

> Dès les traductions de Sophocle par Hölderlin, l'ahmonie [sic] est si profonde entre les *deux* langues que le souffle du langage n'effleure le sens que comme le vent fait vibrer la langue hx [sic] éolienne. Ces traductions st de vrais archétypes: sur elles rôde l'immense danger que court dès l'origine tte traduction: la porte d'une langue si élargie risque de retomber sur le traducteur et de le murer ds le silence. Ses versions de Sophocle furent l'oeuvre ultime de H. En elles, on voit le sens s'effondrer d'abîme en abîme jusqu'à risquer de se perdre ds les gouffres sans fond du langage. (Hoppenot, 462–63)
> [In Hölderlin's translations of Sophocles, the ahmony between the *two* languages is so profound that the breath of language does not touch upon

meaning except as wind makes language vibrate hx aeolian. These translations are real archetypes: the immense risk run by every translation from
the beginning preys on them: the door of a language thus enlarged may close
again on the translator and wall him up in silence. H.'s versions of Sophocles
constituted his ultimate work. In them, one witnesses meaning collapse from
abyss to abyss, until it risks losing itself in the bottomless depths of language
(My emphasis).]

One detail of this translation proves to be fundamental. By translating "the harmony of *all* languages" as "the harmony" (or, rather, "ahmony") between "*two*
languages," Blanchot arrives at a conception of pure language that differs radically from the one Benjamin expresses. In Blanchot's article:

> The example of Hölderlin illustrates the risk that is run, in the end, by the
> man fascinated by the power of translating: the translations of *Antigone* and
> *Oedipus* were nearly his last works at the outbreak of madness. These works
> are exceptionally studied, restrained, and intentional, conducted with inflex-
> ible firmness with the intent not of transposing the Greek text into German,
> nor of reconveying the German language to its Greek sources, but of unifying
> the two powers—the one representing the vicissitudes of the West, the other
> those of the Orient—in the simplicity of a pure and total language ("Translat-
> ing," 61).

Benjamin's vision of the lost language of paradise, an idea derived from Jewish
mysticism, becomes in Blanchot's text the union of the Greek and the German.
This is an eminently Heideggerian topos, which played a considerable role in
the context of the cultural and intellectual aspirations of the National Socialists.
Blanchot's thinking, clearly, is not oriented toward the claim that Germany was
destined to realize the heritage of Greece, a claim that so strongly influenced
the ultimately murderous vision of an absolutely supreme, neopagan Germany,
opposed principally to the Jewish and, to a lesser degree, Christian tradition.
Nevertheless, his "translation" of Benjamin's pure messianic language into a
pure Greco-German language, in an article in which Blanchot praises Benjamin's essay, is surprising. Although inspired by Benjamin's remarks on Hölderlin
and his translations of Sophocles, the divergence between the end of Blanchot's
article, which concludes with praise for the German poet, and the final passage
of Benjamin's essay is crucial. It pertains to all three aspects of translation that
I have been analyzing: the distinction between translation and translator, the
status of the poetic work in relation to its translation, and the ultimate aim of the
authors' philosophies of language.

In a stance prefigured by his insistence on the role of the translator as an individual rather than on translation as a phenomenon, Blanchot glorifies Hölderlin
in the last paragraph of his article. He turns him into a mythological hero who
"s'avançait témérairement vers ce centre où il croyait trouver rassemblé le pur

pouvoir d'unifier et tel qu'il pût donner sens, en dehors de tout sens déterminé et limité" [was fearlessly advancing toward the center in which he believed he would find collected the pure power of unifying, a center such that it would be able to give meaning, beyond all determined and limited meaning] ("Traduire," 73). Blanchot here espouses a central value of modernist poetics: the transgression of conventional meaning resulting in a singular literary creation. His insistence, however, on the "power to unify" and the revival of "meaning" is foreign to the Benjaminian conception of translation as a medium through which all meaning leads to its own abolishment, ending in a pure language that no longer means or expresses anything.

The greatest divergence between Blanchot and Benjamin occurs with Blanchot's omission of the latter's final paragraph, both in his notes and in his article. "Translating" ends with an emphasis on what Benjamin, in his penultimate paragraph, describes as the danger of Hölderlin's translation. For Blanchot, the courage to confront this risk marks the conclusion of his text: Hölderlin is the one who "avec le pouvoir unificateur qui est à l'oeuvre dans toute relation et dans tout langage . . . [s]'expose en même temps à la scission préalable, l'homme prêt à traduire est dans une intimité constante, dangereuse, admirable, et c'est de cette familiarité [avec le danger] qu'il tient le droit d'être le plus orgueilleux et le plus secret des écrivains—avec cette conviction que traduire est, en fin de compte folie" ("Traduire," 73) [with the unifying power that is at work in every practical relation, as in any language, . . . (is) expose(d) . . . to the pure scission that is always prior(;) the man who is ready to translate is in a constant, dangerous, and admirable intimacy—and it is this familiarity (with danger) that gives him the right to be the most arrogant or the most secret of writers—with the conviction that, in the end, translating is madness ("Translating," 61)].

Blanchot's radicalization of the danger Benjamin describes of losing oneself in the bottomless depths of language contrasts fundamentally with the final passage of Benjamin's essay, which Blanchot does not address.

Having portrayed the dizzying descent from abyss to abyss faced by the translator who follows Hölderlin's example, Benjamin continues as follows: "Aber es gibt ein Halten" ("Aufgabe," 21), a sentence that Gandillac translates as "Mais il y a un point d'arrêt" [There is, however, a stop] (275). In fact, in this context, the German word "Halten" suggests much more: Something holds and holds back, preventing this fall into a bottomless gulf and saving one from madness. Whereas Blanchot speaks of a "scission préalable [prior scission]" ("Traduire," 73), Benjamin's essay envisions a return to the very depths of a monotheistic "one." This return manifests itself "[w]o der Text unmittelbar, ohne vermittelnden Sinn, in seiner Wörtlichkeit der wahren Sprache . . . angehört" ("Aufgabe," 21), a condition vouchsafed in holy scripture alone, which would be "übersetzbar schlechthin" ("Aufgabe," 21) and thus without difference, tension, or mediation.

Here are Benjamin's final words: "The interlinear version of the Scriptures is the prototype [*Urbild*] or ideal of all translation" (Translator, 263) [Die Interlinearversion des heiligen Textes ist das Urbild oder Ideal aller Übersetzung] "Aufgabe," 21). This concept, which comes from the kabbalistic Jewish tradition of a primary unity before the breaking of the vessels—and contrasts sharply with a "prior scission"—forms the messianic core of Benjamin's philosophy of language. It rests on the idea that God's word, which reverberates through biblical Hebrew, passed immediately, "without any mediating sense" (Translator, 262) [*ohne vermittelnden Sinn*] into a human language. Between Hölderlin and the Bible, the Greco-German and the Jewish, on one hand, and between the primacy of a scission and of monotheistic truth, on the other, Blanchot and Benjamin clear paths going in opposite directions. It remains to be examined whether Blanchot, in translating Benjamin literally as well as figuratively, remains faithful to his own vision of the task of the translator, which involves exposing one's own language to the alterity of the other.

# 8 Ideas of Prose: Benjamin and Agamben

> And the entire lengthy volume, [which] the hand of the scribe had crammed with characters, was nothing other than the attempt to represent the perfectly bare writing tablet on which nothing had yet been written.
>
> Giorgio Agamben[1]

> The white page is poisoned. The book that doesn't tell any story kills. The absence of story signifies death.
>
> Tzvetan Todorov[2]

WHOEVER HAS ONCE—in a dream or daydream—dwelled in the redeemed world and whoever, like a figure in a fragment by Franz Kafka, has had a near-death experience from which he returns, certainly has rich stories to tell. One can learn many a thing from him, contends Kafka, but what really occurs after death or—in our case—after the end of history—and whether this is a realm where stories are still being told, that he cannot tell.[3] Anyone who considers messianic redemption itself as nothing but a story that has lost its relevance would consider it futile to speculate on the nature, the language, the very existence of stories in a redeemed world. Paradoxically, such a death certificate would only confirm the continuing life of this *grand récit* in that it announces, like all messianisms, the end of an age-old story—the story of the eschatological imagination itself. If, however, we accept Walter Benjamin's dictum that every story legitimately invites the question "How does it continue?"[4] then asking about the fate of stories after the end of times is as legitimate as wondering what follows the *grands récits* themselves. One can see a possible variation of this continuation in the current reception of Walter Benjamin's ideas about the relationship between language, epic forms, and messianic expectations.

Giorgio Agamben performs one of the most radical recoveries of Benjamin's messianic thinking to date. Agamben's references to Benjamin, which permeate his work from his early theoretical studies on aesthetics and language to his later juridical and political texts, forcefully wrench Benjamin's ideas away from the context of their former *milieu,* especially from Gershom Scholem and

Theodor W. Adorno, as well as from his later readers, especially Jacques Derrida. Agamben considers that the constitutive inability of Derridean deconstruction to reach closure helped perpetuate the prevailing dismal condition of humanity through an attitude that he terms "a petrified or paralyzed messianism."[5] Agamben rejects Derrida's exhortation of an endless "expectation without expectation" and his definition of the messianic as an existential structure of infinite deferral and radical openness toward an incalculable, unpredictable future. In opposition to Derrida, Agamben recovers aspects of Benjamin's messianic thinking that foreground the urgency to terminate deferral. Agamben's approach significantly affects his reading of Benjamin's reflections on messianic language.

Between 1982 and 1992, Agamben wrote several essays on Benjamin's messianism that emphasize a redemptive reversal occurring at a "point of indifference," an empty spatial and temporal spot where beginning and end collapse into each other and the course of history as a Hegelian "bad infinity" is brought to an end. A recurrent motif of these essays is a critique of various traditions of thought that rest on the structure of an infinite deferral. Most specifically in the essay "Language and History: Linguistic Categories and Historical Categories in Benjamin's Thought," originally published in Italian in 1983,[6] Agamben addresses Benjamin's messianic concepts of a universal history and the universal language that corresponds to it. Utilizing Benjamin's understanding that history arose along with meaning, Agamben develops Benjamin's idea of a pure language in correlation with the end of history. In the course of his argumentation, Agamben rejects various manifestations of the structure of deferral that, he believes, run counter to Benjamin's messianism. At first sight, these opposing theories, which range from kabbalistic speculations to contemporary French thought, seem to have little in common, but they all imply a form of "infinite task," an *unendliche Aufgabe*.

Agamben, along with Benjamin, rejects the attempt artificially to construct a universal language as Ludwig Zamenhof did in 1887 with Esperanto. According to Agamben, Benjamin rejected this language because it conceived of language as a sign system based on an infinite conservation of signification and meaning. Benjamin based his rejection mainly on political grounds, viewing Esperanto as a false construction because it prematurely claims universality before universal justice—the only authentic manifestation of redemption—is established. Agamben's mistrust of Esperanto is more linguistic-philosophical in nature. Another avatar of infinite deferral negated by Agamben is a hermeneutics of infinite meaning, for which universal language is merely a regulative ideal. Agamben objects to Hans-Georg Gadamer's view that "all human speaking is finite in such a way that there is laid up within it an infinity of meaning to be explicated and laid out."[7] Agamben rightly refers to Benjamin's own critique of an approach to interpretation as an "infinite task" (*Potentialities*, 56). Agamben succinctly describes Benjamin's idea of textual interpretation, the "mortification of the work" (*Potentialities*, 57) that ought to occur in the face of the danger of the respective historical moment as the opposite of a Gadamerian hermeneutics directed toward the merging of the horizons of past and present. It remains questionable, however, whether Agamben's alternative to Gadamer, which he derives from Martin Heidegger, namely a definitive "saying of the work" (*Potentialities*, 57) that captures its essence stripped of mediating comments and philological explanations could—and should—for Benjamin, be practiced in an unredeemed world.

The third possible interpretation of universal language rejected by Agamben stems from the tradition he traces from the Kabbalah via Gershom Scholem to Derrida and deconstruction. Common to them is the primacy of writing and its infinite deferral of true meaning. Instead, Agamben insists on the messianic necessity to conclude the "infinite task" and reach the point where language will finally be free of all presupposition and mediation, emptied of all meaning, and saying nothing but itself. In all these examples of Agamben's rejection of infinite deferral, it remains unclear whether the correspondence between pure language and messianic redemption is one of precondition, analogy, causality, or any other mode of relation.[8] As Benjamin suggests in "Theologico-Political Fragment,"[9] this other mode of relation will come into being only with the coming of the Messiah and his coming represents the absence of relation itself.

In my following analysis of Agamben's reading of a passage by Benjamin, I shall point out the correlation between Agamben's rejection of deferral—generally associated with Jewish messianism and explicitly described by Scholem as the characteristic mode of Jewish existence in a *"Leben im Aufschub"* [life in deferral][10]—and his transformation, if not outright effacement, of the ethical and political dimension of Benjamin's messianism.

## Preamble: Hegel's Aesthetics

Agamben's "Language and History" interprets a single passage from Benjamin's paralipomena to his "On the Concept of History." Focusing on the link that Benjamin establishes between "pure language" and "universal history," Agamben retraces the correspondences that Benjamin posits between the genres of narration, history, and redemption. These correspondences derive from a revision of Hegel's theory of aesthetics. Hegel's traditional triadic scheme places the epic, which encompasses human experience in its unity and totality, at the beginning. The epic, the most ancient account of history told in the form of heroic song, was later sublated into poetry, which, in turn, was sublated into "disenchanted"[11] and no longer integral prose. In Hegel's progressive scheme, prose aims at regaining the original totality corresponding to the ancient epic, the genre for recounting universal history. Benjamin viewed the idea of a constantly progressing and developing history, which ultimately attains pure self-consciousness, as in crisis just as much as continuous narration. His messianic thought, although also modeled on the triad of Paradise, Fall, and impending Redemption, is marked by discontinuities, which also characterize his theory of narration. In modern times the genre of a continuously flowing, all-encompassing narrative has lost its validity. Henceforth, narration must either signal the impossibility of its own continuity or mark its status as a mere model for the historiography of a future messianic age.

Benjamin gave no clear answer to the question "what the situation of a 'redeemed humanity' might actually be, what conditions are required for the development of such a situation, and when this development can be expected to occur" [in welcher Verfassung sich die 'erlöste Menschheit' befindet, welchen Bedingungen das Eintreten dieser Verfassung unterworfen ist und wann man mit ihm rechnen kann].[12] Instead, he recovers scattered messianic fragments that point to anticipatory forms of this future state. These include allusions in Benjamin's work to various experiences and figures: whether Proust's *mémoire involontaire* or a *leibhaftige Geistesgegenwart* [embodied presence of mind], the *flâneur* or the collector, the translator or the materialist historian, Kafka's seemingly insignificant assistants or the righteous man. This heterogeneous group includes the chronicler and his secularized alter ego, the storyteller. Benjamin's essay "The Storyteller" [Der Erzähler][13] contains few messianic echoes, but the note written in preparation for his "On the Concept of History" provides clues about the condition of redeemed mankind that also touch on the question of narration in a messianic world:

> The messianic world is the world of total and integral actuality. In it alone is there universal history. What goes by the name of universal history today can only be a kind of Esperanto. Nothing can correspond to it as long as the confusion originating in the Tower of Babel is not smoothed out. It presupposes the language into which every text of a living or dead language must be translated in full. Rather, it is itself this language. Not, though, as written, but as festively celebrated. This celebration is purified of every ceremony; it knows no celebratory songs. Its language is the idea of prose itself, which is understood by all men, as is the language of birds by Sunday's children.[14]

Other versions of this fragment in Benjamin's paralipomena to "On the Concept of History" end with the following remark: "The idea of prose coincides with the messianic idea of universal history. (Compare the passage in The 'Storyteller.')" [Die Idee der Prosa fällt mit der messianischen Idee der Universalgeschichte zusammen (siehe auch Erzähleraufsatz)].[15] The most extensive variant of the note contains an additional reference to "the types of artistic prose as the spectrum of universal historical types—in 'The Storyteller'" [die Arten der Kunstprosa als das

Spektrum der universalhistorischen—im "Erzähler"].[16] It may not be an exaggeration to see in Benjamin's note a prism that encompasses all the messianic sparks relating to history, language, and narration that are scattered in his work.

Benjamin's fragment projects the state of redeemed humankind as a comprehensive, fulfilled presence of language and history. Only in a messianic world, only at the end of time, and from its end can history be recounted in its entirety. Benjamin is here criticizing the narrative historicism of the nineteenth century, which deluded itself in claiming that it could still relate history in an epic form.[17] Benjamin considers that this concept of history creates the illusion of an intact world, sides with the victors, and does not take the oppression of humankind into account. The prerequisite of a rightful and just universal history, the prerogative only of redeemed humankind, is the healing of the confusion of tongues through a universal language "understood by all men." This attitude recalls Benjamin's early essays "On Language as Such and On the Language of Men" [Über Sprache überhaupt und über die Sprache der Menschen][18] and "The Task of the Translator" [Die Aufgabe des Übersetzers].[19] Integral actuality—the fulfilled concurrence of all events—finds expression in a language freed of mediation and difference, of writing and signs, a language of immediacy that will eventually liberate nature from its mute sorrow and reconcile it with humankind. With the concept of the "idea of prose," which refers to Benjamin's doctoral thesis, "The Concept of Criticism in German Romanticism" [Der Begriff der Kunstkritik in der deutschen Romantik][20] and the reference to the storyteller essay, this passage, in addition to the essays on language, echoes two early texts that are less about language than about epic forms. But how can the messianic hope for immediacy and "integral actuality" accord with narrative, which always also presumes tension, difference, deferral, and mediation?

## White Light

Benjamin's earlier-cited comment linking prose forms and universal historical types[21] recalls a passage in the storyteller essay, in which Benjamin depicts history as "the creative indifference between all forms of the epic" [die schöpferische Indifferenz zwischen allen Formen der Epik].[22] If one regards history in these terms, Benjamin continues, "written history would bear the same relationship to the epic forms as white light bears to the colors of the spectrum" [würde sich die geschriebene Geschichte zu den epischen Formen verhalten wie das weiße Licht zu den Spektralfarben].[23] Benjamin's concept of "creative indifference"—the possibility of creatively reconciling polarities and contrasts—signifies an alternative, romantically inflected form of sublation that circumvents Hegel's idea of progress and avoids its dialectical loss of the concrete. The white light of history writing, in which all epic forms are inherent just as all poetic forms are inherent in prose, merely has the semblance of uniformity. The purity of this light would not be an emptiness or absence of colors, but instead an absolute fullness. Benjamin elucidates this figure of thought, echoing Hegel's definition of types: "For if . . . the writing of history constitutes the creative matrix [in the original: *schöpferische Indifferenz*] of the various epic forms (just as great prose constitutes the creative matrix of the various metrical forms), its oldest form, the epic, by virtue of being a kind of common denominator [in the original: *eine Art von Indifferenz*], includes the story and the novel.[24]

This vertical stratification, in contrast to Hegel, preserves all the lower forms unimpaired in the higher ones. Benjamin considers that the epic contains both the novel and the story, but in distinguishing between story and novel, he clearly views the former, the secularized form of the chronicle, as pointing ahead to a messianic, "full" prose. The "idea of prose" that Benjamin introduces in his note as a form of universal history appears as the last in this series of sublations. It is attained not through a Hegelian teleological advance but in messianic fulfillment. In the "idea of prose," the potentials of all the forms absorbed in it continue to have an effect. Accordingly, in the all-encompassing light of the messianic idea of universal history, which coincides with the "idea of prose," the story is preserved as one of the colors of the spectrum.

The metaphor of the white light and the spectrum, of the invisible fullness of its constituent colors, corresponds, in Benjamin's dissertation on Romanticism, to the definition of the Romantic "idea of art" as an "absolute medium of reflection" [*Reflexionsmedium*].[25] There, prose is called "the idea of poetry" [die Idee der Poesie].[26] For the Romantics, it represents the highest form of poetry, containing all its potentialities and liberating poetry from its codifications. In prose, "all metrical rhythms pass over into one another" and "combine in a new unity" [gehen sämtliche gebundenen Rhythmen ineinander über" und "verbinden sich zu einer neuen Einheit][27] that is characterized by "sobriety" [*Nüchternheit*] and corresponds to a successful "disenchantment" of the epic and its festive songs. If, in Benjamin's dissertation, prose is the "idea of poetry" in which all poetic forms are liberated, then the messianic "idea of prose"—corresponding to the model of "creative indifference"—is its highest stage. It is "universal history," which contains within itself all varieties of art prose, just as the "white light" of "written history" contains the spectral colors of all epic forms. It encompasses everything that has ever occurred and frees it from its codified bonds, indeed from its own artificiality. This messianic feast of freedom contains no festive songs, therefore, and does not return intact to the heroic songs of the epic: it is sober and "general," like the prose described in Benjamin's dissertation. This "idea of prose" encompasses all other forms of art and, as universal narrative, takes in and preserves all the experience of creation. This concept in Benjamin's early writings of redemption as encompassing even the most insignificant creature prefigures his later political concerns, his care for those whom the victors' canonized historiography has omitted and forgotten.

## Scheherazade and the Dying Man

Two opposing figures vouch for storytelling in the storyteller essay referred to in the addendum to Benjamin's note. One, Scheherazade, comes from the literary realm. She is the one who invents a new story whenever her tale comes to a halt, and this trait resides, in one form or another, in every storyteller. The second, opposite, figure is taken from life: the dying man. In Benjamin's exposition, both figures take on a messianic dimension that brings them into line with the idea of a universal history at the end of time. Scheherazade, while embodying that "unmessianic" movement of narrative that defers the end, is, for Benjamin, also the guardian of epic memory, creating the web that all stories weave together in the end. The narrative of the dying man, on the other hand, comes into being as retrospection. Benjamin writes, "his lived life" [gelebtes Leben] constitutes the stuff of his stories. The storyteller, like the dying man, possesses the gift of "being able to recount his *entire* life" [sein ganzes Leben erzählen zu können].[28] Universal history is the collective analogy to that narrative: It relates the *entire* history of all creatures on earth from its messianic end point. As with the dying man, even if he is "the poorest wretch," the storyteller recovers the past in its totality, thus erasing all hierarchical differences.

Scheherazade and the dying man together embody messianic figures who preserve in the spectrum of the "idea of prose" the dual motion of deferral and retrospection, infinity and closure, hope and memory. The concept of the "idea of prose" contains not only the pure, perfect, and in itself complete *idea*, but also *prose* as the general, the manifold, and worldly story of all creation. In Benjamin's messianic world, a web of stories spun from the matter of "lived life" [gelebtes Leben] accomplishes, in his words, the *restitutio in integrum* of the past. At the conclusion of the storyteller essay, Benjamin calls the storyteller the "advocate of all creation" on the day of the Last Judgment. His integral prose strives to preserve the particularity of each individual phenomenon in its entirety and do justice to all creatures. It would be a language of names to the extent that it no longer denotes arbitrarily but evokes and vivifies authentically what it names: Benjamin founded his messianic ethics of narration on the desire for a complete narrativity, which, with this highest form of attentiveness, calls things by their name.

## The Enjambment and the Expressionless

Agamben's piece "The Idea of Prose," in his volume of poetic-philosophical short texts with the same name, offers an initial insight into the difference between the two writers' ideas on the subject.[29] In this short text, Agamben, just as Benjamin does in his early study of art criticism in the Romantic period, derives the essence of prose from its relation to poetry. Whereas Benjamin, in line with Schlegel, calls prose the "idea of poetry" and, using the metaphor of white light, envisions "all the possibilities and forms of poetry" in it, Agamben situates the relationship of prose and poetry at the interface *between* them. He describes the specificity of poetry as the divergence between rhythm and meaning. The location of this divergence is the enjambment, the uninterrupted continuation of a syntactic unit from one line or couplet of a poem to the next, which Agamben calls "the distinguishing characteristic of poetic discourse."[30] It is the point where poetry and prose are both most radically different, yet conjoined to the point of being almost indistinguishable. In the enjambment, verse introduces the syntax of prose and, paradoxically, becomes poetry at the very point where it disavows the metrical language of poetry. At this point, the "idea of language," which is "neither poetry nor prose, but their middle," occurs.[31] Unlike Benjamin's metaphor of the white light that contains, even though invisibly, the fullness of all spectral colors, this middle—a mere interruption in the flow of the poetic sentence, a blank space on the page—is empty.

Agamben elucidates the relationship between language and history in terms of the discrepancy between the original language of names and the historically mediated, always already transmitted and hence inauthentic, language of communication between human beings. In Agamben's explication of Benjamin's note, names always precede all speech as original signs and cannot be grasped or circumvented. In contrast, thought without presuppositions is impossible in a language of signs. The mediation to which names are subject throughout history determines an endless chain of presuppositions, which circumscribe and constrict thought and human beings.

Agamben grafts this concept of language as an imaginary prison onto Benjamin's philosophy of history. Because history came into being at the same time as the fall of language from its original, unmediated state, the end of history coincides with the end of the communicative language of signs and the restitution of the Adamic language of names. To Agamben, Benjamin's "idea of prose" aims at the messianic end of a history understood as fate and therefore as unfreedom. This corresponds in many respects to Benjamin's understanding of history in his note. Because Agamben, however, does not take into consideration the reference to the storyteller essay and the significance of prose as epic form, he identifies the "idea of prose" entirely with the "idea of language." His perception of the term thus leads to an aesthetic of emptiness and an ethics of disconnectedness, to which Benjamin would hardly have subscribed. The differing views of the "expressionless" [*das Ausdruckslose*] in Agamben and in Benjamin support this contention.

In his essay on Johann Wolfgang von Goethe's *Elective Affinities*, Benjamin links the "expressionless"—a feature of language that has no meaning in itself but interrupts a falsely harmonious continuity—to Friedrich Hölderlin's concept of the caesura. For Hölderlin, this hesitation in the poetic meter produces a "counterrhythmical interruption" [*gegenrhythmische Unterbrechung*], a resistance to the flowing rhythm of the hymnic poetry.[32] Whereas Benjamin insists that this interruption serves to rupture the illusion of wholeness, Agamben considers it as the event itself. In "Idea of the Caesura," another short text in *Idea of Prose*, Agamben refers to the same Hölderlin passage about the caesura as Benjamin does and comments: "What does the interruption of the rhythmic transport in the poem reveal? . . . The rhythmic transport, which bears the momentum of the poem, is empty and bears only itself. It is the caesura, which as *pure* word, thinks this emptiness—for a while. . . . The poet . . . awakes and for a moment studies the inspiration which bears him; he thinks only of his voice."[33] This reading of the Hölderlin quotation, which flows into an awareness of the voice, shows traces of Agamben's earlier book *Language and Death*, whose subtext is Heidegger's *On the Essence of Language* [Das Wesen der Sprache].[34]

In Agamben's book, voice plays a crucial role, and it reveals the origins of his own ethics, implied in his understanding of the "idea of prose": "The Voice, as we know, says nothing; it does not mean or want to say any significant proposition. Rather, it indicates and means the pure taking place of language and it is, as such, a purely *logical* dimension." In this sense, Agamben continues, language as Voice is "the original ethical dimension in which man pronounces his 'yes' to language." This very affirmation of language "opens up to man the possibility for the marvel of being and the terror of nothingness."[35] This ethics also determines Agamben's later interpretation of Benjamin's "idea of prose." There, pure "saying" is not only the task of the philosopher, but also becomes the ethical task as such: "It is . . . the actual construction of this relation and this region [of pure language] that constitutes the true task of the philosopher and the translator, the historian and the critic, and, in the final analysis, the ethical engagement of every speaking being."[36]

Agamben's "idea of prose" calls for an integral actuality, that is, a fulfilled now-time without tension, displacement, or deferral. Whereas Benjamin's "*Jetztzeit*" contains worldly splinters pointing to a messianic fulfillment, Agamben's "now" suggests an attempt to imagine a "pure" interruption, free of all mediation, conception, and precondition, uninfected by a world that presents itself as one continuous catastrophe. The urgency, however, which Agamben constantly conjures up, stands in curious contrast to the emptiness to which he simultaneously appeals. Significantly, his thinking eschews the revolutionary thrust of Benjamin's idea of interruption. Agamben's hypostasis and, one might say, "defunctionalization" of the interruption itself creates a break in the bridge between Agamben's linguistic philosophy and his political thought. No path leads from "the marvel of being and the terror of nothingness" to an ethics and politics of justice. That impasse lies in an approach that overlooks paths in favor of cuts, thresholds, and empty spaces that no longer stand in any relation to what they interrupt. Ultimately, it becomes a matter of the theoretical enthronement of discontinuity itself.

The messianic forces that, for Benjamin, interrupt the time continuum and point toward a redeemed world are, for Agamben, rendered absolute and empty to the degree that they are no longer redeeming bearers of hope and signals for the cessation of a false continuity. Instead, interruption becomes an end in itself, eliding the experiential content and the worldly bearings of Benjamin's messianic figures. His sparks and splinters, poetic metaphors of a profane illumination, whose luster indicates the path of redemption, become abstract locations of discontinuity: the threshold, the limit point, the interface, "the in-between" as such. Perhaps, in an increasingly complex postrevolutionary age, their emptiness seems to be the only possible configuration for saving the radicalism of Benjamin's political-theological legacy, but the very thing that is to be saved—worldly life itself—is in danger of being lost.

## Coda

For Benjamin, the origin of storytelling is imbued with the authority of the dying man, whose stories derive from the material of his "lived life." In "Idea of Matter," the first text in *Idea of Prose*, Agamben indicates the place from which stories emerge. The text starts with a description of "the decisive experience" that is "so difficult to talk about." It is, Agamben continues, "not even an experience. It is nothing more than the point at which we touch the limits of language. . . . Where language stops is not where the unsayable occurs, but rather where the matter of words begins. Those who have not reached, as in a dream, the wooden substance of language . . . are prisoners of representations, even when they keep silent."[37]

Agamben illustrates the liberation from this imprisonment by a comparison with a near-death experience: "It is the same for those who return to life after a near-death experience. They did not really die (otherwise they would not have returned), nor have they liberated themselves from the necessity to die one day. But they have freed themselves from the representation of death. That is why, when asked to tell what happened to them, they can say nothing about death, but they find rich material to tell stories and relate exquisite tales about their life."[38]

To have been there, near the place of death, liberates from representation and its presuppositions. The stories generated by this experience, however, derive not so much as in Benjamin from the stuff of lived life but from "the matter of the word."

A fragment from Kafka's diaries—obviously the model for Agamben's text—speaks of the near-death experience and its relation to storytelling. For Kafka, too, "whoever has once experienced near-death, can tell terrifying things about it, but how it is after death, that he cannot say."[39] The inability to tell, however, has less to do with the limits of language and more with the limited experience of death of the returnee. He has, Kafka contends, not even been closer to death than anyone else, he has merely lived something exceptional and it is not this exceptional but common life that has become more valuable to him. It is the same with everyone who has experienced something exceptional. Moses, for example, certainly experienced something extraordinary on Mount Sinai, but rather than surrendering to this exceptional experience, he rushed down the mount and had valuable things to tell and loved the humans to whom he fled even more than before. One can learn a lot from both the one who returned from near death and the one who returned from Sinai, but the decisive one cannot learn from them because they themselves have not experienced it. And if they had experienced it, they would not have come back.[40]

The rupture, the exceptional, is, for Kafka as for Benjamin, mainly to be seen in relation to the everyday, the common, the lived life. The place of the rupture, of the exceptional, the revelation—whether death or Sinai—is as manifold as it is indifferent in and of itself. Whoever has been there has "obviously valuable stories to tell," but we cannot learn "the decisive"—*das Entscheidende*—from them. "But," Kafka adds, "in truth, we don't even want to know it."[41]

# 9 Reading Scholem and Benjamin on the Demonic

The night is the source of the demonic. The "new heaven" is the heaven without night and messianic time is, in Hebrew, called "the Days of the Messiah" for good reason. It is only in lament that darkness shines.

Gershom Scholem[1]

THE AMBIGUITY OF the term "demonic" between, on the one hand, the Greek idea of a powerful, mostly benevolent spirit or force, and, on the other, the incarnation of evil as imagined in monotheistic religions, still plays a role in contemporary controversies where fundamental worldviews are at stake. An association with the indistinct and the elusive, the irrational and the uncontrollable, and, ultimately, with ambiguity itself reinforces this role. The demonic is almost by necessity invoked in ways that only partially encompass its multifarious significance. The issue becomes especially complex when those meanings of the demonic that suggest stark contrasts—as positive force or satanic evil—appear at a hair's breadth from each other or even seem to be inextricably intertwined. Such instances of the demonic occur, not surprisingly, in the context of the Kabbalah.

The significance of the demonic in the writings of German-Jewish thinkers of the early twentieth century, particularly those who invoke the Kabbalah in their reflections on history, politics, and language, is a touchstone of their positioning on the threshold between tradition and modernity. It plays a paradigmatic role in controversies about Walter Benjamin and, even more so, Gershom Scholem, who both allude to the Jewish mystical tradition in their reflections on modernity, particularly in elaborating their respective views of history. Scholem, Benjamin's first reader as well as the primary influence on the Jewish dimension of his work, is one of the crucial figures in the debates about Benjamin's relationship to theology and Judaism. Scholem also is a contentious figure in his own right in discussions about the origin and manifestation of modernity in Jewish history and thought. His frequent use of the term "demonic" in various contexts is an essential part of these debates, which touch upon his ideas of history and myth, Judaism and Zionism, and of modern Judaic studies. His understanding of the term also affects the portrait he drew of Benjamin and his thought. Two particularly significant examples of contemporary reactions to these aspects of Scholem's writings, the one articulated by Giorgio Agamben, the other by the leading Israeli Kabbalah scholar Moshe Idel, illustrate the various meanings of the demonic in these controversies.

In "Walter Benjamin and the Demonic. Happiness and Historical Redemption,"[2] Agamben takes Scholem to task for describing Benjamin as a melancholic thinker with a dark and desperate vision of history. He is particularly critical of Scholem's interpretation of the angel in Benjamin's autobiographical sketch "Agesilaus Santander"[3] and in "On the Concept of History"[4] as a figure that "hides dark and demonic traits" (*Potentialities*, 138). For Agamben, Scholem thereby "casts a melancholic light on the entire horizon of Benjamin's reflections on the philosophy of history" (*Potentialities*, 138). In about the same period—the last decade of the twentieth century—Moshe Idel, who is often considered Scholem's successor, critically depicts the latter as one of the "desolates." He uses this term throughout his book *Old Worlds, New Mirrors* to designate "the new Jewish elite"[5] consisting of early-twentieth-century German-Jewish writers and thinkers such as Franz Kafka, Leo Strauss, Ernst Bloch, Benjamin, Freud, and others. Idel characterizes these figures as absorbed with all-encompassing and "noteworthy concerns with melancholy" (Idel, *Old Worlds*, 9). In this context, Idel, like Agamben, criticizes Scholem for his "demonic reading of history" (Idel, *Old Worlds*, 102–5).

Although Agamben continuously invokes the Kabbalah and even explicitly refers to Idel's work (*Potentialities*, 165), the Italian thinker and the Israeli scholar could not be further apart in their general views of politics, history, Zionism, and Judaism, or in their understanding of Benjamin. Moreover, their motivations for criticizing Scholem's melancholic view of history, which they both relate to the demonic, are diametrically opposed. The similarity of their negative assessment of Scholem's melancholic view of history as demonic and of Scholem's associating Benjamin with this view thus represents an intriguing phenomenon that invites an exploration of their respective critiques and a comparison with Scholem's own use of the term.

## Giorgio Agamben: Melancholy and Eudaimonia

Agamben explains that he entitled his essay "Walter Benjamin and the Demonic" because he intended "to complete and, in a certain sense, also rectify the interpretation offered by the scholar of Jerusalem" (*Potentialities*, 138)—a somewhat portentous designation for Scholem. Agamben wants to rectify Scholem's reading of Benjamin's angel, and, beyond this specific instance, Scholem's approach to history. Agamben directs his criticism most explicitly against Scholem's interpretation of "Agesilaus Santander," objecting mainly to Scholem's tendency to "make

Benjamin's entire text seem immersed in a demonic light" where "a Luciferian element is present in every detail" (*Potentialities*, 140). Although Agamben announces that the central aim of his essay is "to trace the fundamental (and for now provisional) lines of Benjamin's ethics" (*Potentialities*, 138), the target of his critique and the foil of his own argument is Scholem's view of Benjamin's "melancholy, indeed desperate view of history" (*Potentialities*, 144). Agamben maintains that Scholem's interpretation of the angel in "Agesilaus Santander," and also the "angel of history" as a "melancholic figure, wrecked by the immanence of history" is "clearly at odds with Benjamin's own text, which ties the figure of the angel precisely to the idea of happiness" (*Potentialities*, 144). Countering Scholem's interpretation of Benjamin's angel as a figure pertaining to the demonic associated with darkness and melancholy, Agamben posits that Benjamin derived his theory of happiness from the Greeks, more particularly their linking "of the demonic [*daimonion*]" to happiness, as is evident in its derivation from "the Greek term *eudemonia*," which designates the highest good (*Potentialities*, 138).

Agamben contests Scholem's portrait of Benjamin's angel as a "melancholic and Luciferian figure of shipwreck" (*Potentialities*, 145) with a series of counterarguments intended to establish Benjamin's orientation toward happiness in the sense bestowed on it by the Greeks. Agamben's primary argument aims at refuting Scholem: Quoting Benjamin, Agamben states that the angel "wants happiness: the conflict in which lies the ecstasy of the unique, new, as yet unlived, with that bliss of the 'once more,' the having again, the lived" (*Potentialities*, 138). Agamben, however, fails to do justice to Scholem and, in many ways, to Benjamin as well. The angel's *wanting*, his wishing and striving for happiness, in no way contradicts the melancholy permeating Scholem's reading of Benjamin and his angel. The "shipwreck" of history in Benjamin's idea of the angel is nothing but the impossibility of actually fulfilling his redemptive mission of rescuing the past as it presents itself to the angelic visionary. The heap of rubble [*Trümmerhaufen*][6] piling up in front of the "angel of history" signifies an unredeemed world in which its initial wholeness has, in the words of the Kabbalah, been shattered into pieces [shevirat hakelim] and, in historical terms, has piled catastrophe upon catastrophe.[7]

Agamben does not differentiate between the angel's *wish*—expressed in the ninth thesis "On the Concept of History" as its vain attempt to "awaken the dead and to restore what has been shattered"[8]—and the *fulfillment* of this wish, a fulfillment that Benjamin relegates to future messianic times. This blurring sets the stage for Agamben's problematic polemic against Scholem, whom he accuses of interpreting Benjamin's view of history as dark and melancholic. Agamben correctly invokes Benjamin's "Theological-Political Fragment"[9] where it is "the order of happiness—and not the messianic order—that has the function of a guiding idea for the profane-historical order" (*Potentialities*, 144). He errs, however, when he deduces from this orientation that "the angel cannot be the melancholic and Luciferian figure of a shipwreck" but "rather must be a bright figure who, in the strict solidarity of happiness and historical redemption, establishes the very relation of the profane order to the messianic that Benjamin identified as one of the essential problems of the philosophy of history" (*Potentialities*, 145). Agamben's analysis leads to an interpretation of Benjamin's "angel of history" as a figure opposed to a melancholic allegory and an embodiment of "humankind's most difficult historical task and most perfect experience of happiness" (*Potentialities*, 148). It is, however, highly unlikely—and possible only through a blurring of the distinction between potential and fulfillment—that the angel in Benjamin's ninth thesis, who is kept from restoring the wholeness of the world by the storm of progress, stands for ultimate bliss. It is, indeed, not the common understanding of happiness that Agamben has in mind, but a very particular one that invokes an aspect of the demonic that he—as will be shown below, erroneously—believes to be opposed to Scholem's melancholy: the impulse for redemptive destruction.

In support of his argument, Agamben rejects Scholem's evidence of the demonic nature of Benjamin's angel in "Agesilaus Santander"—its "claws and wings," pointing instead to the Greek figure of Eros and its iconography featuring precisely these attributes. For Agamben, the angel is, therefore, "not a demon in the Judeo-Christian sense, but a *daimon* in the Greek sense" (*Potentialities*, 141). Agamben also refers to the section "Demon" in Benjamin's essay on Karl Kraus[10] where "the demonic light" shining on the Austrian critic "illuminates the face of Socrates" (*Potentialities*, 148). Agamben, however, fails to consider Benjamin's ambivalent use of the term "demonic" in this context: In Benjamin's essay, there is, indeed, a "demon *in* Kraus," which manifests itself in his genius, but the demon is also something that must be overcome. Benjamin admires Kraus for performing a "genuinely Jewish *salto mortale* by which he tries to break the spell of the demon."[11] Similarly, Agamben insists on the Greek origin of Benjamin's view of the demonic by quoting his idea that it is in tragedy that "the head of genius lifted itself for the first time from the master demon" (*Potentialities*, 149–50), but here, too, the demonic is, for Benjamin, rather an antagonist, and tragedy its antidote. Agamben's argument does not do justice to Benjamin's ambivalence toward the demonic. This is even more evident in Agamben's critique of Scholem.

In addition to his Greek references, Agamben invokes possible Jewish sources of the demonic such as the female figure of Lilith or the *shehinah*, the kabbalistic idea of divine glory, "which designates the sphere of redemption" (*Potentialities*, 142). He emphasizes, however, the distinction between a negative and melancholic Jewish demonic and a Greek *daimon* signifying a dialectically destructive-redemptive, profane-historical order for which happiness is the "guiding idea" (*Potentialities*, 144). Agamben nevertheless—although purely theoretically—pleads for a fusion of "ancient pagan and Neoplatonic" with Jewish motifs derived from apocryphal and antinomian kabbalistic texts. In his actual discussion, he concludes that Benjamin's angel "is not a demonic figure" in Scholem's (Jewish) melancholic sense but a positively "destructive figure" (in the Greek sense) that fulfills history by bringing it to an end (*Potentialities*, 153). This end, Agamben intimates, would coincide with "the power of destructive justice, which consumes the historical totality of phenomena" (*Potentialities*, 157).[12] Agamben thus ignores Scholem's own attraction to a dialectic between destruction and redemption that lies at the core of his writings on Jewish mysticism. In addition, Agamben pushes his own anarchistic celebration of the destructive impulse so far that it does not allow for melancholy as an open-ended, incomplete, and infinite expression of despair about history as voiced by Scholem and, to some extent, by Benjamin too.[13]

Agamben's critique fits his general intellectual and political outlook, which, in many ways, accords with Benjamin's insistence on a (revolutionary) necessity to interrupt the "empty, homogenous time of modernity." Agamben, however, radicalizes Benjamin's view in ways that transform crucial elements of the latter's approach to history, Judaism, and ultimately to politics. Whereas Benjamin's politics displays a tension between urgency and patience—a tension that also characterizes his idea of Jewish messianism—Agamben's messianism, modeled on the Apostle Paul, focuses on the abrogation of the existing order in view of an event, the coming of Christ, that has already happened and that has transformed the present into a "time that remains." Scholem's melancholic view of history and his bleak interpretation of Benjamin's angel seem, in Agamben's eyes, a paradigmatic example of the "paralyzed messianism" that he rejects in all notions of history and politics that are oriented to the idea of an "infinite task."[14] The destructive power of the "happy daimon" would then be, for Agamben, its welcome antidote.

## Moshe Idel: Desolation and Plenitude

Although Moshe Idel also objects to Scholem's melancholy, he bases his stand on premises that differ from Agamben's and he has other alternatives in mind. Idel, like Agamben, criticizes Scholem's melancholic view of history as it applies to his interpretation of Benjamin's angel. Whereas Agamben wants to "save" Benjamin from Scholem and his melancholic reading of the angel as a negative demonic figure, Idel sees Benjamin, along with Kafka, as the main inspiration for Scholem's negative vision of history. Idel expands Scholem's "demonic view of Jewish history" to his understanding of history in general by invoking his friendship with Benjamin. As in the case of Agamben, Idel refers to Scholem's reading of Benjamin's angel, both the angelic figure in "Agesilaus Santander" and the "angel of history" of Benjamin's Ninth Thesis in "On the Concept of History." After quoting the text of this thesis in full, Idel draws parallels between "Scholem's giant of Jewish history" and Benjamin's interpretation of Paul Klee's *Angelus Novus* as a "metaphor for the very essence of history" (Idel, *Old Worlds*, 105). Idel speaks of a "gap" that closes between Scholem's "demonic and frightening giant as a metaphor of Jewish history and Benjamin's angel of history in general," and he criticizes both for their "basically negative" vision (Idel, *Old Worlds*, 105). For Idel, Scholem's understanding of history as a "constant failure" corresponds to Benjamin's view of history as "one single catastrophe" (Idel, *Old Worlds*, 105). For both Benjamin and Scholem, Idel writes, "the figures related to the past [the "demonic giant" and the "angel of history"] are concerned with death. None of them sees the future" (Idel, *Old Worlds*, 105). For Idel, this future has a name and a face that encompass the revival of a new and fruitful Jewish scholarship (of which he, Idel, is now one of the most prominent figures). Primarily, Idel rejects the desolates' pessimism because they do not recognize the promise of Zionism and its potential for a revival of Judaism. Idel's critique of Scholem's view of the demonic must undoubtedly be seen in this light.

Idel is also, however, opposed to Agamben's critique of Scholem's melancholy, a critique inspired by an antinomian Kabbalah and a Greek "happy daimon." Idel regards Scholem as too close to pagan and other external influences: He contrasts Scholem's gnostic penchant for the demonic—the idea of a destructive force intervening in history—with a more genuine and joyful Judaism expressed in a different, namely performative and ritualistic, understanding of the Kabbalah.

Idel most succinctly sums up his pervasive critique of Scholem's melancholy in "Scholem's Reading of Jewish History as 'Demonic'" (Idel, *Old Worlds*, 102–8). In this text, Idel links the two contexts in which Scholem speaks most explicitly of the demonic—the first is where Scholem elaborates his concept of history, and the second is Scholem's critique of the *Wissenschaft des Judentums* (Science of Judaism), a German movement led by a group of nineteenth-century Jewish scholars who advocated a radically historicist and rationalist approach to Judaism and worked toward emancipation and ultimately the assimilation of the Jews into their enlightened bourgeois environment. In connection with the first context, Idel addresses Scholem's idea of history and describes the main influences on it: the Lurianic Kabbalah's vision of humanity's all-encompassing exile, Benjamin's vision of history as an ongoing catastrophe, and, in Scholem's later work, the experience of the Holocaust. In the second case, in criticizing the *Wissenschaft des Judentums*, Scholem portrays the movement and its members as apologetically attempting to justify Judaism through an emphasis on its rational, "respectable" aspects and a repression of its kabbalistic, subversive "other side." Idel's own position, however, suffers from an oversimplification of Scholem's critique and his use of the term "demonic" in these contexts.

Idel backs up his critique of Scholem's melancholic view of history by quoting two key passages from Scholem's essay "Reflections on the Science of Judaism," written in Hebrew in 1944.[15] In them, Scholem uses the demonic not only to describe the founders of this movement, in particular, Moritz Steinschneider (1816–1907) and Leopold Zunz (1794–1886), but also to shed light on Jewish history as such: "The removal of the pointedly irrational and of demonic enthusiasms[16] from Jewish history, through an exaggerated emphasis upon the theological and the spiritual—this is the fundamental sin that outweighs all others. The frightening giant, our history, is called upon to render an accounting of itself—and this great creature, filled with explosive power, compounded of vitality, wickedness, and perfection, becomes limited and reduced in stature, and declares itself to be naught. The demonic giant is no more than an innocent fool" (quoted in Idel, *Old Worlds*, 103).

Idel does not quote the rest of this passage, in which Scholem's critique and his understanding of the demonic becomes clearer: This "demonic giant," an allegory for the fiery forces [*dämonische Glut*] inherent in Jewish history, has, at the hands of the rationalist scholars of the *Wissenschaft des Judentums*, turned into "a simple fool, who fulfills the duties of a solid citizen who believes in progress, and every decent Jewish bourgeois could unashamedly bid him good-day in the streets of the little city, the immaculate city of the nineteenth century."[17] Scholem clearly ascribes a positive meaning here to the term "demonic," which he uses to describe the forces that have been rendered tame and mediocre by the scholars of the *Wissenschaft des Judentums*. Idel, however, denies this affirmative view of the demonic and, in his interpretation of these sentences, distinguishes between the "demonic and wicked on the one hand, the powerful and even perfect on the other hand" (Idel, *Old Worlds*, 103). He also explicitly rejects David Biale's suggestion[18] that Scholem's sense of the demonic—and, therefore, his view of the "demonic giant of history"—is not purely negative. Idel quotes but immediately questions Biale's statement that Scholem used the term in a "more positive sense than normal usage suggests. Like Goethe's interpretation of the word '*daemonisch*,' Scholem conceives of demonic irrationalism as a creative force: Destruction is necessary for future construction" (Idel, *Old Worlds*, 104).[19] Although admitting that Biale's interpretation constitutes an "important insight," Idel rejects its gist by quoting the passage from Scholem's Hebrew essay from 1944 describing the founders of the *Wissenschaft des Judentums*: "The 'chthonic' aspect of the deeds of the great scholars of the Science of Judaism emerges with frightening power in three figures, whose demonic side has not been properly evaluated. . . . they are truly demonic figures . . . they also have an intense Other Side. Suddenly, while reading their words, you feel as if you are gazing into the face of the Medusa . . . and you see before you giants who, for reasons best known to themselves, have turned themselves into gravediggers and embalmers, even eulogizers" (quoted in Idel, *Old Worlds*, 104).

Idel considers the "negative tone" of this quotation as "quite evident" (Idel, *Old Worlds*, 104). Because Scholem uses similar vocabulary to describe the forces prevalent in Jewish history and in the *Wissenschaft des Judentums*, Idel sees "no reason to substantially attenuate the negative valence of Scholem's description of the frightening giant when he uses it as a metaphor for Jewish history" (Idel, *Old Worlds*, 104).

Idel undoubtedly correctly assesses that for Scholem, "the demonic in history is strongly related to the demonic in nineteenth-century Jewish scholarship," but he wrongly concludes that the term is, for Scholem, "unqualifiedly negative" (Idel, *Old Worlds*, 104). Idel's contention that Scholem uses the term "demonic" in a thoroughly negative sense—an argument Idel presents in order to support his portrait of German Jews as melancholic desolates with a "saturnine proclivity" (Idel, *Old Worlds*, 9)—is unconvincing. As Peter Schäfer has shown (and as Idel, referring to Schäfer, admits in a footnote [Idel, *Old Worlds*, 271]), Scholem, who, in his 1944 essay often used the Hebrew term "demonic" [*demoni*] negatively, uses the Greek word "daimonion" [*ha daimonion shebakhem*] when he characterizes the scholars of the *Wissenschaft des Judentums* as "demonic figures." In the same text, Scholem also explicitly admits that he has "always been attracted to [these scholars]," precisely because "they have the *daimonion*" and the "*sitra ahra*,"[20] the [Other Side] (Schäfer and Smith, 127), which Scholem considers as two manifestations of the "force of 'destruction' . . . without which no lasting reconstruction is possible" (Schäfer and Smith, 137). Schäfer explains, however, that these nineteenth-century scholars were, in Scholem's eyes, "incapable of keeping the balance between destruction and construction and, deploying only the destructive forces, failed to participate in *tikun olam*," the kabbalistic term for repairing the world (Schäfer and Smith, 137).

In his explication of Jewish history, Scholem uses the term "demonic" in a fashion similar to his use of the term in the context of his analysis of *Wissenschaft des Judentums*. The "sin" of the enlightened, apologetic scholars was precisely to have negated the powerful irrational forces inherent in Jewish history and, as can be gleaned from other passages in Scholem's essay, in history as such.

It is worth noting that Idel fails to mention another passage in Scholem's Hebrew essay from 1944 in which he attacks—as well as expresses his fascination with—the scholars of the *Wissenschaft des Judentums*. In this essay, where Scholem refers to the demonic forces of history in a positive sense and criticizes those who obliterate it, he also assesses the state of Jewish studies in Palestine at the time in which he wrote the essay. He accuses his fellow Judaic scholars in terms similar to those he uses in his polemic against the German nineteenth-century scholars, although the formers' "sin" now appears in the guise of Zionist nationalism: "All these plagues are now clad in national attire. From the rain in the eaves. After the void of assimilation [the sin of the *Wissenschaft des Judentums*], there emerges another emptiness, the one of the big-mouthed nationalist phrase. . . . In both cases, the true forces that are reigning in this world, the truly demonic (*daimonion*) remain out of the picture that we have created" (quoted in Schäfer and Smith, 134). Beyond confirming Scholem's positive use of the term "demonic," which here clearly refers to the Greek meaning of *daimon*, this passage reveals Scholem's critique of a secularized nationalism that was spreading among the scholars of Judaism in the Palestine of the 1940s. This may also explain why Idel, who barely hides his Zionist agenda, does not mention this passage. As other passages in *Old Worlds, New Mirrors* indicate, Idel's Zionist outlook underlies his charge that, even as the world—and particularly the Jewish one—was falling apart in Europe, the desolates failed to see that a new, future oriented, optimistic new world was opening up in Palestine.[21]

Idel's critique of Scholem's "demonic view of history" serves an additional purpose. In the introduction to *Old Worlds, New Mirrors*, Idel states that his study aims at correcting what he considers a false and obsessive fixation on the "tiny elite" of German-Jewish modernists at the expense of the more positive mentality of the Jews from Eastern Europe. Not only were the latter less infected by Western modernity, but also they were less melancholic. In the first pages of his book, Idel writes: "The majority of the Jewish population in that period . . . would have found it difficult or impossible to relate their own beliefs and practices to the abstractions, universal missions, negativities and religious paradoxes elaborated by a minuscule Central European Jewish intelligentsia" (Idel, *Old Worlds*, 11). Unlike the "desolates" such as Benjamin and Scholem who, Idel continues, all were "under the profound influence of Kafka's negativity" (Idel, *Old Worlds*, 11), the Eastern European Jews, with their "joy and divine immanentism," embodied an antidote to the demonic understood as melancholy. Idel praises their "traditionally Jewish emphasis on *plenitude* of life and language" (Idel, *Old Worlds*, 64).

Paradoxically, Agamben's and Idel's critique of Scholem meet at this point. So much separates the Italian philosopher and the Israeli Kabbalah scholar: different views of the Kabbalah, of the relationship between Scholem and Benjamin, and last, but not least, of the demonic. Whereas Agamben emphasizes its primarily Greek and positive sense, Idel regards it as negative and, "after all, as religious a term as 'divine'" (Idel, *Old Worlds*, 108). Although Agamben and Idel share a negative view of Scholem's melancholy and of the other desolates, Agamben is motivated by a quasi-apocalyptic anarchism, whereas Idel is impelled by an alternative approach to Judaism and the Kabbalah.

An explanation for the unlikely correspondence between Agamben's and Idel's views lies in their shared aversion to the idea of "an infinite task" and "a life lived in deferral and delay," which Scholem calls the essence of Jewish existence. This similarity between the Italian philosopher and the Kabbalah scholar goes hand in hand with their common attraction to some form of closure. Agamben heralds a radical destruction dialectically related to fulfillment and happiness; Idel celebrates fullness and plenitude considered as characteristic of Judaism, and he emphasizes the kabbalists' unification with the divine. Both views are indeed incompatible with melancholy and its sense of an ongoing incompleteness.

## The Demonic and Lament

Scholem's references to the demonic throughout his writings are, to say the least, ambivalent, if not outright contradictory. They cover the entire range of meanings from the Greek *daimon* and Goethe's *Dämonischen* to the monotheistic meaning of evil incarnate. The origin of this inconsistency lies in Scholem's daring—antirabbinic, antirationalist, and antinationalist—understanding of the Kabbalah as an intrinsic and most precious element of the Jewish tradition and simultaneously as the most promising force of a yet to be realized Jewish modernity. Scholem's exposition thereby becomes an arena where the various meanings of the demonic clash against one another and, in that collision, paradigmatically enact the ambiguity that the term denotes.

We should not understand Scholem's demonic view of Jewish history and history in general and his interpretation of Benjamin as indicating merely helpless despair; rather, we should view it in terms that do justice to Scholem's shifting use of the demonic as containing elements of both the Greek and the Jewish tradition. Similarly, his approach to the Kabbalah must be regarded as an attitude that encompasses both a destructive and a performative dimension. The most illuminating elaboration of this position can be found in the last of Scholem's "95 Theses on Judaism and Zionism" (1918), dedicated (but never actually given) to Benjamin on the occasion of his twenty-sixth birthday and quoted as a motto above: "The night is the source of the demonic. The 'new heaven' is the heaven without night and it is not without reason, that in Hebrew one speaks of messianic times as 'the days of the Messiah.' It is only in lament that darkness shines" (Schäfer and Smith, 295; my translation).

Scholem's enigmatic "thesis" links the demonic and what Agamben and Idel perceive as melancholy through lament. The aphorism starts with an utterly Romantic image: the night as the dwelling place of the demonic. At this point, the valence of this word—a powerful, benevolent force or an impersonation of evil— remains unresolved: Does the night designate a somber darkness or the potential for a (magical) transformation (as in the messianism proper to Romanticism)?[22] The image becomes clearer in what follows: The "new heaven" of enlightened modernity represses this night along with the demonic that emerges from it. According to the traditional Jewish view, messianism performs a similar act, but for different reasons: In messianic times, there will, indeed, no longer be a night, because the demonic will have lost its destructive-redemptive function. In both contexts, the demonic proves to be identified with a powerful and irrational force, but beyond doubt a positive and, as Agamben suggests, a dialectically liberating one as it frees humanity by destruction (*Potentialities*, 150–51). Contrary to Agamben's view, however, this force does not preclude melancholy in the here and now: In lament, regarded as an expression of mourning, the demonic arising from the darkness of the night illuminates it, or, rather, turns darkness itself into light. In this as yet unredeemed world, Scholem's dark, demonic light constitutes, in Benjamin's terminology, one of the sparks that prefigures messianic times and participates in bringing it about, but without denying—or rather precisely by acknowledging—that darkness is still reigning on earth. We can see a parallel between Benjamin's melancholic angel—who seeks happiness and the *tikun* of the world but is unable to accomplish this redemptive task—and Scholem's lament, which is both a melancholic and radiantly lucid expression of unfulfilled yearning for redemption.

PART IV

# Exile, Remembrance, Exemplarity

# 10  Paradoxes of Exemplarity: From Celan to Derrida

"One can become a Jew, just as one can become a human being; one can Judaize. . . . I consider this commendable."[1] This sentence in Paul Celan's preliminary notes for his "Meridian" speech, delivered in 1961 on the occasion of receiving the Büchner Prize, the highest literary distinction in Germany, paradoxically describes a universal human capacity in terms of a particular culture, tradition, or ethnic group. Instead of resolving this paradox, Celan reinforces it in the subsequent elaborations on this odd verb *"verjuden"*: "Verjuden: es ist Anderswerden"—"Judaizing: that is, becoming other." Beyond the provocation of invoking in a positive sense a word referring to an age-old antisemitic myth signifying the contamination of something—most often a place or an institution, but also an entire society—by Jews, Celan's sentence is problematic because it posits a universal potential—the "becoming other" of *"man*," of anyone—in the name of a particular—the Jew. This discursive procedure seems questionable in both logical and ideological terms and calls for careful and skeptical scrutiny.

Attributing characteristics and values associated with Jewishness to Jews and non-Jews alike partakes of a long and loaded tradition. In "'The Jew Within': The Myth of Judaization in Germany,"[2] Steven Aschheim reconstructs the history of "the strange doctrine of 'Judaization'" from the inception of Christian theology to the Third Reich, finding its most prominent representatives in the late nineteenth and twentieth century in figures such as Richard Wagner and the Nazi ideologues. *Verjudung*, in Aschheim's words, connoted a condition in which Jews were not only considered poisonous for German society but also in which the "Jewish spirit" ostensibly had "seeped through the spiritual pores of the nation to penetrate and undermine the German psyche itself."[3] As Aschheim points out, this myth and its consequences, which, in the extreme, led to the desire to purge an entire society of any manifestation of Jewishness, was made possible by the "detachability" of the "Jewish spirit" from actual Jews, who were considered both the carriers and the symbol of a variety of traits considered despicable and dangerous to the German body politic. Above and beyond the stereotypical associations with rootlessness, materialism, and parasitism, the Jew became both the agent and the metaphor for the feared erosion of the German nation's unity and cohesion. Precisely this option of detaching Jewish attributes from actual Jews, however, allowed for a reversal of the myth of Judaization in late twentieth-century thought.

In their works, several—mainly French—postmodern thinkers such as Jean-François Lyotard and Maurice Blanchot attached a positive value to attributing presumably Jewish characteristics to non-Jews, and they associated it with a subversive power apt to undermine an oppressive existing order. Jewish critics such as Alain Finkelkraut, Jonathan Boyarin, and Daniel Boyarin have strongly criticized this reversal, objecting to this backhand universalizing of the Jew and insisting on the need to retain the distinction between "real" and "figural" Jews in order to preserve the latter's historical and cultural particularity. Celan's notes, while seemingly affirming a universalizing troping of the Jew, articulate a third possibility that is equally distant from universalism and particularism, a figure of thought that ultimately aims to undermine the boundary between these options.[4]

The complexity arising from Celan's lines pertains to what Jacques Derrida, in his "Philosophical Nationality" seminars conducted in the 1980s and 1990s, calls the "paradox of exemplarity." In those seminars, discussed in depth by Dana Hollander,[5] Derrida explores "discourses of national affirmation" that yield statements of this sort: To be most particularly French is to be most devoted to the universal value of equality.[6] She cites another example given by Derrida—Fichte's claim that Germanness is the exemplary expression of "freedom of the spirit."[7] How—and, above all, to what effect—Derrida asks, can authors of such statements invoke a particular entity in their articulation of universalist values such as equality or freedom? Derrida indicates that beyond their nationalist chauvinism, such statements are paradoxical at their core: In both cases, an irresolvable tension between a specific nation and a claim to universal attributes puts the particularity of this nation into question.

Derrida points out that a similar structure underlies the role assigned to Europe in the discourses of Edmund Husserl and Martin Heidegger: These two philosophers regard it as "world civilization" and "culture" as such, as the "telos of all historicity: universality."[8] This idea of Europe implies that in order for Europe to be most itself—a world civilization—it must open itself to its other, to humanity in general. As Hollander states: "Europe as a cultural project striving to universalize its particular heritage would then consist in equating the European project with the very project of denying its specific identity."[9] In Derrida's words: "It is necessary to make ourselves the guardians of an idea of Europe . . . that consists precisely in not closing itself off in its own identity and in advancing itself in an exemplary way towards what it is not."[10]

Derrida identifies a similar paradox in the Jewish claim of election. Implicitly referring to Franz Rosenzweig and Emmanuel Levinas, Derrida defines the Jewish claim of being "elected" as "having been chosen as a guardian of truth, a law, an essence, in truth here, of a universal responsibility."[11] He then proceeds to explore the boundaries of this claim.

Derrida is understandably critical of such statements and speaks of exemplarism as a "formidable temptation."[12] In a kind of counter-reading, however, that turns these statements on their head, Derrida goes beyond objecting to such claims and reveals a redemptive dimension in the paradox inherent in them. For Derrida, such statements become instances in which "national affirmations" are neither simply particularistic, as they take place in the name of universal philosophical values, nor simply universalist because they make their claims in the name of cultural particulars. Instead, they draw both the particular and the universal into a logical impasse that opens up closed identities and destabilizes petrified dichotomies within and between established discourses. They thereby undermine the oppositions between positions bent on strengthening particularist identities and those that encourage the dissolution of differences in the universal. Despite their seemingly paradoxical and contradictory nature, statements of "national exemplarity" would thus present an alternative that eschews both the egocentric chauvinism of particularism and the disregard for cultural differences characteristic of universalist discourses. Derrida regards what he calls "the German-Jewish phenomenon" as an especially powerful expression of this dynamic.[13]

In "Interpretations at War: Kant, the German, the Jew,"[14] a reading of Hermann Cohen's *Deutschtum und Judentum*, Derrida formulates the "paradox of exemplarity" explicitly in the German-Jewish context: "What happens when a people presents itself as exemplary? . . . In what sense and how, since the *Aufklärung* . . . has . . . the German-Jewish pair been doubly exemplary of this [paradox of] exemplarity?"[15] In response to this question, Derrida forges a link between the privileged status of the German and the Jewish: the "German" as an exemplary site of the elaboration of a nationalism with a universal mission and the "Jewish" in the experience of the election of a people with a universal responsibility.[16] In intertwining these two self-images and their respective "paradoxes of exemplarity" into each other, the German-Jewish pair becomes the very site of self-difference, a mode of being, thinking, and writing that invokes Jews but is not necessarily embodied by them.

Associating Jewishness with universally available values and ideals has for a long time been considered a prerogative of German-Jewish thinkers in the Enlightenment tradition, who searched for what Aschheim aptly calls an "honorable synthesis,"[17] a way of accommodating their Jewish particularity with a universalist ethics grounded in imperatives addressed to a common humanity. From the early twentieth century, German-Jewish thinkers have, indeed, regarded the Jew as a kind of noble "other"—a paradigmatic stranger for Georg Simmel, a conscious pariah for Hannah Arendt, a representative of a spirit free of preconceptions for Walter Benjamin, and a figure independent of the "consensus of the compact majority"[18] for Freud. While adopting a similar vision of the Jew as both an outsider and one who disturbs the established order in a positive manner, Derrida attempts to undo the self-laudatory dimension of these more or less hidden manifestations of exemplarism. Pursuing this paradox to its ultimate logical impasse, he declares: "If the self-identity of the Jew or of Judaism were to consist of this exemplarity, that is, in a certain non-self-identity"—meaning the German-Jewish situation par excellence—"then the more one dislodges self-identity, the more one says 'my own identity consists in not being identical to myself, in being foreign, non-coincident with myself, etc.,' the more one is Jewish! And at that moment, the word, the attribute 'Jewish' . . . the logical proposition 'I am Jewish' thus loses all assurance, is swept up in an ambition, a claim, an outbidding (surenchère) without end!"[19]

The exemplary discourses of national affirmation that concern us here assert the most universal philosophical values in the name of the most particular, national-cultural, or linguistic entities. Thus, they have the structure of an aporia. Far from seeing in such an aporia a mere dead end, however, Derrida argues that these discourses lead to a relentless *mise en abîme*, an unending experience of undecidability, an "outbidding without end" that corresponds in its logical structure to the groundlessness of the figure of noncoincidence with itself. This figure, as we have seen, is regarded as Jewish, an attribute that is, in turn, being put into question by that very groundlessness and so on, ad infinitum. It is in this very structure of infinite regress that Derrida sees an opening toward an ethical stance no longer grounded in or aiming for a stable identity, but, on the contrary, emerging from and oriented toward this vertiginous dynamic itself.

To understand this dynamic better, it may be helpful to consider a critique of Derrida's views formulated by Jonathan Boyarin. In *Thinking in Jewish*,[20] Boyarin is critical of Derrida's blindness to the particularity of Jewish difference, which, for him, is constituted by the Jews' "diasporic experience" and the specific historical legacy generated by this mode of existence. "Allegorizing all difference into a univocal difference," Boyarin writes, "is to be blind to concrete particularity."[21] He claims that the Jews invoked by Derrida—but also by other French thinkers such as Lyotard and Nancy—stand for an abstract, "paradigmatic other" because of their importance for European modernism. Boyarin points out that Freud, Benjamin, Kafka, Adorno, Arendt, Celan, and the like are not "the Jews" as such. They are not representative of actual Jews but are, for these French thinkers, figures that embody the abstraction of self-difference. Boyarin traces the role of the Jew as ultimate disturber of the universal, which he equates with Christianity, back to the apostle Paul, for whom, paradoxically, becoming a "good Jew" meant precisely renouncing one's specific difference. Not only does positing the figure of the Jew as the "paradigmatic other" ignore the Jews' concrete specificity, but also, according to Boyarin, the very act of allegorizing is problematic because it divests those with historically grounded identities of their difference. "Real Jews," Boyarin concludes, "end up being a trope"—from the Greek τρόπος (*tropos*)—"a turn, a change"—and lose all reference to their specific historical and cultural experience. It is thus crucial how one regards the operation of troping the Jew and whether one can approach Jewishness figuratively while at the same time doing justice to the particulars of the Jewish historical experience and cultural tradition.

Jonathan Boyarin's critique does not adequately do justice to Derrida. Circumventing both conceptual fixation and factual description, Derrida introduces the historical concrete in a performative mode of writing that has far-reaching consequences. As neither a historian who stays with the particular nor a traditional philosopher who aims at universal abstractions, Derrida thematizes—and in his mode of writing, enacts—the passages and breaks that occur when actual experiences, specific situations, and particular linguistic forms turn into general possibilities. Derrida continuously shifts registers between philosophical conceptualization and personal narration. The importance Derrida attaches to the particular way of articulating general content—a characteristic generally attributed to literary texts and explicitly invoked by Derrida—has significant implications for his approach to the "paradox of exemplarity." As his reading of Yosef Yerushalmi's *Freud's Moses* will show, the seemingly contradictory logic of attributing universal values to a particular national affirmation can be a source of awareness that the universal always and necessarily articulates itself in a specific narrative mode, a particular idiom, and from within a specific historical, cultural, and existential situation.

## Freud—Yerushalmi—Derrida

Attempts to reveal the Jewish dimension of the great figures of German-Jewish literature and thought such as Kafka, Benjamin, or Freud are a privileged locus of exemplarism. Numerous studies exploring the Jewish dimension of the lives and works of these figures emphasize their universal relevance precisely in light of their existence as Jews in a foreign, often hostile, environment. Their existence as both participants and outsiders has become an emblem of universal modernity. Because of the correspondences between the split or multiple identities acquired by Jews in such contexts and the multilayered structure of the self uncovered by psychoanalysis, investigations into the Jewish dimension of Freud's life and work are a particularly fertile ground for such reflections. These studies range from the most straightforward recovery of a "Jewish Freud" to the most sophisticated and subtle reflections on the implications of this approach itself. Many of these studies take literally Freud's answer to the question "What is left to him that is

Jewish after he has abandoned all common characteristics of his compatriots?" He famously replied: "A very great deal and probably the essence." Those who then go on to search for this Jewish "essence" in his life and writings will collect and aggrandize all things Jewish in Freud and emphasize their universal significance. These instances of exemplarism are, in many ways, inspired by Freud's own attributions of universal values to national characteristics such as the Jewish primacy in the "*Fortschritt in der Geistigkeit,*" the advance in spirituality or intellectuality, which, although paired with a repression of drives and its ensuing pathologies, is taken as praise of Jewish matters.

Yosef Yerushalmi's book on Freud, written in the early 1990s, is probably the most famous and, in many ways, the most subtle example of "reading Freud Jewish."[22] In *Archive Fever*, Derrida expresses his admiration for Yerushalmi's book but criticizes passages in which he succumbs to the temptation of exemplarism. Derrida, as Hollander points out,[23] dwells on one of Yerushalmi's remarks to Freud in a fictive address in which Yerushalmi implies that "Freud's thinking lacks 'the anticipation of a specific hope for the future.' . . . It is on this question of hope or hopelessness," Yerushalmi adds "that your teaching may be at its most un-Jewish."[24] Derrida draws a parallel between this claim—the attribution of "Jewishness" to hope—and a claim Yerushalmi makes in an earlier book, *Zakhor*, that "only in Israel and nowhere else is the injunction to remember felt as a religious imperative to an entire people."[25] He reacts to Yerushalmi's statement in an overtly personal and astonishingly emotional tone: "I would have liked to spend hours, in truth an eternity, meditating and trembling before this sentence." This trembling represents both a poignant response to and a critique of these claims: "How can one not tremble before this sentence?" Derrida continues:

> I wonder, while trembling, if they are just, the sentences that reserve for Israel *both* the future *and* the past *as such*, *both* hope . . . and the duty of memory. . . . (Unless, in the logic of this election, one were to call by the *unique* name of Israel all the places and the people who would be ready to recognize themselves in this anticipation and in this injunction.) Because if it is just to remember the future and the injunction to remember . . . , it is no less just to remember the others, the other others and the others in oneself, and that the other peoples could say the same thing—in another way.[26]

Despite his criticism of Yerushalmi's exemplarist claims, Derrida affirms Yerushalmi's mode of approaching Freud—a highly personal perspective that concludes with a fictive monologue, a direct address by Yerushalmi to Freud, "which in reading, contesting, or in calling to Freud, repeats in an exemplary fashion the logic of *Freud's Moses*. The strange result of this performative repetition . . . is that the interpretation of . . . the Jewish legacy can only illuminate, read, interpret, establish its object, namely a given inheritance, by inscribing itself into it."[27]

Derrida insists that the question of Freud's Jewishness, and indeed of the meaning and significance of Jewishness as tradition and legacy, cannot be approached from a neutral, indifferent perspective but only as a performative act by a specific speaker inscribed in a particular situation. Fully acknowledging the discomfort—*das Unbehagen*—that he experiences in the face of attempts to identify Freud as Jewish, to identify hope and memory and psychoanalysis as Jewish, Derrida nevertheless does not advocate submitting to universalist demands. Instead, Yerushalmi's confrontation with *his* Jewishness brings out an acknowledgment of the weight of Derrida's own—and in the end anyone's own—legacy. Each person, Derrida suggests, bears his or her inheritance and faces it as legacy that can and must be faced from within one's life.

Derrida eschews both a homogenizing universalism and the self-celebration of identitarian particularism. Furthermore, far from obliterating the concrete historical experience, Derrida, in fact, confronts the appeal to Jewish exemplarity from within his own situation and through his own particular mode of writing. Derrida intermingles personal memories of his childhood in Algiers with his early experiences of antisemitism, experiences he describes as the autobiographical origin of his critique of national affirmations and of the "temptation of exemplarism" itself. His own mode of writing is indeed another way of approaching those questions. Derrida's oscillation between philosophical speculations and personal narrative performs the transition—the "becoming other"—from particular experience to universal possibility and thereby approaches the realm of literature, of poetry, of Paul Celan, to whom we shall now return.

## The Poem, the Jew

In light of these reflections, we can now return to the beginning, to Celan's notes that state, "*Man kann verjuden*," and read it as an exemplary instance of the "paradox of exemplarity." Here is the full quote:

> One can become a Jew, just as one can become a human being; one can Judaize, and, I would like to add, from experience: today most of all in German . . . Judaize. One can Judaize; this is, admittedly, difficult, and—why not admit this too?—many a Jew has failed in it; that is precisely why I consider it commendable. . . . Judaize: it is the becoming other. . . . Not because the poem speaks of irritation, but because it unshakably remains itself that the poem becomes irritation—that it becomes the Jew of literature. The poet is the Jew of literature—one can Judaize; this admittedly happens rarely, but sometimes it does happen.[28]

Celan's lines seem full of contradictions. They indeed articulate the "paradox of exemplarity" in its most succinct form. They unmistakably invoke a particular— "the Jew"—to describe a universally accessible condition of "becoming other," and they run into the logical impasse described by Derrida: Would not this "becoming other" at the moment when the process succeeds undo the identity suggested in the very word ver*Juden*? But there is more: "One can become a Jew, just as one can become a human being" [in the German original: Man kann zum Juden werden, wie man zum Menschen werden kann]. Can one really "become a human being," and if so, how can this "universal" question serve as an analogy to becoming a Jew? Even more paradoxically, how can the poem be praised for remaining just like the Jew, "unshakably itself," while at the same time signifying the process of "becoming other?"

In bringing into play the word "*verjuden*," Celan both speaks of *and* performs a transformation: He invokes a vocabulary of exclusion and discrimination and simultaneously turns this historically loaded, negative term—a term indicating an abject contamination by the Jew and "his spirit"—into an affirmative metaphor for transformation, for "becoming other." "*Verjuden*" thus comes to stand for an affirmation of the other in one's midst. Beyond the provocative reversal of an antisemitic insult, Celan's use of "*verjuden*" performs an ingenious crossing of the universal and the particular: One—anyone—can "become other," can be transformed, can relinquish his or her closed selfhood. At the same time, however, the metaphor's vehicle, the verb *verjuden*, retains in its resonance the singularity of its idiomatic use at specific moments in German-Jewish history. Far from dissolving the concrete particular, the universal possibility—that "*man*," "one," "anyone" can Judaize—is attained here through reference to a particular situation experienced at definite times and in a specific place, to a particular usage by a group of people and its language, German, which designates another particular group, the Jews, as intruding, unwanted strangers. In his preparatory notes to the Meridian speech, Celan links the process of *Verjudung* explicitly to the effect of poetry, its unsettling of common discourse, its power to transform the one it addresses, and its own openness to being transformed by the addressee through his or her experiences, language, situation, and individual reading. Celan enlists the power of poetic language in order to invert a murderous trope directed against the stranger into a metaphor of a positive self-estrangement performed by poetry itself.[29]

The striking, and, in many ways, dizzying imbrications of particular and universal are, in turn, achieved in a radically particular, idiomatic language. Just as "*verjuden*" ultimately cannot be translated without losing its distinct reference to the German myth reconstructed by Aschheim, so too, the only way in which the opening words of Celan's notes (where "becoming Jewish" is identified with "*zum Menschen werden*") make sense is if the universal "*Mensch*" is understood in its particular Yiddish signification as an "ethical human being." Similarly, the uniquely German word "*verjuden*" is untranslatable and, at the same time, designates the very act, the ideal of translation: the becoming other while remaining "unshakably itself." Celan thereby enacts the "endless outbidding" described in Derrida's "paradox of exemplarity." It both characterizes the poetic gesture as such as a universal possibility, while at the same time keeping the memory of—and remaining true to—a singular experience and situation and to a speaker inscribed in it, in the language of poetry.

Although Celan indeed reverses the value of the term *verjuden* and translates it as "becoming other," he is far from mystifying Jewishness as the ultimate, essential otherness. Instead, he writes in a somewhat jocular tone: "One can become Jewish. Admittedly, this is difficult and many a Jew has failed in it."[30] If a Jew can fail to "become Jewish," then a gap opens up between the literal use of *Jude* in *verjuden* and its self-conscious meaning of "becoming other" as a trope. This gap in which *verjuden* changes into something "commendable" transforms the insult into an appeal for responsibility, for accomplishing the impossible yet urgent task of remaining "unshakably oneself"—and of remaining, in the old Christian vocabulary, "*verstockt*," refusing assimilation—while letting oneself be infiltrated and contaminated by the other. The meaning generated here is central to matters German-Jewish: In finding words for an interrelationship that negates both self-identity *and* dissolution, both insularity *and* assimilation—even dialogue between separate entities, on the one hand, *and* symbiosis, on the other— Celan opens up alternative ways of envisaging the German-Jewish phenomenon. The painful history of this pair remains ineradicably inscribed in the word *verjuden*; yet, at the same time, this word itself is transformed and inverted through an act of poetic renaming into a universal name for the very act of ethical transformation itself.

What are the implications for the German-Jewish situation? Can these insights be applied to other situations or used as a model or metaphor for other intercultural and interethnic relations? Can literature play a role in answering this question? Celan's note, although in many ways unsettling, is an exemplary instance in which literature demonstrates its potential to undo dichotomies such as the universal and the particular and even reach beyond a mere reversal of the habitual ways in which these terms and their relationship are regarded. Like Derrida, Celan does not resolve the contradictions of these paradoxes at a conceptual level, but he engages in an existential confrontation with them that ends up in a commitment and a responsibility to be taken up individually, in a very specific situation.

Celan says this in German, from within his own experience, from his situation as a Jewish poet writing in the language of the perpetrators in the aftermath of the Holocaust. He says it with all the ambivalence of the painful memory captured in the word and the faint hope for a different future. He gives this memory and this hope a name recalling his inheritance, his experience, his history. Celan says it in German, a poisoned German that is not his language but a language that he makes his own through a poetic act of bitter remembrance and playful irony. "It is in this way that," as Derrida writes of his own Jewish legacy, "the oscillation and the undecidability continue, and I would dare say, must continue to mark the obscure and uncertain experience of heritage. "In any case," he continues, "I have been unable to halt this experience in me, and it has conditioned the decisions and the responsibilities that have imprinted themselves upon my life."[31] Similarly, the oscillation at work in Celan's "*Man kann verjuden*," its oscillation between singular inheritance and universal significance, endures and is imprinted in his poetry as it was in his life.

# 11  Two Kinds of Strangers: Celan and Bachmann

THE PUBLICATION OF the correspondence between Paul Celan and Ingeborg Bachmann in 2008 represented a major event in the world of German letters. The Jewish poet whose parents were murdered in the Holocaust and the Austrian daughter of a National Socialist met and fell in love in Vienna in 1948. They began exchanging letters and sent each other poetry until Celan's suicide in 1970. The fascination exerted by their epistolary exchanges undoubtedly derives from what one of the editors of their correspondence describes as the "exemplary ways in which their speaking and writing address the problem of writing and authorship after Auschwitz."[1] Indeed, their letters afford insights into the biographical, historical, and affective context in which Bachmann's and Celan's poetry came into being and provide numerous clues that illuminate their dark and difficult verses. Their correspondence becomes especially meaningful where it implicitly, and at times explicitly, addresses the very question of their exemplarity as poets after the Holocaust. In such passages, their personal relationship, its significance for the historical moment in which it took place, and the very matrix of their poetry come together. After preliminary reflections, I shall examine a single moment in the early period of their correspondence that illustrates the weight and complexity of their encounter.

Characterizing poets and their work as exemplary evokes the traditional role of poets as spokespersons for a larger community—for a group, a people, for humanity as such. It raises questions about the relationship between the singular subjectivity out of which poems emerge and the claim to more universal significance that is inherent in them. This relationship also contrasts sharply with the way in which subjectivity and general meaning relate to one another in letters, an exchange of personal missives steeped in the specific circumstances and contingencies of individual lives. Letters are essentially a private dialogue held in communicative language that presupposes the possibility of sharing a common world. Once published, they constitute a semiprivate realm, suspended midway between a subjectivity addressing a specific other, and a generality that the letters cannot claim and will never achieve. Poetic language follows a contrary logic. Poetry draws from the radical singularity of a lone subjectivity, while simultaneously conveying an equally radical claim to the general realm. The correspondence that Ingeborg Bachmann and Paul Celan exchanged over three decades reveals not only the meeting—and the clash—of two existences but also two approaches to the poetic word and its ways of relating to the world.

Speaking of the poet as the "place-keeper of the human voice" [Statthalter der menschlichen Stimme] in *The Writing Self*, Bachmann invokes a continuity between the poetic word and the language of universal humanity.[2] According to this outlook, the poet's "I" guards the ultimate but tenuous possibility of voicing truth through an embodied, speaking self. In contrast, for Celan, poetry performs a radical descent into individuation, into the particular and the singular, into what he calls "his innermost straits." [*allereigenste Enge*][3] Only there, and by way of a paradoxical inversion, does he address another—a "possibly altogether Other," as he writes in "Meridian." "I am you, when I am I," a verse from an early poem, captures this figure of inversion: It performs an antithetical turn in which the radically singular "I" midwifes meaning for the unspecified you—any you—by turning away from it.[4] In this inversion, the "I" "sets itself free," as it is not constrained by a notion of the other's expectations, interests, and imagined requirements. It liberates itself from the presuppositions and the historical ballast of common language and, finding what Adorno calls the "unsaid, the ungrasped, the as yet unsubsumed,"[5] accedes to a different and unprecedented meaning. These different poetic figures underlie Bachmann's and Celan's respective poetics and intersect in striking ways with the terms of their epistolary exchange and, possibly, their encounter altogether.

On August 20, 1949, in one of his first letters to Bachmann, Celan describes their encounter in antithetical terms: "Perhaps I am mistaken, perhaps it is so that we are evading each other *in the very place* where we would so like to meet, maybe we are both to blame."[6] In the following sentence, Celan hints at a discord that lies deeper than an emotional fear of greater intimacy. Partly revoking his generous suggestion of a shared and mutual guilt, he continues: "Maybe we are both to blame. Except that I sometimes tell myself that my silence is perhaps more understandable than yours; for the darkness that imposes it upon me is older" (*Correspondence*, 13). The wording remains elusive, but the reference is easily recognizable. The vocabulary of guilt and judgment pervades Celan and Bachmann's early correspondence, whether used explicitly or thinly disguised in suspicions and allegations, in accusations, misgivings, apologies, and pleas for exoneration. There is no doubt about who is on trial: "Your silence was certainly different from mine," Bachmann responds, and she adds: "For me, you are you; you are not 'to blame' for anything" (*Correspondence*, 16). The imbalance is striking, but its cause is not spelled out.

In their early letters, the imbalance in their relationship is at its most salient in the multiple inquiries and attempts to measure the proximity to and distance from each other. In endless variations, Bachmann affirms her closeness: "I long for you. . . . What shall I do? You are so far away from me. . . . For me, it is always about you" [Immer geht's mir um dich] (*Correspondence*, 10; translation modified). "You will conclude from this that I'm very distant from you. I can only tell you one thing; as unlikely as it seems even to me: I am very close to you" (*Correspondence*, 17). Celan asks, "How far away or how close are you, Ingeborg? Tell me, so that I know whether your eyes will be closed if I kiss you now" (*Correspondence*, 14). Bachmann, in a letter preceding Celan's question, writes, "I'm trying not to think of myself, to close my eyes and cross over to what is really meant" (*Correspondence*, 8). Closing her eyes, she leaves her own self behind and crosses the divide that lies between her and her lover in a desire to merge with what he really means. What, indeed, does he mean?

In May 1948, in Vienna, during the initial weeks of their encounter, Celan writes the poem "Praise of Distance," which includes the lines "Disloyal only am I true. / I am you, when I am I."

| Praise of Distance | Lob der Ferne |
|---|---|
| In the wells of your eyes<br>live the Madsea fishermen's nets.<br>In the wells of your eyes<br>the sea keeps its promise. | Im Quell deiner Augen<br>leben die Garne der Fischer der Irrsee.<br>Im Quell deiner Augen<br>hält das Meer sein Versprechen. |
| Here, as a heart<br>that abode among humans,<br>I throw off my clothes and the glare<br>    of an oath: | Hier werf ich,<br>ein Herz, das geweilt unter Menschen,<br>die Kleider von mir und den Glanz<br>    eines Schwures: |
| Blacker in black, am I more<br>    naked.<br>Disloyal only am I true.<br>I am you, when I am I. | Schwärzer im Schwarz, bin ich<br>    nackter.<br>Abtrünnig erst bin ich treu.<br>Ich bin du, wenn ich ich bin. |
| In the wells of your eyes<br>I drift on and dream of spoils. | Im Quell deiner Augen<br>treib ich und träume von Raub. |
| A net snared a net:<br>embracing we sever. | Ein Garn fing ein Garn ein:<br>wir scheiden umschlungen. |
| In the wells of your eyes<br>a hanged man strangles the rope.[7] | Im Quell deiner Augen<br>erwürgt ein Gehenkter den Strang. |

The poem's first stanza evokes "the wells of your eyes" where "the sea keeps its promise." The imagery echoes the verses from the opening poem of their correspondence, "In Egypt" (*Correspondence*, 3), written in the same weeks as "Praise of Distance." Both poems call upon the eye of the other—in "In Egypt" a female stranger—to "be the water," to be the tears mourning for "Ruth! Naomi! Miriam!" in order that, in his love for her, the speaker keep his promise to remain loyal to the Jewish dead. The promise is kept, however, only if the "you" remains a stranger to the "I" and does not cross over to identify and become one with him. The eyes that Celan wants to kiss when he asks Bachmann how far or how close she is might be those eyes whose tears commemorate the dead. Yet his question is ambiguous; he believes that their embrace is also a betrayal in both directions and that it creates a situation barring any resolution. In loving the stranger, he is unfaithful to the dead, in thinking of them, he betrays her. This double treason and the disjunction required to perform it seem to be, for Celan, the very condition of the lovers' embrace, although this embrace must not become a union in which the lovers merge into one. On the contrary: Only from within the irresolvable conflict can he address the beloved, commemorate the dead, and write his poetry. When she, the stranger, closes her eyes, however, forgets herself, and "crosses over," he draws a line and praises distance. Meanwhile, in her letters, Bachmann talks of "old misunderstandings that I would so like to do away with" (*Correspondence*, 28), inventing a fairyland with him as a prince from India or "some other remote, dark brown country" (*Correspondence*, 11). She, too, calls him a stranger, takes his "strange dark head between [her] hands" (*Correspondence*, 10), while she imagines castles and calls him "the desert and the sea and everything that is secret" (*Correspondence*, 11). Bachmann writes "I still know nothing about you and often fear for you because of it" (*Correspondence*, 11), but did she, in those early years of their encounter, really recognize how far he distances himself from her, what a vastly different dark brown country he remembered, and that he could love her only as a stranger?

She must have acknowledged or sensed it at times. The middle of the book containing their correspondence displays the facsimile of an early letter by Bachmann with two crossed-out lines that partially conceal a few typed words, a sentence. These words form the ending of one of four letters Bachmann had written over several months in 1951. Just before the crossed-out sentence, Bachmann refers to Celan's poem "Corona," in which he depicts them as a couple watched by others. "Please write to me occasionally. Do not write too vaguely, do not hesitate to tell me that the curtain in front of the window has burnt up again and that people are watching us from the street" (*Correspondence*, 26).

Corona

Autumn eats its leaf out of my hand:
    we are friends.
From the nuts we shell time and we
    teach it to walk:
then time returns to the shell.

In the mirror it's Sunday,
in dream there is room for sleeping,
our mouths speak the truth.

My eye moves down to the sex of my
    loved one:
we look at each other,
we exchange dark words,
we love each other like poppy and
    recollection,
we sleep like wine in the conches,

like the sea in the moon's blood ray.


We stand by the window embracing,
    and people look up from the
    street:
it is time they knew!
It is time the stone made an effort to
    flower,
time unrest had a beating heart.
It is time it were time.

It is time.[8]

Corona

Aus der Hand frißt der Herbst mir
    sein Blatt: wir sind Freunde.
Wir schälen die Zeit aus den Nüssen
    und lehren sie gehn:
die Zeit kehrt zurück in die Schale.

Im Spiegel ist Sonntag,
im Traum wird geschlafen,
der Mund redet wahr.

Mein Aug steigt hinab zum
    Geschlecht der Geliebten:
wir sehen uns an,
wir sagen uns Dunkles,
wir lieben einander wie Mohn und
    Gedächtnis,
wir schlafen wie Wein in den
    Muscheln,
wie das Meer im Blutstrahl des
    Mondes.

Wir stehen umschlungen im Fen-
    ster, sie sehen uns zu von der
    Straße:
es ist Zeit, daß man weiß!
Es ist Zeit, daß der Stein sich zu
    blühen bequemt,
daß der Unrast ein Herz schlägt.
Es ist Zeit, daß es Zeit wird.

Es ist Zeit.

Reading Celan's poems as though they were addressed to her with the immediacy of letters, Bachmann seems to affirm a situation in which an outside gaze
penetrates their embrace. The next sentence, the one that has been crossed out in
thin, regular wavy lines of black ink, adopts this external point of view of people looking into the window from outside: "Whether or not we place our tracks
together, our lives do have something exemplary, don't you think?" (*Correspondence*, 27). Exemplarity depends on an external point of view, and Bachmann
must have sensed that Celan would disapprove of this perspective, particularly
when they are seen as "exemplary" representatives of the German and the Jew.
And she was right.

In spite of the loving tone of the letters featuring this crossed-out passage, Celan responds in a tone of cold and dry intellectual distance, with what, despite its elusiveness, amounts to a momentous accusation:

> It is difficult to reply to these letters, Ingeborg; you know that, in fact, you know it better than I do, as you can look upon the situation we are now in from a side that was decisive (not to say responsible) for its creation. . . . I—not least through your overtly persistent silence—am faced with problems whose solution only produces a further problem: one of the kind that comes about because one keeps feeding them with sense and significance until, finally, one stands before them as an absurdity, incapable of asking how one got there (*Correspondence*, 30).

Facing an unresolvable problem created by Bachmann's words of love, which he deems to be "whispered carelessly into the distance" (*Correspondence*, 31), Celan thwarts the very possibility of a solution, delegitimizing even the question to which it could respond. It is tempting to fill in the gaps of these sentences, to endow them with sense and significance, reading into what he calls the "solution to the problem" either a wholehearted rejection of Bachmann or an equally complete acceptance of her love. The first case would amount to abandoning his lover, the second to breaking his oath to the dead. It remains unclear which of the two solutions he had in mind, but what indubitably emerges from these lines are an impasse and a prohibition against solving the problem. In Celan's description of this problem, neither in their hearts nor in their thoughts can they follow a linear and continuous path to the place where they so much wanted to encounter each other. They cannot reach it through a steady resolution of their dissonances and conflicts because, for Celan, the place marked by their encounter must remain unattainable, at least in words. In his most passionate letter, he writes: "Ich wollte ja auch stumm sein mit Dir" [I also wanted to be silent with you] (*Correspondence*, 86; translation modified), but in the other letters, little of this wordless embrace remains. In his letters—and in his poetry—the gap between the "I" and the stranger may not be crossed; it must remain a token of the wound that divides their pasts. His sharpest words, therefore, address the lines that Bachmann, in a premonition that testifies to her sensitivity, tried to make illegible. In these blackened words and in Celan's response to them, the lovers' existential and poetic discord coincides. Celan continues:

> If I were not involved, how fascinating it would be, and how fruitful, to follow these moments of reaching beyond oneself on both sides, this dialectically heightened indistinctness of our realities, which have been fed with our blood nonetheless! But I am involved, Inge, and so I do not have an eye for what, in that carefully crossed-out, yet not completely illegible passage in one of your letters, you call the 'exemplarity' of our relationship. And how indeed should I make an example of myself? This sort of approach has never been my concern;

my eye shuts if it is ordered to be nothing more than an eye, but not *my* eye. If this were not the case, I would not write poems (*Correspondence*, 30).

In terms that, for all their subtlety, could hardly be harsher, Celan simultaneously denounces two seemingly contradictory aspects of what he perceives to be Bachmann's way of relating to him: her understanding of their love as a total union in which their respective "I" dissolves and her invocation of a detached view of them from the outside. Refuting both perspectives, while radically affirming his own, singular, and subjective "eye" as the only point of view available to him, he specifies the site of his poetic voice at the end of the passage. If their love is a "reaching beyond oneself on both sides," a genuine forgetting of oneself, a "crossing over," he cannot have it. With this response, he violently disrupts the gesture of reaching beyond, toward her, rejecting any merger with a "you." His insistence on seeing solely with "his [own] eye" also repudiates the viewpoint of a "they," an outside perspective that would turn them and their embrace into a spectacle, and an exemplary one at that. In a shocking reference to the blood defining their respective existences, he invokes an organic metaphor for their distinctive origins, as well as for the violent past that divides them. With almost cruel sarcasm, he denounces her vision of their love as a "dialectically heightened indistinctness of our realities," that is, an uplifting synthesis that sublates (in the Hegelian sense) their differences, which are rooted in these origins and this violence. That notion would subsume and efface all that is specific and singular about them. It would transgress his imperative of seeing only with his *"own* eye" and obliterate the difference between their life experiences. It would erase the separation between them and the necessary distance for him to ensure that she remain the stranger, the one with and against whom he could live the truth of his existence.[9]

It is significant that Celan misreads the words that Bachmann wrote before crossing them out: He reads "das 'Exemplarische' *unserer Beziehung*," the exemplarity of our relationships [sic], whereas she wrote "our exemplary lives"—"Unsere Leben haben doch etwas sehr Exemplarisches" (*Correspondence*, 30).[10] Celan had to reject Bachmann's suggestion that they are representatives of the German and the Jew after the war because it would turn their singular existences into emblematic lives on opposite sides of the divide after the catastrophe. Celan's misreading, however, explains the violence of his reaction: if not only their individual lives but also their relationship itself are perceived as exemplary, then their tangible embrace would, indeed, enact the ultimate union between the Nazi's daughter and the survivor's son, erasing all differences and distinctions and closing all gaps and wounds. Concomitantly, it would restore the possibility of poetry's capacity to speak in the name of one harmoniously unified human voice. In responding to Bachmann that he does not have *"an* eye," only *"my* eye," which he identifies as the *raison d'être* of his poetry, Celan rejects this possibility.

Instead, he specifies the terms of his own poetic speech, an unsolvable, irreconcilable inversion, where his "I am you, when I am I" becomes the expression in which his personal, historical, and poetic credo come together. Nevertheless, precisely in the context of this discord with her, she is and remains, as he will write to her later, "the foundation of my life" and "the justification of my speaking" [Du bist der Lebensgrund, auch deshalb, weil Du die Rechtfertigung meines Sprechens bist und bleibst] (*Correspondence*, 86; translation modified).[11] Bachman's expunction of her words in which she calls their lives exemplary, and Celan's refusal to regard their relationship in these terms, is what we must see when we stand on the street, looking at their shadows in the window.

# 12 Exile as Experience and Metaphor: From Celan to Badiou

"The Lord shall bring thee, and thy king which thou shalt set over thee, unto a nation which neither thou nor thy fathers have known" (Deut. 28:36; KJV). This verse—one of the most succinct of the numerous diverse and variously interpretable accounts of collective exile in the Hebrew Bible—is part of the list of curses (which are really threats) pronounced on the people of Israel near the end of Deuteronomy. The tirade, which begins with the words "But it shall come to pass, if thou wilt not hearken unto the voice of the Lord thy God . . ." (Deut. 28:15; KJV), follows a list of promised blessings if the people follow the divine commandments. Among those blessings is the promise of a place of their own, a home "in the land that the Lord sware unto thy fathers to give thee" (Deut. 6:10; KJV). Like the expulsion from Paradise and the restless wandering of Cain (who fears that he will be killed in exile by anyone who finds him [Gen. 4:14]), exilic displacement appears here as punishment, as a sorrowful state. An ambiguous verse immediately follows the threat of having to live in a foreign land, among a foreign people: "And thou shalt become an astonishment, a proverb, and a byword among all the nations whither the Lord shall lead thee" (Deut. 27:37; KJV). The divergent translations of this line indicate the extent of this ambiguity. In Luther's version, for example, the words not only convey a curse and a punishment but, in connoting abjection and humiliation, do so in the most unforgiving terms: "Und wirst ein Scheusal [a horror] und ein Sprichwort [parable] und Spott [mockery] sein unter allen Völkern, dahin dich der Herr getrieben hat" (Deut. 27:37). Luther's harsh language undoubtedly reflects his hostile view of the Jews, whom he regarded as strangers who lived stiff-necked and unrepentant among the nations. The Hebrew wording, however, ולשנינה בכל העמים אשר־ינהגך יהוה שמה והיית לשמה למשל, allows for a less severe reading.

Martin Buber's translation differs notably from Luther's uncompromising tone. In Buber's German version of the Hebrew Bible, entitled *Die Schrift*, which he translated together with Franz Rosenzweig, the verse reads: "Da wirst du zu einem Staunen, / zu Gleichnis und Witzwetzung, / unter allen Völkern wohin Er dich treibt."[1] With the exception of the curious, onomatopoeic neologism "*Witzwetzung*," this rendering is closer to the English King James translation (see above). Buber, evidently seeking to soften the threatened punishment, describes

the situation of the exiled and displaced as both leading toward a new awareness and neutralizing, if not reversing, the negative judgment imposed upon the
rootless people living among other peoples. In this rendering, the astonishment
that the strangers arouse also implies wonder and, perhaps, even admiration.
Moreover, unlike Luther's "mockery" [*Spott*], the neologism "*Witzwetzung*,"
adapted from the expression "die Zunge wetzen" [to sharpen the tongue, in the
sense of whetting or sharpening a (rhetorical) blade], focuses on the perpetrators
and suggests their murderous violence against the Jewish victims. Most notable,
however, is Buber's translation of the Hebrew משל (mashal) as "*Gleichnis*" [from
"*gleich*," meaning identical or similar], a term that evokes not only a parable but
also a metaphor. This rendering of משל as a neutral term—as a rhetorical figure of
speech or as a concept—does not exclude the meaning of the deterrent example
implied in the biblical curse. It does afford, however, the possibility of regarding
Jewish displacement both in literal and in metaphorical terms, thereby granting
the singular Jewish fate a universal range and significance.

Some biblical passages that deal with exile and displacement invite interpretations in the metaphysical-existential realm, others in the political one. Even if
these two dimensions sometimes overlap, they touch upon fundamentally different levels of meaning.[2] The expulsion from Paradise lends itself to an understanding of exile as a universal *conditio humana* in the alienation of man from nature,
from fellow man, and from God. By contrast, the passage in Deuteronomy in
which the cursed and expelled people become an exception among other, settled,
nations that have their own respective homelands refers to a specific group, the
Israelites, and wields political connotations of subjugation and powerlessness.
Throughout the centuries, the Jews have, indeed, become the epitome of the displaced, wandering, and exposed stranger, the rootless intruders. The modern
philosophical and theoretical discourse that I address here, however, often attributes a positive quality to this state, portraying the Jew as an example embodying
the forfeiting of sterile fixity, oppressive dominance, and ownership associated
with territorial emplacement.

A positive understanding of Jewish exile is by no means exclusively a feature
of modernity. After the Jews' expulsion from the Iberian peninsula, the Lurianic
Kabbalah extended and deepened the metaphysical understanding of exile as a
form of consolation. According to this view, the vessels of the world had been
broken and God himself had gone into exile together with his people; as a result,
the fate of Israel in all its terrible reality had, in fact, become "at bottom a symbol
of the true state of being, yes even . . . of divine Being."[3] In this strand of thought,
so influential in modernist and postmodern theory, the condition of the Jewish people in exile corresponds to the human condition after the expulsion from
Paradise; similarly, it stands in symbolic opposition to the illusion of those who
believe they can create a home on earth and who even claim particular territory

as their property. Jewish exile, regardless of its negative (as the epitome of a reprehensible rootlessness) or positive associations (as a bearer of insight into the existential homelessness of humankind on earth), has over the centuries become the symbol and metaphor prefigured in Buber's translation of מושל in the Book of Deuteronomy.

In modernity, Jewish exile, beyond being a theological, historical, and political issue, became a polyvalent discursive theme, a literary motif, and a loaded philosophical concept. As an embodiment of ignominious rootlessness, it appears in the antisemitic depictions of the wandering, homeless outsider rejected by the nations of the earth.[4] Although the metaphorization of Jewish displacement in this context has played a part in anti-Jewish discourse, it also has led to a reversal or subversion of such discourse among many modernist Jewish authors, including Franz Rosenzweig, Walter Benjamin, Hannah Arendt, Lion Feuchtwanger, and Siegfried Kracauer. Rosenzweig famously criticizes those who are more attached to the land than to the very life of their people as a nation.[5] The Jews are, for Rosenzweig, a people that truly becomes itself only in exile, first in Egypt and then in Babylon. Neither dwelling in a Jewish homeland nor settling in a particular place, as do other nations, the Jews retain and preserve the freedom and mobility of the wanderer. The Jew is a faithful agent of his people only when he dwells in foreign lands and longs for the home he has left behind—in short, when he remains a stranger and outsider in the land in which he resides. Rosenzweig remains to this day one of the best-known pre-Holocaust philosophers with a positive approach to Jewish exile conceived as a critical alternative to territorial nationalism.[6]

In the post–World War II period, this gesture demonstrated particular critical potential. Understandably, after the years of National Socialism, the idea of the Jew as a homeless, eternal wanderer reactivated the notion of an intellectual rootedness imbedded in the law, the word, and the letter as an alternative to a national or geographic rootedness. The old motif of the wandering Jew viewed as being disruptive of all nationalisms underwent a transformation. Those who allude to the centuries-old narrative of Jewish displacement seek, on the one hand, to reverse the inimical view of the rootless Jewish people and, on the other, to propagate a universally valid alternative, and even counterforce, to ideologies of "blood and soil" and, ultimately, to all nationalist identity politics. The simultaneity of these concerns raises fundamental questions: How can one present Jewish exile as a positive, indeed exemplary, displacement and extraterritoriality in light of the history of Jewish suffering, which includes a long and bloody history of suffering *because of* the lack of a proper place? Moreover, how can one formulate a concept of nonidentity that is closely linked to not identifying with a place through recourse to a particular identity without at the same time—on the Jewish side—invoking a discourse of national self-affirmation or—on the non-Jewish side—slipping into an appropriating heteronomy?

Many writings from the second half of the twentieth century feature a motif of an exemplary and positive Jewish homelessness in numerous variations and modalities. These include works by thinkers such as Jean-Paul Sartre, Emmanuel Levinas, Maurice Blanchot, Bernard Henri-Lévy, Jean-François Lyotard, Philippe Lacoue-Labarthe, Jean-Luc Nancy, Edward Said, George Steiner, and Jacques Derrida and numerous literary analyses.[7] Some of these thinkers speak about an actual, existing Jewish people with a history and tradition carrying the *message* of or—and already this is a major difference—*embodying* rootlessness as a universal value. Some references to Jewish rootlessness are purely metaphorical; in such cases, specific manifestations of Jewishness are not only superfluous but even a hindrance to or in conflict with the dissolution of a localized identity. Different situations—which vary with the speaker, location, and time of occurrence—and different levels of metaphorization—from model and example to symbol and metaphor—produce starkly different conceptions. A fundamental difference exists between non-Jews' praise of Jewish exile as a model of a political stance worth emulating, on the one hand, and turning a heteronymous and ahistorical mythologem into a universal symbol, on the other. Similarly, one should distinguish between the victims' reversing the significance of exile as a compensatory rehabilitation of humiliation and suffering and using the concept of exile as a metaphoric screen upon which to project external ideological agendas.

On the Jewish side, envisioning a "positive" Jewish exile as a source of consolation—that is, attempting to give meaning to a painful historical experience—is not the same as deploying the figure of exile for purposes of identity politics. The universalization of Jewish exile is a precarious discourse that requires careful scrutiny: It threatens to degenerate into either (on the Jewish side) questionable self-affirmation of one's own collective identity or (on the non-Jewish side) usurping appropriation of a particular tradition, whose cultural and historical particularity is at the same time denied.

George Steiner undoubtedly represents a prime example of questionable universalization of Jewish exile by a Jewish thinker after 1945. In his article "A Kind of Survivor," which is dedicated to Elie Wiesel, Steiner writes:

> The rootlessness of the Jew, the cosmopolitanism denounced by Hitler, Stalin . . . is historically an enforced condition. . . . But though uncomfortable in the extreme, this condition is, if we accept it, not without a larger meaning. . . . Nationalism is the venom of the age. . . . *Even if it be against his harried will, his weariness, the Jew—or some Jews at least—may have an exemplary role. To show that whereas trees have roots, men have legs and are each other's guests.* . . . Even a Great Society is a bounded, transient thing compared to the free play of the mind and the anarchic discipline of its dreams.[8]

Moshe Idel criticizes Steiner's position for being unhistorical and falsifying the Jewish tradition and history; Idel applies his charge to using the modern idea of

Jewish exile as a whole. In a polemical analysis of Steiner's oeuvre, Idel criticizes his notion of a "Jewish spirit" as essentialism and illegitimate metaphorization. He argues that Steiner's recourse to the topos of Jews as "People of the Book" is not only a false transfiguration[9] that fails to do justice to Jewish life in terms of ritual and community, but also an idea that lives on only as a construct of modern intellectuals that has no genuine relationship to living Judaism. He criticizes Steiner's view of Jewish exile in similarly harsh terms: "Few Jews," states Idel, "ever imagined peregrination as more than a simple curse, reminiscent of the wandering Cain. To say otherwise is, from a historical point of view, sheer distortion or anachronism. Jews were no more enamoured of the concept of the *homo viator* than were medieval Christians or Muslims."[10] This critique, however justified historically, implies a general rejection of any continuation of the Jewish tradition under the conditions, demands, and values of modernity. Rather than examining the historical accuracy of Steiner's claim, I shall consider his statement in terms of its rhetorical gesture.

Steiner's rhetoric is seductive. For him, the Jew's specific historical situation, that is, as a rootless individual, represents a universalist—and apparently universal—ethics. These ethics, however, explicitly directed against Heidegger's "rhetoric of dwelling" and sense of home,[11] would have to reject the notion that the Jews are the exemplary nation of the rootless, an idea that this ethics, in fact, retains. Evidently aware of the problem, Steiner relativizes it with the interjection of the words "at least some Jews." If not the Jew as such, but merely "some Jews," embody the state of rootlessness, then it remains an open question whether the reference to Jews is still meaningful. Do Jews freely choose this role and must they uphold it, or does it befall them *as Jews*, in the name of an unexamined adherence to the Jewish people or its tradition? Furthermore, in Steiner's exposition, a violent historical uprooting to which he himself refers, evolves seamlessly into the admirable rootlessness of the free-floating intellect. This portrayal thereby also casts doubt on the range and tendency of Steiner's polemic: His blurring of the distinction between enforced exile and cosmopolitanism and his self-affirming idea of an exemplary role for his own people weaken his polemic against the poison of an exclusive nationalism.

Emmanuel Levinas presents a concept of Jewish exile that is more complex than Steiner's. Levinas's thinking in many ways focuses on an ethics of uprootedness. The core of his philosophy, namely, the constitution of ethical subjectivity in the exposure to the other, is presented in terms of a model of (metaphorical) exile: *La face de l'autre*, the face of the other, forces the subject out of his self-absorption and shatters every notion of autonomy. In his philosophical texts, Levinas limits the description of this concept of subjectivity to abstractions of exteriority. In his "confessional" or "Jewish" writings, however, particularly in *Difficult Freedom*,[12] this universal structure corresponds to the biblical message in the story of Abraham, who, unlike Odysseus, does not return home. Hearkening to the call of God, of the absolute Other, Abraham leaves his own land to journey to a foreign one. In his essay "Heidegger, Gagarine et nous,"[13] Levinas draws an explicit analogy between the structure of subjectivity and the Jewish foundation myth of Abraham's departure from the land of his forefathers. For Steiner, the message of Judaism is opposed to Heidegger's notion of dwelling, which the latter conceives as a response to the thrownness of man. Levinas directs his praise of Jewish rootlessness, for which he uses the terms "exile" and "exteriority" interchangeably, against Heidegger's idea of a bond to a place, that is, to what Heidegger calls soil, a rootedness that Levinas ascribes to paganism and regards as "nationalism in terms of its cruelty and pitilessness." Contrasting Judaism/Jewry to Heidegger's pagan rootedness, Levinas characterizes Jews as a deterritorialized community, one enlivened rather than deracinated by groundlessness and displacement: "The constitution of a real society is an uprooting—the end of an existence in which the 'being-at-home' is absolute."[14] For Levinas, a detachment from this bond is the basic condition of all ethics and politics: "One's implementation in a landscape, one's attachment to *Place*, without which the universe would become insignificant and would scarcely exist, is the very splitting of humanity into natives and strangers." In other words, the "spirits of the Place," the *genii loci*, are dangerous.[15]

"Judaism," Levinas writes, "has always been free with regard to place."[16] For Levinas, this negation of rootedness lies at the core of one of Judaism's universal messages. He turns this message into a fundamental distinction between Judaism and Christianity that, with its different approaches, correlates with the distinction between spirit and letter. In Levinas's view, Christian doctrine not only retains pagan residues, but also adheres to a false conception of Jewish loyalty to the letter. In his view, such loyalty refers "not [to] the subordination of the spirit to the letter, but the substitution of the letter for the soil."[17] When Levinas identifies this counterposition to rootedness as the actual message of Judaism, the contradiction between the universalist tendency of his philosophical writings and his privileging of the Jewish tradition of thought in his confessional writings becomes quite evident. He draws a clear distinction between the idea of Jewish exile as suggested by the Abraham story and Heidegger's concept of thrownness that portrays existence as fate. Abraham, as Levinas sees him, assumes of *his own free will* the responsibility of departing from the land of his forefathers. Levinas, unlike Steiner, thus distinguishes emphatically between voluntary uprooting, which he affirms, and historical enforced exile.

In Levinas, as in Steiner, the universalization of Jewish exile entails a contradictory discourse of national self-affirmation. For other thinkers, such as Sartre, Blanchot, and Lyotard, it repeatedly assumes features of a questionable appropriation of a philosophical notion dedicated to surrender of ownership—particularly a territorial one—that is associated with domination and ultimately with the violence of exclusion. The positive inversion of the old stereotype of the rootless Jew finds expression in Sartre's work in his determination of consciousness as a mode of being that is "for-itself" (*pour-soi*). Contrary to the "in-itself" (*en-soi*), consciousness is inherently marked by self-distance, which Sartre, referring explicitly to Jewish exile, describes as "diasporic."[18] In his *Anti-Semite and Jew: Reflections on the Jewish Question*,[19] Sartre notoriously defined Jewishness as a characteristic ascribed to the Jew by a hostile external perspective, thereby denying Jews any autonomy, tradition, or self-determination.[20] He nevertheless made a considerable contribution to the inversion of Jewish exile into a universal mode of existence. In his work, Sartre approaches but ultimately avoids a metaphorical appropriation of Jewish exile: In his definition of consciousness, rather than implying a direct equivalence between universal human consciousness and Jewish exile, he merely sketches a structural analogy.[21]

The case of Blanchot is different. He, partly under the influence of his friend Levinas, effects a complex bond between literature and Jewishness. In contrast to Levinas's thought, for Blanchot the placeless, rootless Jew is no longer the bearer of a message to humanity; instead, he is explicitly a metaphor in which the Jews' active participation, even their actual presence, disappears. In an implicit dialogue with Levinas, Blanchot shifts, ever so slightly yet nonetheless significantly, Levinas's conception of a universally valid "ethic of rootlessness" proclaimed by Jews, and he transforms it into a "poetics of wandering" that he associates metaphorically with Jewish exile.[22] Blanchot, like Levinas, opposes Jewish exile to the pagan fixation on place and dwelling. Whereas Levinas argues against attachment to soil from an ethical perspective, Blanchot does so in the name of literature, which for him stands for a language that resists any use or function. Such language is without foundation or *telos*; its routes are detours without goal or purpose, and therefore Blanchot considers that one can describe it with the metaphor of the Jewish people wandering in the desert.[23]

Commenting critically on Blanchot's equation, Levinas notes that in the desert, the Jews also entered into a covenant with God and became a nation. This criticism hardly undermines Blanchot's metaphorical construction: In his theory of literary language, figurative discourse does not depend on any external reality. In Blanchot's view, such discourse is, therefore, more authentic than the conceptual language of philosophy because it admits referential failure from the start. Considered as a performative and destabilizing act, a metaphor is itself a form of deterritorialization. It is not surprising that Blanchot characterizes the ethics of uprootedness that Levinas ascribes to Jews as "nomadic," thereby eliding the suffering associated with exile that runs through Jewish history: "If Judaism is destined to take on a meaning for us, it is indeed by showing that, at whatever time, one must be ready to set out, because to step outside is the exigency from which one cannot escape if one wants to maintain the possibility of a just relation: the exigency of uprooting; the affirmation of nomadic truth."[24]

In his reflections on uprootedness, Blanchot explicitly admits his indebtedness to Levinas. He asserts, however, as Sarah Hammerschlag explains, that Jewish resistance to place "appears now as a series of tropes, metaphors for human tendencies that can be disengaged from their proper referent."[25] In replacing displacement and exile with the nomadic, Blanchot elides "a mode historically associated with Judaism."[26] Jewish displacement, or rather placelessness, becomes a pure metaphor of the negation of any identity and belonging whatsoever, a "necessity of foreignness" [*exigence de l'étrangeté*], an exteriority of speech which, according to Blanchot, "unfolds in the prefix of the words exile, exodus, exteriority and *étrangeté*."[27] The sliding shift of these concepts is itself what Blanchot would term a performative act, one subverting the foundations of referential language. Metaphor is itself "similar to" the exiled Jew: a disturbing stranger, an intruder in a foreign context. It is "*impropre*" in the sense of "out of place" [un*eigen*tlich], that is, itself astray and confusing the order of identities: the Jew as metaphor, the metaphor as Jew. In this circular argument, the very exteriority that Blanchot promotes is at risk of being lost.

As metaphor of the "non-selfsame," the nonidentical Jewish exile has its apotheosis in Lyotard's *Heidegger et les "juifs."* In his distinction between "juifs" and Juifs (the latter capitalized and without quotation marks), Lyotard differentiates between the exilic "jew" as metaphor for nonidentity and the historical Jews. Lyotard most succinctly expresses his understanding of the term "jews" in his description of the "fate of this non-nation of survivors. Jews and non-Jews whose being together is owed to no authenticity of an original root, but to the sin of a never-ending anamnesis."[28] Lyotard considers that Jews who describe themselves as such are bad "jews," insofar as they claim an identity for themselves yet do not fulfil, as good "jews" should, the commandment of remembering a sublime unsayability, an "immemoriality" of the radically [divine] Other. Instead, such bad "jews" insist on a referential or narrative recourse to their particular history.[29] Lyotard later retracted this approach, ascribing it to the haste and urgency with which he wrote the text at the time of the Heidegger controversy. In later writings, he replaces his earlier metaphorization of the Jew as "jew" with a rather stereotypical praise of Jews as the "people of the letter."[30] He compares their injunction and practice of endless commenting on and interpreting of texts to the eternal wandering of exile in that such acts never definitively arrive at a goal. In other words, Jewish exegesis of scripture implies a structure of nonarrival at a fixed place. Although in his later writings Lyotard rehabilitates capitalized Jews and their tradition, his writings as a whole obliterate the historical experience of exile and obscure its hardships.

Paul Celan's work presents a powerful alternative to the dichotomy between Jews and "jews" and between "bad" real Jews attached to identity and territory and "lettered," wandering "jews." In his poems and reflections on poetry, he questions and unravels the destructive effect of metaphorization, thus preserving the perception of the singularity of specific phenomena. In a letter to Peter Szondi, he writes, "This whole metaphor-trend comes from the same direction: something is turned into a figure of speech in order to get rid of it, something is visualized that one doesn't want to believe, acknowledge."[31] One could see Celan's statement as parallel to Jonathan Boyarin's criticism of Derrida, that is, as a critique of the loss of the specific due to turning Jews into a metaphor. Celan, however, more in line with Derrida's approach and in contrast to Boyarin, unhinges the tropes and metaphors so that, even in their negation, they oscillate between connotations, acquiring universal significance while preserving the singularity of the Jewish experience of exile.

In a poem written on April 9, 1966, which concludes the cycle "Eingedunkelt," or "Darkening Light" (published in 1968), Celan envisions Jewish exile in terms similar to those of the other authors considered here. As did other thinkers who regard the Jew as the embodiment of displacement, Celan associates both rootedness and belonging to a place with Heidegger and, beyond that, with the "blood and soil" ideology of National Socialism. Celan, too, associates the alternative to this dangerous rootedness with the text and letter. He, however, does not envision either transfiguration or self-affirmation. Simultaneously, he blocks the paths to appropriation and, above all, enacts an irrefutable resistance to the forgetting of suffering, in particular, the suffering from displacement.

| | |
|---|---|
| Mit uns, den | With us, those |
| Umhergeworfenen, dennoch | thrown about, nevertheless |
|     Fahrenden: |     traveling: |
| | |
| Der eine | The sole |
| unversehrte, | unscathed, |
| nicht usurpierbare, | nonappropriable, |
| aufständische | defiant |
| Gram.[32] | grief.[33] |

In a short, two-part sentence lacking any verbs, Celan speaks as "we" (or "us") and says what or how it is "with us." The intertextual reference to Heidegger's "Being-with" [*Mitsein*] becomes more explicit in the second line, where he defines the collectivity to which he refers: The we/us are the "thrown about, nevertheless." "We" are, and also are not, the Heideggerian thrown, those thrown into the world as beings. "We" are, more precisely, "thrown about"—thrown from one place to the next, displaced, hunted, and expelled. "We" are, above all, those who

"nevertheless," despite the trauma of persecution and expulsion, eschew searching for a homeland and resist the yearning for a dwelling that would ward off the
existential condition of thrownness. "We" are those who "nevertheless" defy that
consolation, who turn the passivity of having been thrown by fate and history
into a self-determined action: "We" become the travelers [*die Fahrenden*], who as
such could be Rainer Maria Rilke's "*fahrendes Volk*," the circus people, the art-
ists and vagabonds, those unsettled and unplaced, melancholy yet of their own
free choice, nomadic wanderers. Celan's travelers, however, derive their significance from the resistance evoked in the "nevertheless"; they are the expelled and
hunted who nevertheless withstand the temptation of remaining in place, who
resolutely travel as resistance against emplacement. This resistance rests on the
only unrelenting, undiminished certainty that remains:

> The sole
> unscathed
> nonappropriable,
> defiant
> grief.

The insurmountable, defiant, grief uniting anger and mourning binds these travelers and accompanies them. It does not stand for them metaphorically nor does
it define an identity; rather, it is *with* them. It is neither to be used nor to be appropriated (as a metaphoric undoing of particularity would have it); it stands upright
amid all movement. As in the poem "At no time, lasting grief," written two years
later, it defies the "mimeticists," who "no matter how lettered," never wrote a
word "that rebels." [34] The sorrow evoked in "With Us" is as defiant as the letter of
this poem in which *Gram*, grief, and *grammaton*, the Greek word for letter, come
together in the concrete and singular reality of the poem that is open to all fellow
travelers who are touched by it.

## Coda

Discourse touching upon Jews and place has taken on an increasingly political
tone in the context of recent developments in continental thought. Today's thinkers conduct an affirmative discourse of exemplary Jewish exile in the context of
a critique of Zionism. In this discourse, the critique of the Jew who identifies
himself as Jewish and resists the universalization of the metaphorical "jew" is
taken to its radical conclusion. Simultaneously, the metaphor is charged with
the concreteness of contemporary political reality: The idea of exile as the core
of Jewishness is marshaled against its current Zionist "falsification." This line of
thought appears in numerous thinkers of otherwise often divergent views, such
as Judith Butler and Alain Badiou.[35] In her book *Parting Ways*, Butler,[36] who
otherwise questions any identity based on essential characteristics, attributes to

the Jews as such a propensity for living in exile. Similarly, in her recent article "Who Owns Kafka?" she avers: "The exilic is proper to Judaism and even to Jewishness."[37] Butler correlates this characteristic with Kafka's mode of writing, which she calls "a poetics of non-arrival." She counterposes this characteristic to the Zionist self-perception of an arrival and homecoming of Jews in the land of Israel: "What I hope to show is that a poetics of non-arrival pervades [Kafka's] work and affects, if not afflicts his love letters, his parables about journeys, and his explicit reflections on both Zionism and the German language."[38] Butler convincingly describes Kafka's writing in terms of an infinite deferral. But she not only presents her own political interpretation of this mode of writing and its alleged incompatibility with Zionism (as ultimate "arrival") as incontrovertible, she also arrives at a fixed and immutable position. Butler's harnessing of Kafka onto a set political "location" thus contradicts her praise of his "writing of non-arrival."

One of today's most prominent contemporary continental philosophers, Alain Badiou, makes pronouncements that are even more dubious. In his polemics against Jewish particularism conducted in the name of a universalism inspired by the apostle Paul, Badiou calls for abolishing the word "Jew," which he considers to be an invention of Hitler. No longer solely concerned with the surrender of a particularist identity, Badiou does not regard the Jew as either the exemplary embodiment of exile or the metaphor of deterritorialization par excellence. Instead, the Jew is—rather astonishingly—the name of "a new *place*" yet to be created ["*un nouveau lieu à créer*"].[39] This place refers to a "new Palestine," but because, for Badiou, "Palestine represents not only a local situation but stands in as a symbol of all humanity,"[40] it also carries a wider meaning. In line with the ideas of the Apostle Paul, whom Badiou calls the ultimate Jew ["juif entre les juifs"],[41] the Jew is supposed to stand for a "universalism of the Jewish site" [un universalisme de site juif],[42] in which, paradoxically, as Paul proclaimed in his new doctrine, there are "neither Jews nor Greeks" any longer. Badiou's universalism thus requires divesting the Jew of any historical, national, ethnic, or religious particularity. The consequences of this postulate are remorseless: "If we have to create a new place" [Si nous avons à créer un nouveau lieu], Badiou writes, "this is because we must create a new Jew" [c'est parce que nous avons à créer un nouveau juif].[43] Satisfying this imperative would not only solve the question of the reality, metaphoricity, or exemplarity of Jewish exile; it would solve the "Jewish Question" altogether.

# 13 Winged Words and Wounded Voices: Geoffrey Hartman on Midrash and Testimony

> Emotionally and intellectually I am with Emerson, but empirically and spiritually I'm closer to the point where Midrash and Kafka intersect.[1]

Elements of the Jewish tradition continue to inspire late-twentieth-century visions of modernity in the writings of Geoffrey Hartman, an American scholar and literary theorist of German-Jewish origin. They also point to the role literature can play in upholding the tension between Judaism and other forms of Western thought.

In his seminal essay "Midrash as Law and Literature," from which the above lines are drawn, Geoffrey Hartman positions himself between the Romantic vision of a cosmic unity resting on poetry and nature and the discontinuity and fragmentation constituting the common ground of Jewish commentary and modernist literature. The tension between these two poles underlies some of Hartman's most inspired and inspiring writings. It is only in his poetry that Hartman occasionally allows the yearning for unity and wholeness to erupt unfettered:

> The heart pleads one cry.
> Not this or that
> Not more or less
> But all. All.[2]

This first of Hartman's "Five Elegies," a poem published in *The Eighth Day* in 2013, evokes a metaphysical primal scream, a yearning for totality and unity that is enacted in the verses' structure, sense, and sound. The chiasmus uniting the "one cry" in the first verse with the final monosyllabic "all" enfolds in a choking embrace the "this or that," the "more or less," the multiplicity of differentiated, fragmentary, and incomplete phenomena. The poem is an elegy, not a hymn. Far from affirming the existence of such a cosmic unity, it conjures it up in words that implicitly lament its absence. The closing cry for "all," a majestic sentence of its own, is nothing but an awesome echo resounding in the void. It follows the most compact descriptions of the price to pay for such an absolute: the discarding of "this or that," of what is concrete, defined and tailored to the human measure of "more or less." This negation of specifics dismisses—along with "this" and "that," with "more" and "less"—the "or," which signifies not only disjunction, uncertainty, and hesitation but also the possibility of an alternative, of an escape from closure.

The Romantic vision is among Hartman's first and primary objects of study. Even as his interest moves to other fields, this vision remains, often as foil or touchstone, an object of longing. It leaves its traces in his critical and theoretical writings through many decades, resisting ever-shifting onslaughts: Modernism, deconstruction, and a concern with literature of trauma bring to the forefront the fragmentary and contingent, the unsynthesizable and ruptured. Unlike most of his fellow travelers in the heyday of literary theory, however, Hartman never fully espouses difference, deferral, and endlessly disseminating flights of meaning.

Arguably, the most intricate challenge to both his romantic longing and his allegiance to deconstruction is Hartman's encounter with Judaic texts. As a "raider of the lost ark" (*Third Pillar*, 85), he seeks to rehabilitate the treasures buried by age-old anti-Judaic foes. "Sneaking through the wall like a thief in the night," (*Third Pillar*, 85), he enters the grounds guarded by Jewish orthodox sentinels who ward off all intruders. The treasure that he conquers and transmits to us lies in the ingenious strategies employed for this simultaneous adventurous raid on several fronts. His main challenges in this rescue operation are conceptual.

In "Midrash as Law and Literature" (*Third Pillar*, 85–101), Hartman contrasts Jewish scriptures—the Hebrew Bible, Talmud, and midrashic commentary—with various concepts of unity, continuity, and totality and the traditions resting on such oneness. He addresses the Greek tradition, in particular the Aristotelian poetics of unity, the patristic exegesis that subsumes all textual contradictions and loose ends under a single and coherent foreshadowing of the kingdom of Christ, but, foremost, the Romantic vision of the cosmos as a unified whole, the "all" cried out in Hartman's elegy.

In his essay on Midrash, this vision is represented by Ralph Waldo Emerson, the author of the famous line "I am nothing; I see all."[3] A quote from Emerson's journal provides Hartman with the starting point of his contrast between romantic wholeness and Jewish fragmentation: "Away with this Jew's rag-bag of ends and tufts of brocade, velvet, and cloth-of-gold; let me spin some yards or miles of helpful twine, a clew to lead to one kingly truth."[4] Dismayed by this disparaging comment about the Jews, Hartman feels torn between loyalty to the Romantic poet and a defense of Jewish texts. Emerson's unity of all, mainly of man, nature, and poetry stands in contrast to the endless heaping up of exegetic possibilities, of possible roads to take, none of them ending up in necessary finalities. Hartman's conflicted allegiance may explain his dual approach in countering Emerson: He argues, on the one hand, that there is nothing wrong with rag-bags, bits and pieces, "this or that" and, on the other, that rag-bags are in truth the most refined of textures, with their own binding power. These somewhat divergent claims lead to formidable insights about how it is possible to relate closure and infinity, "all" and "this or that" without reconciling them.

The allusion to the "Jew's rag-bag," Hartman begins his defense of Jewish texts and commentary, does not "need to be an insult." True, the Torah displays no formal unity defined along the lines of Aristotle, nor do Midrash and Gemarah strive for the Church fathers' single-minded exegesis with its unambiguous, all-inclusive interpretation that dissolves all inconsistencies and contradictions. The Jewish commentator, the *darshan*, tries to "redeem the text's negative features (incoherence, ellipses, the disparity of historical fact and religious expectation)" and aligns them with already existing religious values. He refrains, however, from claiming any higher, God-ordained unity, regarding the incongruities and gaps as faithful renderings of *human* complexity. Even when rabbinic commentators resort to homiletic or moralistic demonstrations based on combinatory letter-counts—a practice justified by the sacredness of the Hebrew language—they receive the credit for the ingenuity of their hermeneutic discoveries, which are not taken as proof of a single, transcendent truth. Consequently, the "infinity of meaning" suggested by rabbinic Midrash is closer to the contingent ramshackle of daily life than to a mystical understanding of language as an emanation of the divine name. Furthermore, Hartman regards the fragmentariness of midrashic commentary as both the linguistic correlative of a metaphysical condition—the expulsion from Paradise or the kabbalistic "breaking of the vessels"—and of a historical trauma, the destruction of the Temple in Jerusalem. Feigned unity or harmony would be an embellishing lie or, even worse, a betrayal of Jewish memory.

Hartman also follows a different logic, however, that insists on demonstrating that the Torah and its commentary do form a unity, albeit unlike that of Greek poetics, Christian supersessionist allegoresis, or, above all, the Romantic "all." The Torah, in contrast to the Aristotelian unity of the classical work of art, lacks unity of place and time. It thus invites, or even welcomes, commentary, a nontotalizing exegesis. Together, Torah and Midrash constitute a renewable, performative unity of an absolute—the "letter-pure" scripture—and the creative freedom of interpretation. Midrashic hermeneutics has room to roam; yet, in preserving the sacred archtext, it does not fall prey to freestanding arbitrariness.

In uplifting formulations permeated with puns and paronomasias, Hartman speaks of Midrash as a literature that is yoked to the divine word but is more down to earth than are any of its contemporary scriptural genres. In refusing to treat "the sacred texts as a mysterious void" (*Third Pillar*, 92), Midrash translates scripture into a "language of common words adapted to human capacities" (*Third Pillar*, 94).

This simultaneously sacred and mundane aspect of Midrash also characterizes Hartman's reflections on testimony after the Holocaust. Although seemingly
unrelated, Hartman's writings in the two domains, the Jewish textual tradition
and remembrance of the Jewish catastrophe, exhibit a similar tension that underlies and reveals his idea of Judaism and its relation to literature and commentary.
This tension can be described in terms of the "point where Midrash and Kafka
intersect." The fragment from Kafka's diaries quoted in full in chapter 8 illustrates this junction:

> One can learn a lot from both the one who returned from near death and the
> one who returned from Sinai, but the decisive—das *Entscheidende*—one can-
> not learn from them because they themselves have not experienced it. And if
> they had experienced it, they would not have come back. But in truth, we don't
> even want to know it.[5]

Kafka draws an analogy between the most dreadful and the most elevating
experience—the confrontation with death and the face-to-face with God—and
reflects on the relationship between these experiences and ordinary life. In Kafka's
text, both encounters with the absolute provoke the individual paradoxically to
turn to the ordinary rather than to surrender to totality; they also deepen the
concern for common humanity. Furthermore, although one cannot experience
either of these encounters to the utmost, they do generate "valuable things to tell,"
and there is an implied link between these told "things"—stories or texts—and an
intensified care for common life.

Hartman's reflections on testimonies by those who escaped death in the
Holocaust and on revealed scriptures of the Jewish tradition display a similar
pattern. In both cases, his approach underscores the tension between, on the one
hand, an attraction to an unnamable absolute that eludes representation, disrupts the quotidian, and escapes human grasp and, on the other, a humanizing
impulse directed at the intelligible, the moderate, and the concrete that embraces
the impure diversity of everyday life. For Hartman, as for Kafka, both the survivor who has almost faced death and Moses, who has almost faced God, return
from the abyss and the heavenly heights with "valuable things to tell" from their
encounter with another realm. Hartman maintains, however, that this otherness
cannot fully be reached, and one should not surrender to its lure. Instead, the
words derived from the experience of the extraordinary—whether testimony or
scripture, the living voice of the witness or the dictate of the divine—come down
to us as audible or written texts. As is true for Kafka, Hartman attributes their
value not so much to their otherworldly origin as to their impact on the specific
particulars of ordinary existence. In this sense, these texts are themselves media-
tors of the encounter between the unnamable absolute and the human realm.
The thrust of Hartman's "Jewish" writings is revealed in the role textuality and

commentary play in conveying these experiences: More than mere means of transmission, they are complex reenactments of what has been experienced. A recurrent metaphor in his writings on both testimony and scripture is struggle.

## Testimony and the Struggle with Trauma

In a key sentence from "Testimony and Authenticity," a chapter in *Scars of the Spirit*, Hartman speaks of the struggle between testimony and trauma.[6] His essay reenacts this opposition in juxtaposing two approaches to language, speech, and discourse in the aftermath of the Holocaust: The first considers the Holocaust as a trauma that has shattered the human instruments to record the events of horror, disabling or delegitimizing any retelling or representation other than an invocation of abysmal silence attuned to a horror beyond words. The second, while admitting the limitations and insufficiencies of speech to do justice to the horror of the events, nevertheless encourages the recovery of individual voices and the recording of details of the survivor's specific experiences. Hartman structures his essay with a series of oppositions between these two views: He starts by praising Victor Klemperer's diaries, in which he recorded "a plethora of telling details that convey the nightmare" (*Scars*, 85). He then turns to Primo Levi's famous statement that the only true witnesses are those who could no longer witness,[7] those who, as in Kafka's text, actually do not come back: "the submerged, the dead" (*Scars*, 86). Hartman's discussion opens up the dichotomy by contrasting Jean-François Lyotard's and, more extensively, Giorgio Agamben's responses to Levi with those of the psychiatrist and child survivor of the Holocaust Dori Laub. In discussing Lyotard, the thinker of a postmodern sublime escaping representation and communicative speech who applies his vision of the *differend*—a manifestation of unsayability—to Holocaust testimony, and Agamben, the philosopher of liminality who considers the concentration camps' muselman and his utterly passive and mute existence on the threshold between the human and the nonhuman, the "integral witness," Hartman rejects their location of authentic testimony in extreme passivity and abysmal silence. This approach, he contends, neglects and devalues actual survivor witnesses, substituting an eloquent muteness for an empirical exploration of their experiences. He prefers the approach of Laub, who, while acknowledging the effect of trauma, nevertheless wishes to restore the "damaged or deeply buried ability to speak" (*Scars*, 88). Hartman distances himself, however, from the implications of Laub's view that the human is limited to communicative language.

Just as Kafka, in his last lines, resolutely turns his back on the absolute, which he claims—"we don't even want to know," Hartman, too, explicitly sides with the actual, the specific, the spoken testimony. Although actual survivor testimony necessarily remains impure, mixed, thwarted, and open to both factual error and banalization through the use of common speech, Hartman refuses the totalizing gesture of situating authenticity in the void, the silence, the absence at the core of trauma. Concomitantly, he portrays the appropriate addressee of the survivor's testimony as a caring and gentle person rather than a "hypnotized" listener (*Scars*, 88), overwhelmed by the power of what he or she hears.

In an attempt to retain this intensity even as he castigates those who devalue actual testimonies in favor of an abstract emphasis on the breakdown of speech, Hartman conceptualizes testimony itself as a clash between ordinary speech and awesome and sublime silence. The potential to capture *in vivo* the disruption in speech—rather than the rupture *of* language or its limits as such—makes video recordings of survivor testimonies Hartman's preferred medium of Holocaust remembrance. These recordings, Hartman maintains, "capture the survivor's defining struggle with trauma or loss" (*Scars*, 96). He contends that the struggle itself is transmitted to the listener. As in the most powerful post-Holocaust art and poetry, the voice of survivor testimony, however broken, "devious, self-deceiving, elliptical and occasionally erroneous" is nevertheless—and one could add precisely because of these imperfections—"eminently interpretable" (*Scars*, 88). This hermeneutic turn averts both the indifference to the specific resulting from theoretical abstractions emphasizing trauma and silence and the danger of representation's smoothing out of rupture. Framed in the vocabulary of commentary and interpretation, testimony becomes text. Simultaneously, the risk of the listener's identification with the survivor deriving from the testimony's illusion of presence and immediacy is transformed into the challenge of entering the bond of what Hartman calls a "testimonial alliance" (*Scars*, 88). In this bond, the witness's wounded voice, his struggle between silence and speech, projects onto the listener's own struggle between a self-forgetting enthrallment with what he hears and the mediated attentiveness of care.

At first sight, Hartman's attitude to testimony does not seem intrinsically Jewish. His approach to these wounded voices and the winged words of the ancient Judaic tradition converge, however, in his insistence on the interpretability of testimonies, on intimacy rather than identification or distance, on the inscription of the absolute into the ordinary, and on the description of a struggle against a dehumanizing silence.

## Midrash and the Struggle with the Angel

"Winged words" (*Third Pillar*, 112) is Geoffrey Hartman's synonym for angels, and it is with angels that man struggles. Hartman calls angels "Hermenunculi" (*Third Pillar*, 112), a neologism inviting both awe and smiles, as well as interpretation: It evokes homunculi, humans created by alchemists. As carriers of the hermeneutic act, Hermenunculi are doubtlessly manmade, but they also allude to Hermes, the messenger of the gods. Both witty and inspired, this word captures the struggle between the ordinary and the absolute that pervades Hartman's writings on Midrash. In the first chapter of *The Third Pillar*, "The Struggle for the Text," Hartman defines the terms of this confrontation as a combat between the voice of the divine—its unity, totality, and absoluteness—and human speech, a combat that he sees as paradigmatically enacted in midrashic commentary. The parallels between this struggle and the one between testimony and trauma are striking, with the notable difference that the otherness that threatens to burst into the human world stems, in the case of Midrash, not from the abyss but from heavenly heights. It is, nevertheless, no less a threat to the human. The forces unleashed from those heights are too overwhelming to leave room for man and his earthly concerns. This struggle does not demand a victory that implies the elimination of the other. It is, rather, a struggle for words, for a response to the voice from above in a humanized language. It is a struggle for words that would diminish the risk of being stricken by a force too strong, too present, too grand, so blinding and deafening that it shatters the fabric of worldly experience. These sublime forces, undoubtedly, appear so attractive and tempting—an ecstatic soaring up to higher realms or, in a more passive mode, the opening up and subjection to a divine call. Manifestations of these forces such as the *bat kol*, the celestial voice, and its effects on the person who succumbs to it, an ecstasy and trance expressed in a language without meaning and eschewing the structure of the interpretable sign, elevate and illuminate those who experience it, like lightning or a *coup de foudre* (*Third Pillar*, 133). Their intensity intoxicates, causing rapture and self-forgetting. They also risk paralyzing the listener into silence.

Midrash, the subtle and vivacious response to scripture's otherworldly claims, deflects the forces of this divine call by demanding interpretation. It thereby disciplines and tames ecstatic flights toward the formidable Other. Midrash presents an alternative response to the challenge of absolute otherness, one that leads from the experience of a supernatural disruption to an ethical alterity that leaves the reader both "instructed and roused" (*Third Pillar*, 145) and, in the juncture of the two, anchored in the realm of the human. Hartman's writings on Midrash, however, also present a countermovement to this humanizing claim: They describe hermeneutic attentiveness as a source of creativity that discloses in common words "the presence of a sacred name or alphabet" (*Third Pillar*, 94), turning exegesis into a form of prayer. This two-directional movement endows the Jewish *via hermeneutica* with an extraordinary potential of safeguarding an intellectual, aesthetic, and ethical intensity without succumbing to the totalizing dangers of the ecstatic and the sublime. This duality pervades all Hartman's writings on Midrash and invites comparison with his approach to testimony.

As in Hartman's views on testimony, the oscillation between these two attractions—the absolute and the prosaic—comes to rest on the side of the human.

Hartman maintains that in counteracting dread, fear and trembling, and the shocking suddenness of a radical, transformative event, Midrash calls upon a vocabulary of intimacy, familiarity, and proximity that thwarts both excessive distance and cohesive fusion. Just as testimony must keep at bay identification with the survivor witness, so, too, the reader of scriptures, in the midrashic approach, wards off the desire for unification—this time with the divine, which, in Judaism, forbids the merging of man and God.

Hartman's distrust of the hypnotized listener of testimony corresponds, in his writings on Midrash, to his distrust of the "reader overcome by the magic of the recorded experience or its literary vapors" (*Third Pillar*, 108). Just as a caring interlocutor is led to interpret rather than sanctify the testimonial gaps, the reader of Midrash is encouraged to adopt an interpretive rather than an ecstatic approach. The "testimonial alliance" between the survivor and his listener has its equivalent in Hartman's writings on Midrash: It is "the covenantal relation" (*Third Pillar*, 88) that binds God and man. Hartman is as suspicious of invocations of a *mysterium tremendum* in defining spirituality as he is of assigning the monopoly of authenticity in testimony to the absolute silence of trauma. In an echo of his emphasis on the interpretability of testimony, Hartman expresses sympathy with the process by which, in Midrash, the initial shock of revelation leads to "questions and problems" (*Third Pillar*, 145) that address human minds and lives.

At the same time, a comparison between Hartman's writings on testimony and those on Midrash reveals a significant difference in the method of resolving the tension between the absolute and the humanizing in these two realms. In his reflections on survivors' recollections, Hartman focuses on the way the absolute of traumatic silence is introduced into the survivor's speech: He performs a dialectic integration of the unsayable absolute with common language. As a result, the gaps and ruptures—traces of the abysmal horror—are contained in and by speech. Occasionally, his writings on Midrash describe a similar process, as when he states that midrashic hermeneutics creates a unity that preserves the sacred archtext but fits it into the human order. More often this closure never really occurs in Hartman's midrashic writings, where the pull toward the absolute is both hemmed in and given room to soar.

Rather than synthesizing the two polar attractions in his writings on Midrash, Hartman brings the earthly and heavenly together in continuous juxtapositions, simultaneities, and double movements without closure that do not shy away from paradox or contradiction. He frequently uses oxymoronic formulations—a "glorious patchwork" (*Third Pillar*, 86), a "conservative mode of transgression" (*Third Pillar*, 109)—and repeatedly speaks of a "balance of strangeness and similitude" (*Third Pillar*, 114) or a sublime voice that also tells "a very human story" (*Third Pillar*, 90). Midrash's inventiveness redeems the gaps to create a higher unity but at the same time effects a rectification toward the earthly and the human.

Hartman sees an inflection toward the human in the dual meaning of the Hebrew word "*ruach*," which signifies both the heavenly spirit and the wind. "*Ruach*," Hartman writes, "never forfeits its quality as *a tremendum, yet* as a speaking and intelligible voice it moves towards a pathos *at once* human and sublime" (*Third Pillar*, 140). Often the content of the argument in which the struggle between earthly and heavenly plays out affirms the supremacy of the common mode, but its articulation speaks another language that undermines the content of the thought. The seduction of poetic beauty, which—pace Kant—is never entirely separable from the sublime, perhaps, exerts too great a pull on Hartman's aesthetic sensibility: He neither can let go of it; nor would he confine it to a dialectic closure. At its most captivating, Hartman's prose is poetic in ways that often clash with the embrace of the common, the moderate, the tame and ordinary it purports to affirm.

According to Hartman, angels, who entice "the imagination to dangerous extraterrestrial flights" (*Third Pillar*, 111), symbolize the ultimate temptation to turn from the earthly to the sublime and heavenly. Commentary and midrashic exegesis engage in the struggle with these angels and keep those who "seduce ecstatic believers into manic and ultimately self-destructive acts within textual bonds" (*Third Pillar*, 113). Repeatedly referring to Jacob's story, Hartman devotes a chapter of *The Third Pillar* to a Midrash commenting on Jacob's encounter with an angel. In the Midrash, two rabbis discuss the biblical passage featuring the angel who, after having wounded Jacob, asks the latter to release him: "Let me go, for the day breaketh" (*Third Pillar*, 124). Debating possible meanings of this request, one of the rabbis surmises that God creates new angels every day: They utter one song of praise and then depart forever. In Hartman's own midrashic commentary, angels must die because they sing their praise in the fullness of God's presence: "If the angels are created for song, they also die of song, of ecstatic praise. Their single moment of song is also their swan song" (*Third Pillar*, 128). Imagining angels as perishable, Hartman writes, "is a warning light," a "caution for the rabbinic imagination, which is tempted by ecstasy, by turning away from earthly to heavenly, to return to the text, away from thoughts about life or death in God" (*Third Pillar*, 128). At the end of this story and its commentary, at the end of Hartman's text, the angel has become humanized and Jacob, who acquires the new name Israel, is touched by the divine. The struggle engenders the name of a tribe both winged and wounded.

# Epilogue: New Angels

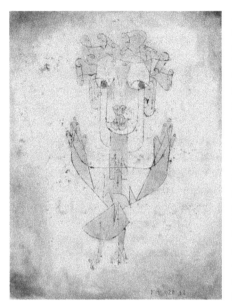

A Klee painting called *Angelus Novus* shows an angel looking as though he is about to move away from something at which he is staring intently. His eyes are wide open, his mouth is gaping, his wings are spread. This is how the angel of history must look. Where *we* perceive a chain of events, *he* sees one single catastrophe, which keeps piling wreckage upon wreckage and hurls it at his feet. The angel would like to stay, awaken the dead, and make whole what has been smashed. But a storm is blowing from Paradise and has got caught in his wings with such violence that the angel can no longer close them. The storm drives him irresistibly into the future, to which his back is turned, while the heap of rubble before him grows skyward. What we call progress is *this* storm.[1]

[Kafka] sacrificed truth for the sake of its transmissibility: its aggadic component.

    Walter Benjamin[2]

H‍IS WINGS READY for flight, Paul Klee's *Angelus Novus* looks as though he wants to return to the precarious stance lent to him in Walter Benjamin's "Angel of History," an allegory[3] that turned him into the most prized emblem of German-Jewish thought.[4] But the fame that blows in his wings from countless theoretical, literary, and visual reproductions blocks his path of return and drives him inexorably forward. In Benjamin's allegory, the angel's horrified gaze and his silence expressing unspeakable outrage bear witness to the victims of history and all that its victors have destroyed and forgotten. In the present, the angel himself has become entangled in his triumph, inspiring a myriad of poems, stories, artworks, performances, exhibitions, posters, and dozens of book covers.

The angel is invoked and parsed in sundry contexts and used for very diverse and often questionable purposes. From whence is he coming and whither is he going? Over the generations, thinkers have traced the angel's genealogy back to a variety of origins. Benjamin's correspondence with Gershom Scholem about Klee's *Angelus*, as well as his other texts featuring angels, such as his essay on Karl Kraus[5] and the autobiographical sketch "Agesilaus Santander,"[6] emphasize talmudic and kabbalistic sources. Later critics, particularly Giorgio Agamben, highlight other sources, such as Christian, Persian, and Islamic angelology, preanimist myths, and surrealist literature.[7] In the same way, the angel's meaning and function have multiplied in markedly divergent directions, variously transforming the image in ways that reflect the fate of German-Jewish thought as such. The reception of Benjamin's allegory sheds light on the changing approaches to this thought and points to the persistence, but also the tenuousness, of its legacy.

In the original controversies surrounding Benjamin's "angel of history," interpretations oscillated between a theological and a political understanding of this figure. Early readings depicted it as an echo of talmudic tales, a prophet or witness of the Jewish catastrophe, or a messianic figure longing in vain to awaken the dead and restore wholeness to the broken vessels of a primordial unity.[8] Contesting such theological or mystical interpretations, Marxist critics viewed the angel as the ultimate embodiment of the powerless materialist historian, testifying to the violence and destruction perpetrated by capitalist modernity. The most convincing interpretations of Benjamin's allegory, supported by its immediate context, his theses "On the Concept of History," which he wrote shortly before his death in 1940, reconcile the two approaches. These readings regard the angel as a messianic-revolutionary figure derived from the Jewish tradition and conveying a modernist rupture with historicism and its belief in continuity and progress.[9]

In the context of a deconstructionist approach that subverts dichotomies and closed hermeneutic frameworks, a second phase of interpretations of Benjamin's allegory rejected attempts to identify a single true meaning of the angel or to embed the figure in a particular tradition. These readings focus instead on Benjamin's views of transmission and on the positive and productive aspect of the angel's silent paralysis, interpreting this interruption of continuity as enabling new and potentially infinite meanings. These critics portray the angel not as staring backward in a fixed gaze but as looking beyond the frame of the painting and transcending the contextual boundaries of Benjamin's allegory. The angel thus represents a paradigm of transmission, in which reader and viewer, in the words of the Israeli art critic Ariella Azoulay, do not have "the passive role of saving and preserving a closed and sacrosanct relic" but rather "the active role of the destroyer, of the apostate, the exterminator."[10] They are invited to disregard the origin and status of the image in order "to tell the picture anew." Out of the destruction of its frame and meaning, Azoulay writes, "countless new angels can emerge."[11]

New angels have, indeed, emerged. After the deconstructive dissolution of the hermeneutic horizon of Benjamin's allegory, recent readings again invoke the "angel of history" in concrete and localized contexts. Some of these interpretations refer to Zionism or, more specifically, the Israeli–Palestinian conflict. Responding to the Israeli filmmaker Udi Aloni's movie about this conflict, *Local Angel*,[12] which was inspired by Benjamin's "Angel of History," Slavoj Žižek and Alain Badiou, in the book accompanying the film, reintroduce the theological and political dimension of Benjamin's allegory. These realms and the constellation between them, however, bear no resemblance to the initial politico-theological readings, particularly their references to Judaism, which now appear in the strange light of the Pauline turn.

In a text titled "What Does a Jew Want?" Žižek praises Aloni's film for including a theological dimension in its political statement. Žižek, who identifies himself explicitly as a Leninist and an "old-fashioned dialectical materialist," sees great political potential in what he calls the "Judeo-Christian tradition," calling its "deepest insight" the "idea of a weak God."[13] The Jewish component of this hyphenated tradition disappears a few lines later when Žižek invokes Benjamin's allegory: "Ultimately," Žižek writes, "my twist is that this famous Benjaminian angel to which the title of the movie refers, is Christ himself."[14] Similarly commenting on Aloni's film, Badiou barely even gestures in the direction of the Jewish tradition. Like Žižek, he praises the film's political agenda and its idea of a God who "is not the god of glory and potency but a weak and suffering god."[15] "Is it possible," he asks wistfully, "to have simultaneously a strong [Palestinian] protest and revolt, and, on the other hand, a god of weakness, pity and compassion, something like a Christian god?"[16] Several lines later, he calls this god "the god who is not the god of one people but the god of everybody." Badiou concludes by situating the vision of Aloni's *Local Angel*, as it concerns the Israeli–Palestinian conflict, "between four figures of messianism: Walter Benjamin, Gershom Scholem, Shabbetai Zvi, and Saint Paul."[17] It is doubtful whether any of the parties most immediately involved in this conflict would gladly adopt this quartet of patron saints to bless their struggle.

Commenting on the "angel of history" in the same local framework of the Israeli–Palestinian conflict, Judith Butler develops a complex, full-fledged critique. Arguing against Zionism in the name of a "different Judaism,"[18] Butler devotes several pages to Benjamin's angel, questioning whether "Benjamin [can] help us think, for instance, about the war in southern Lebanon in the summer of 2006 or the war against Gaza in 2008-9."[19] In a section titled "Storms," an allusion to the storm blowing from Paradise in Benjamin's text, she explores the nature of this destructive storm, asking in what possible sense "is the storm blowing from Paradise? Is paradise sending a message? If so, is it the kind we find in Kafka, the imperial message that never quite does arrive since the messenger is thwarted by an infinitely compressed and impenetrable architecture? If something is being destroyed, is it perhaps forward movement itself?"[20]

Understandably, Butler, as a self-proclaimed progressive thinker, laments the destruction of progress in Benjamin's allegory. In mourning the loss of a "forward movement"—the angel's inability or refusal to "look ahead"—she finds herself in surprising company, albeit at the other end of the table. Moshe Idel, too, in his critique of German-Jewish thought as desolate and melancholic—a critique he phrases in Zionist terms as an obsession with the past and, in the case of Kafka and Benjamin, a failure to participate in the promising future of Jews in Palestine, deplores the angel's backward gaze. In contrast to Butler, however, Idel takes Benjamin himself to task, objecting that his "interpretation of Paul Klee's painting *Angelus Novus* is concerned [only] with death" and "does not see the future."[21] It is, indeed, doubtful that the angel's hopes coincide with Idel's picture of the future.

What of the destructive storm that, surprisingly, blows "from paradise"? Butler's puzzlement at this paradox is justified. She resolves it by regarding destruction itself as a potential harbinger of redemption, a view that certain passages in Benjamin's writings to some extent confirm. It is, however, unlikely that Benjamin's storm called progress has any positive features or that the heap of wreckage at which the angel stares in horror and despair can be considered the collateral damage that results from restoring the "movement forward." More likely, the storm originates in Paradise because the "forward movement" of humanity did, indeed, initially bear a hopeful promise for the future of humanity, albeit a promise thwarted by the actual march of history.

Finally, Butler's suggestion that the storm in Benjamin's allegory is comparable to "Kafka's imperial message" is intriguing, but one wonders how this destructive storm could be truly analogous to Kafka's "thwarted messenger." Unlike the message sent by the dying emperor, Benjamin's storm does arrive, smashing its force into the angel's wings so violently that he can no longer fold them. If a parallel exists between the two stories, it is rather between the demeanor of Benjamin's backward-looking angel and Kafka's figure at the window awaiting the emperor's message. Both face the past, but neither can grasp it: The true message and the primal wholeness remain forever beyond reach. Kafka's "heap of sediment" at the "center of the world" and Benjamin's "heap of rubble" at the feet of the angel point to the remnants of a history gone awry. These piles of wreckage block the path between the angel and Paradise, between the man at the window and the palace of the emperor. In modernity, wholeness has turned into scattered fragments and truth into mere rumor. But rumors of true things persist, and the backward gaze in Kafka's and Benjamin's texts suggests that they still sought sparks and splinters from an obstructed, inaccessible origin. For the German-Jewish thinkers discussed in this book, the fragments of the divine message—its language, its law, and its promise of messianic redemption—are part of the debris from the past that can no longer be transmitted as truth at this late stage of history. It is through the true rumors of literature—Benjamin's allegory, Kafka's parable—that this message can be envisioned as in a dream, when the evening comes. The evening of the Jewish dimension in modernist thought may well have arrived. In Judaism, however, the falling of dusk begins a new day, and, as Benjamin reminds us, the Jews are not permitted to investigate the future.[22]

.

# Notes

## Introduction

1. *Kafka's Selected Stories*, 120.
2. Ibid.
3. Ibid.
4. One can also read Kafka's story, particularly its ending, as a reflection on the role of literature as surrogate of a higher truth that has become inaccessible. (See Vivian Liska, *When Kafka Says We*, 207–8).
5. The expression "so heißt es" [it is said] could indeed refer to the oral Torah. In his German translation of the *Talmud Bavli*, the Babylonian Talmud, Lazarus Goldschmidt frequently uses this expression (*Der babylonische Talmud*, translated by Lazarus Goldschmidt [Frankfurt am Main: Jüdischer Verlag Suhrkamp, 2002]). Originally translated by Goldschmidt between 1930 and 1936. I thank Theodor Dunkelgrün for this insight.
6. *Correspondence of Walter Benjamin 1910–1940*, 565.
7. Ibid.
8. For the purposes of this book, German-Jewish refers to authors who composed their works in German. Writers such as Celan and Kafka, for instance, wrote in German although they were not born in Germany.
9. See Nicolas Birns, *Theory after Theory*, 291.
10. Benjamin, Scholem, and Arendt knew each other well, and all three wrote extensively about Kafka. Celan frequently refers to the writings of Benjamin, Kafka, and Scholem in his poetry.
11. The only other figure Mosès assigns to "critical modernity" is the French neomystical author Edmond Jabès. Scholem is, for Mosès, a borderline case. See Stéphane Mosès, "Le Fil de la tradition."
12. Mosès, "Le Fil de la tradition," 106.
13. *Hannah Arendt: The Jewish Writings*, 466.
14. This statement deserves a commentary that cannot be elaborated here. See Benjamin, *Briefe 1910–1918*, 1: 75–76.
15. Kafka, *Letters to Milena*, letter of May 30, 1920, 19.
16. *Paul Celan–Ilana Shmueli: Briefwechsel*, 96.
17. The considerable scholarly literature addressing these authors as a group—or at least some of them in different constellations—focuses mostly on their "Jewishness" rather than on the echoes of the Jewish tradition in their writings. In those studies, the common denominator between these authors is derived from their historical, social, and political contexts, such as their experience of foreignness, marginality, exile, or antisemitism, or their attitude toward Zionism. The Jewish tradition, particularly theological topics and motifs, is often, and sometimes explicitly, bracketed out.
18. See Liska, *When Kafka Says We*.
19. Obviously, many other thinkers belonging to this group also have dealt with Jewish issues, such as Philippe Lacoue-Labarthe and Jean-Luc Nancy or, in a very different vein, Sarah

Kofman. I discuss the three mentioned here—Blanchot, Lyotard, and Derrida—in this book because they explicitly address elements of the Jewish tradition rather than questions of anti-semitism or the Holocaust. It is noteworthy that Lacoue-Labarthe and Nancy state: "Jewish identity is not an identity. The Jewish people do not constitute a subject and there is no proper Jewish being," but they insist that "anti-Semitism has been (and remains) the de facto fault line of this catastrophic century" (Lacoue-Labarthe and Nancy, "From Where Is Psychoanalysis Possible?")

20. For a succinct overview of some of these shifts, see Aschheim, *Beyond the Border*, 102–11. For one of the earliest studies of this relationship, see Susan A. Handelman, *Fragments of Redemption*. See also Gillian Rose, *Judaism and Modernity. Philosophical Essays*.

21. Jacques Derrida, *Specters of Marx*, 74.

22. Aschheim, "Icons Beyond the Border," in *Beyond the Border*, 82.

23. See Giorgio Agamben, *The Time That Remains*; Alain Badiou, *Saint Paul*; Slavoj Žižek, *The Puppet and the Dwarf*. The considerable literature discussing this new prominence of Paul in recent continental thought includes Ward Blanton and Hent de Vries, eds., *Paul and the Philosophers*; John D. Caputo and Linda M. Alcoff, *St. Paul among the Philosophers*; and Dominik Finkelde, *Politische Eschatologie nach Paulus*; Douglas Harink, ed., *Paul, Philosophy, and the Theopolitical Vision*. For a strong critique of this phenomenon, particularly of Badiou's approach to Paul, see Eric Marty, "Saint Paul among the Moderns," 80–96. See also Sarah Hammerschlag, "Bad Jews, Authentic Jews, Figural Jews," 220–40.

24. Unlike Badiou, Agamben (and to some extent Žižek) insists on a continuity between Paul and the Jewish tradition. Agamben, who, despite his critique of Derrida, is much closer to deconstruction than either Badiou or Žižek, elicits from Paul's "Letter to the Romans" the idea of the non-non-Jew, produced by the "division of the division" between Jews and others. He explicitly distinguishes this universal nonidentity from Badiou's homogenizing understanding of the universal that opposes cultural, religious, or ethnic differences altogether. In their adoption of Pauline thought, all three occasionally manifest overt tendencies of supersessionism. Each adopts the epistemic, ethical, psychological, and cultural features of Pauline Christianity, irrespective of the atheist or agnostic context in which he invokes it.

25. See Moshe Idel, *Old Worlds, New Mirrors*. For another example of this approach, see Yitzhak Melamed's paper, "Salomon Maimon and the Failure of Modern Jewish Philosophy," wherein he writes this in conclusion: "I have argued that the vast majority of modern Jewish philosophers did not have basic competence in classical Jewish literature. This unpleasant fact becomes even more disturbing if we raise the bar slightly and search for modern Jewish philosophers who were both well-informed in classical Jewish literature and good philosophers" (http://www.theapj.com/wp-content/uploads/2013/03/Melamed-on-Maimon.doc, last accessed December 3, 2015).

## Chapter 1 Early Jewish Modernity and Arendt's Rahel

1. Randolph Starn, "The Early Modern Muddle," *Journal of Early Modern History* 6, no. 3 (2002): 296–307.

2. Andrea Schatz, "Peoples Pure of Speech: The Religious, the Secular, and Jewish Beginnings of Modernity," 176.

3. Starn, "The Early Modern Muddle," 299.

4. Deborah Hertz, *How Jews Became Germans*, 218.

5. Adam Sutcliffe, "Imagining Amsterdam," 96.

6. Hannah Arendt, *Rahel Varnhagen*.

7. The first version of Hamburger's essay was written in 1933–34. She revised the essay considerably after the war in light of the Holocaust and republished it in 1968 (Käte Hamburger, "Rahel und Goethe," in *Rahel Varnhagen Gesammelte Werke*, 10: 179–204).

8. Hamburger, "Rahel und Goethe," 204.

9. Hannah Arendt and Karl Jaspers. *Correspondence, 1926–1969*, 727 (no. 134).

10. Hamburger, "Rahel und Goethe," 199.

11. Heidi T. Tewarson, *Rahel Levin Varnhagen*, 5.

12. Ibid., 6.

13. Ibid., 222.

14. Ibid., 5.

15. Ibid., 5.

16. Arendt, *Rahel Varnhagen*, 251.

17. Ibid.

18. Ibid., 250. On other issues, however, Arendt's approach closely resembles what is here designated as the early modern paradigm. This holds true especially for her view of Berlin salons and her idea of emancipation as "an admission of Jews *as Jews* to the ranks of humanity" (Hannah Arendt, *The Jew as Pariah*, 68).

19. David Ruderman, referring to Andrea Schatz in Ruderman, "Introduction," 18.

20. Edith Waldstein, "Identity as Conflict and Conversation in Rahel Varnhagen (1771–1833)," 112.

21. See Liliane Weissberg, "Schreiben als Selbstentwurf: Zu den Schriften Rahel Varnhagens und Dorothea Schlegels," *Zeitschrift für Religions—und Geistesgeschichte* 47, no. 4 (1995): 231–53.

22. Seyla Benhabib, "The Pariah and Her Shadow," 17.

23. For stark examples, see Liliane Weissberg, "Stepping Out: The Writing of Difference in Rahel Varnhagen's Letters," *New German Critique*, no. 53 (Spring–Summer 1991): 146–62; Barbara Hahn, *"Antworten Sie Mir"*: *Rahel Levin Varnhagens Briefwechsel*; and Waldstein, "Identity as Conflict."

24. Waldstein, "Identity as Conflict," 107.

25. Ibid.

26. Arendt, *Rahel Varnhagen*, 85. See also Hertz, *How Jews Became Germans*, 215.

27. Tewarson, *Rahel Levin Varnhagen*, 222.

## Chapter 2 Tradition and the Hidden: Arendt Reading Scholem

1. Hannah Arendt, *Rahel Varnhagen*, 250.

2. Gershom Scholem, *Major Trends in Jewish Mysticism*. Henceforth cited in the text as *Major Trends*, page number.

3. Steven Aschheim, *Beyond the Border*, 109. However, see Susan Neiman's contention that "Arendt's writings are charged with theological language" (Neiman, "Theodicy in Jerusalem," in *Hannah Arendt in Jerusalem*, 69).

4. Arendt, "Jewish History, Revised."

5. Stéphane Mosès, "Le Fil de la tradition est-il rompu? Sur deux formes de modernité religieuse," 107. Cited in the text as "Le Fil," page number.

6. Mosès quotes from Arendt's essay on Benjamin: "Walter Benjamin, 1892–1940," in *Men in Dark Times*. Arendt's essay is cited in the text as WB, page number.

7. Hannah Arendt and Gershom Scholem, *Der Briefwechsel*. Cited in the text as *Briefwechsel*, page number. Not all the correspondence between Scholem and Arendt has been translated into English.

8. Arendt, *Eichmann in Jerusalem*.

9. Seyla Benhabib, *Arendt's Reluctant Modernism*, 45.

10. The extent to which Scholem's own thinking is dialectical is a matter of contention. He repeatedly uses the term in his descriptions of manifestations of Jewish mysticism, but he does so in idiosyncratic ways that forego any synthesis or *Aufhebung* (in the Hegelian sense of sublation). Robert Alter notes in his preface to the 1995 edition of *Major Trends* that for Scholem, dialectical suggests "instability, unceasing change, transformation between opposite poles" (Scholem, *Major Trends*, xviii). As Arendt does, albeit for different reasons, Scholem rejects the materialist and Marxist understanding of the term. While Arendt considers dialectical thinking insufficiently rational, Scholem regards it, in Alter's words, as "a dangerous business because it brackets negation with affirmation, the nihilist denial of value with sublime aspiration" (*Major Trends*, xviii). See also Scholem's description of "Talmudic dialectic" in his diaries: Scholem, *Tagebücher 1917–1923*, 526.

11. Arendt, *Zwischen Vergangenheit und Zukunft*, 175.

12. For a contemporary critique of this Enlightenment view of agency as "individual self-empowerment, or of universal historicity," see Talal Asad, "Agency and Pain," 33. I want to thank Ethan Katz for pointing this out to me.

13. Scholem, "Redemption through Sin," in Scholem, *The Messianic Idea in Judaism*, 78–141.

14. Arendt's depiction of the Sabbateans as an authentic political movement has been contested. As Richard J. Bernstein has pointed out, it says more about Arendt's political convictions and her attraction to spontaneous beginnings emerging in popular movements than about these seventeenth-century Jewish mystics (Bernstein, *Hannah Arendt and the Jewish Question*, 57–58).

15. This runs counter to her later affirmation of the biographical that "always yields a story" (Arendt, *The Human Condition*, 97).

16. Arendt's critique of rabbinic Judaism derives less from any atheism than from her concern for the political, which she considers to be thwarted by religion. Her praise of Hasidism at the end of her text must thus be understood as her hailing of an innovative, rather than a religious, movement.

17. For a summary of this basic attitude running through Arendt's political thought, see Moshe Halbertal, *Concealment and Revelation*, 160.

18. Ibid.

19. Ibid., 161. In this respect, Arendt possibly echoes Georg Simmel's views on secrecy expressed in his essay "The Sociology of Secrecy." I want to thank Ari Joskowicz for this suggestion.

20. Martin Heidegger, *Plato's Sophist*.

21. Elisabeth Young-Bruehl, *Hannah Arendt*, 44.

22. Heidegger, *Plato's Sophist*, 11.

23. Heidegger, *Parmenides*, 16. Moshe Halbertal explains this conflict as a "constant struggle" between "the project of truth as uncovering, which privileges the concealed and hidden" and "the ongoing tendency to disguise and mask our genuine reality" (Halbertal, *Concealment and Revelation*, 156).

24. Eric Jacobson discusses the underlying presence of Heidegger in Arendt's reading of Scholem's *Major Trends* in terms of Heidegger's influence on Arendt's "emphasis on worldly concerns over interpretive ones" (Jacobson, "Ahavat Yisrael," 412). Viewing Heidegger's impact on Arendt's thought in this context is, however, too limited. As Arendt's

affirmation of the "hidden" shows, the impact of Heidegger on her thinking is not restricted to aspects of secularization that can be subsumed under a demystifying shift from religious to "worldly matters." Arendt's sympathetic approach to the hidden in the midst of otherwise primarily "enlightened" concerns also demonstrates that for her, secularization is more compatible with certain ideas and sensibilities associated with Romanticism than is generally assumed.

25. Arendt and Scholem, *Briefwechsel*, 481–83.

## Chapter 3 Transmitting the Gap in Time: Arendt and Agamben

1. Hannah Arendt, "The Gap between Past and Future," in *Between Past and Future*, 3. Further references appear in the text as "Gap," with the corresponding page.

2. Arendt Archive, Manuscript Division Library of Congress, February 21, 1970. Quoted in Mira Siegelberg, "Arendt's Legacy Usurped," 33–41, 34. Hannah Arendt Papers, Manuscript Division Library of Congress. Letter from Giorgio Agamben to Hannah Arendt, February 21, 1970. General, 1938–1976 (Series: Correspondence File, 1938–1976).

3. Giorgio Agamben, "L'Angelo malinconico." The quotation appears in the English translation "The Melancholy Angel" in Agamben, *The Man without Content*, 104–15. Further references to "The Melancholy Angel" appear as MA, with the corresponding page.

4. Arendt, "Walter Benjamin 1892–1940," in *Men in Dark Times*, 153–206. Further references are given as WB, with the corresponding page.

5. It is surprising that Agamben introduces Benjamin into his text via a reference to Arendt's essay on Benjamin. The only passage in this article that mentions Arendt's name is a footnote referring to her essay (Agamben, MA, 128, n. 2).

6. Arendt, *Zwischen Vergangenheit und Zukunft*, 1: 33. This reference is to the German edition of *Between Past and Future*, where this sentence differs from the English version. Arendt herself wrote or translated the German text. See the afterword in this edition, 373–74. The translation comes from "The Gap between Past and Future," in *Between Past and Future*.

7. Agamben, "Benjamin and the Demonic," 153.

8. Ibid., 153.

9. Ibid., 159. Agamben's emphasis.

10. Ibid., 159. It is noteworthy that Agamben, in *Infancy and History*, describes this homeland in different terms—"humankind's original home: it is pleasure" (Agamben, *Infancy and History*, 104).

11. The citation, in my translation, comes from Arendt, *Vom Leben des Geistes*, 200.

12. Arendt, *Vom Leben des Geistes*, 203.

13. Agamben, "Benjamin and the Demonic," 151–57.

14. Both quotations are from Arendt, *On Revolution*, 205.

15. Ibid.

16. I develop this argument more extensively in my book *When Kafka Says We*, 207–212. Arendt quotes this text from the translation by Willa and Edwin Muir in *The Great Wall of China*, adding that she adapted the translation slightly where she deemed it necessary to do so. In a footnote, she adds the original German text ("Gap," 283).

17. The German term appears in *Tagebücher*, 892.

18. Agamben, *State of Exception*.

19. Agamben, *The Time That Remains*.

20. Walter Benjamin, *Gesammelte Schriften* vol. 1, pt. 2: 697.

21. Ibid., vol. 1, pt. 1: 319.

22. Agnes Heller describes Arendt's idea of tradition as paradoxical: How can a radical new beginning simultaneously be transmitted as tradition? "Squeezed between the old and the new . . . humans have been thrown into a world of pull and push, but they can disrupt continuity. Beginning anew as the interruption of continuity is the essence of human action. But only continuity can be interrupted for interruption cannot be interrupted" (Heller, "Hannah Arendt on Tradition and New Beginnings," 20). Such a "division of the division" is, however, at the core of Agamben's thinking. See Agamben, *The Time That Remains*, 23.

23. Heller explains why Arendt rejects a dialectic sublation between continuity and discontinuity: "[Arendt] says that one could sublate this contradiction between continuity and discontinuity only if one told a single story about history. But those who tell a single story about history, the master thinkers of the grand narrative, cannot assume a political perspective" (Heller, "Hannah Arendt on Tradition," 20).

24. Agamben, "Benjamin and the Demonic," 153.

25. Eva Geulen, "Gründung und Gesetzgebung bei Badiou, Agamben und Arendt," 74.

26. Arendt, *On Revolution*, 206.

27. See Mustafa Dikeç. "Space as a Mode of Political Thinking," *Geoforum* 43 (2012): 669–676, 670.

28. Arendt, *On Revolution*, 175.

29. Carl Schmitt, *Political Theology*, 36.

30. Schmitt, *Political Romanticism*, 17.

31. Arendt, *The Human Condition*, 64.

32. See Marcus Twellmann, "Lex, nicht nomos," in *Hannah Arendt und Giorgio Agamben*, 84.

33. Benjamin, in a letter to Gershom Scholem from June 12, 1938, in Benjamin, *Briefe*, 2: 763. Quoted in MA, 114.

34. Benjamin, *Gesammelte Schriften* 1: 704.

35. These messengers are indeed stubborn: In Agamben's volume *Profanierungen*, published thirty-five years after "The Melancholy Angel," they are still preparing for the messianic realm (*Profanierungen*, 29).

## Chapter 4 "As if Not": Agamben as Reader of Kafka

1. Franz Kafka, *Drucke zu Lebzeiten*, 262–63.

2. Ibid., 262.

3. Kafka, *Nachgelassene Schriften und Fragmente*, 2: 34.

4. 1 Cor. 7:29.

5. Giorgio Agamben, *The Time That Remains* (further references appear in the text as Time, with the corresponding page).

6. Jacob Taubes, *The Political Theology of Paul*.

7. Agamben borrows this term from Walter Benjamin's "Theses on the Philosophy of History" in Benjamin, *Illuminations. Essays and Reflections*, 257.

8. Referring to Taubes, Agamben deems Paul's message to be among "the oldest and most demanding messianic texts of the Jewish tradition" (Time, 3).

9. The final part of *The Time That Remains* is devoted to this argument, 138–45).

10. Agamben, *Homo Sacer: Sovereign Power and Bare Life*, 57f (further references appear in the text as *Homo Sacer*, with the corresponding page).

11. See Benjamin, *Illuminations*, 257.

12. The original reads "den Kreuzweg der Wege meines Denkens," in Benjamin *Briefe* 2: 620.

13. Agamben, *State of Exception*, 63f.

14. Benjamin, *Briefe*, 2: 763.

15. Agamben, *State of Exception*, 64.

16. Agamben, *Idea of Prose*, 115–17 (further references appear in the text as Prose, with the corresponding page).

17. Bachmann, *Malina*, 60.

18. Agamben, "Kafka Defended against His Interpreters" (Prose, 137f).

19. *Kafka's Selected Stories*, 129, in *Franz Kafka: Nachgelassene Schriften und Fragmente* (2: 69–70), this sentence, which previously concluded the text, is transferred to the beginning. The editors of the 2002 Fischer version based this decision on an insertion sign in the manuscript at the start of the story. Roland Reuss ("Running Texts, Stunning Drafts," 27) notes, however, that there are not one but two insertion signs in the story, at different places. The sentence's proper place, therefore, remains uncertain.

20. See Werner Hamacher: "It is a truism that every text makes possible an unlimited wealth of interpretations, applications and reactions; what is crucial, however, is that this diversity of readings does not indicate any unfortunate insufficiency on the part of the interpreters, which could be healed at a messianic moment, but, rather, that it is a structural effect of the constitution of language itself, of which every hermeneutic foundation of literary scholarship has to take account" (Hamacher, *Entferntes Verstehen*, 177).

21. Benjamin, *Illuminations*, 139.

22. Ibid., 136.

23. Ibid., 138.

24. Ibid., 139.

25. Ibid.

26. Kafka, *Nachgelassene Schriften und Fragmente*, 2: 38.

27. Benjamin, *Illuminations*, 139.

28. Ibid.

29. Benjamin, *Gesammelte Briefe*, 4: 479.

30. Agamben, *Profanierungen*, 92–93.

31. Ibid.

32. Ibid., 92.

33. Benjamin, *Illuminations*, 139.

## Chapter 5 Kafka, Narrative, and the Law

1. On this passage, see Avivah Gottlieb Zornberg, *The Beginning of Desire*, 110.

2. English version in Franz Kafka, "The Third Notebook," 166. Original: Die Krähen behaupten, eine einzige Krähe könnte den Himmel zerstören. Das ist zweifellos, beweist aber nichts gegen den Himmel, denn Himmel bedeuteten eben: Unmöglichkeit von Krähen ("Das Dritte Oktavheft," 51).

3. Kafka, *Der Prozeß*, 294–95.

4. See, for example, Theodore Ziolkowski, who reads Kafka's work as a paradigmatic exploration of the crisis of the legal system in the early twentieth century; more particularly, the debate about the relationship between law and ethics and the confounding of morality and law. Ziolkowski shows the influence on Kafka's fictional writings of his exposure to contemporary legal controversies such as the disputes between Pure Law and Free Law and the struggle between the conservative values and antiquated laws of the Habsburg Monarchy and the more modern legal system of the German Empire after 1871. Ziolkowski convincingly demonstrates that *The Trial* parodies the absurd procedures of the Austrian system based on Free

Law that make it impossible for the accused to mount a genuine defense; moreover, punishment becomes a direct effect of power. He also describes Kafka's similar dissatisfaction with Wilhemine Germany's Pure Law system of supposedly rigorously rational retribution (Theodore Ziolkowski, *The Mirror of Justice*, 225–26).

5. Examples of readings of Kafka in the context of law and literature studies include Patrick J. Glen's "Essay on Franz Kafka, Lawrence Joseph, and the Possibilities of Jurisprudential Literature" from 2011, in which he insists that Kafka "can provide a glimpse into the real and sometimes surreal world of actual legal practice" (54); he also credits Kafka with showing the need to take the multiple perspectives of the participants in legal procedures into account. A similar and equally didactic justification for reading Kafka in the context of jurisprudence is "Franz Kafka's Outsider Jurisprudence" by Douglas E. Litowitz, who emphasizes Kafka's relevance for a better understanding of the outsider who gets entangled in legal matters without knowledge of its procedures. In "Reading Kafka's Trial Politically. Justice. Law. Power," Graham M. Smith similarly demonstrates how Kafka's legal narratives depict the common man's anxiety in the face of the law's inscrutability; Smith focuses on modern man's vain desire for justice and Kafka's characters' inability to locate, read, or *fix* the law because, although they desire the order it would provide, they reject the necessary sovereign authority that its legitimacy would require. All these examples ignore the specificity of the literary aspect of Kafka's work.

6. Carl Schmitt, *Political Theology.*

7. Letter of July 20, 1934, in Walter Benjamin, *Benjamin über Kafka*, 160; Walter Benjamin, *Gesammelte Briefe*, 4: 459.

8. Derrida, "Before the Law," 195.

9. Ibid, 198.

10. Giorgio Agamben, *Potentialities*, 172.

11. Walter Benjamin, *Benjamin über Kafka*, 20.

12. Ibid, 154.

13. Benjamin, *Selected Writings*, 1: 236–52.

14. Ibid. 2: 498.

15. Rodolphe Gasché, *The Stelliferous Fold*, 278–79.

16. Ibid., 278.

17. Benjamin, *Selected Writings*, 2: 498 (translation altered).

18. Benjamin, *Benjamin über Kafka*, 16.

19. Ibid.

20. Gesammelte Schriften, vol. 2, pt. 3: 1236.

21. Benjamin, *Selected Writings* 2: 815.

22. Benjamin, *Gesammelte Briefe*, 4: 478.

23. Benjamin, *Gesammelte Schriften*, vol. 2, pt. 3: 1246.

24. Benjamin, *Benjamin über Kafka*, 117.

25. This correspondence starts with a letter from Scholem in which he conveys to Benjamin his admiration of the Prague author: "Today, just as ten years ago, his short story 'Before the Law' counts for me as one of the best that exists in the German language" [Seine kurze Geschichte "Vor dem Gesetz" gilt mir heute wie vor zehn Jahren für eine der besten, die es im Deutschen gibt] (*Benjamin über Kafka*, 63). In 1931, Scholem took strong exception to Benjamin's denial that the law is at the heart of Kafka's work and, more particularly, to what he deemed to be Benjamin's "strictly profane" understanding of the law.

26. It was Scholem who initially encouraged Benjamin to include in his Kafka essay a discussion of the "Halakhic and Talmudic reflections as they so pressingly appear in 'Before the Law.'" Scholem did so mainly to please the publisher Schocken, whom he had persuaded to invite Benjamin to submit his Kafka essay (Benjamin, *Benjamin über Kafka*, 19).

27. Ibid., 79.

28. For a succinct reflection on this difference between Scholem and Benjamin, see Handelman, *Fragments of Redemption*, 46.

29. Gershom Scholem to Walter Benjamin, Letter no. 66, September 20, 1934, in *The Correspondence of Walter Benjamin and Gershom Scholem. 1932–1940*, 72.

30. Stephane Mosès, *Angel of History*, 145.

31. Ibid.

32. Letter of September 20, 1934, in Benjamin, *Benjamin über Kafka*, 82. Stéphane Mosès writes that for Scholem, "the law, in the trial appears as a parody of itself: there are tribunals seated in dark attics, penal codes concealing pornographic booklets, judges who do not judge, lawyers who no longer believe in the law, police and hangmen who resemble mediocre provincial actors. This arcane and unfathomable justice," Mosès concludes, "is the reverse image of divine justice and the perfect representation of Scholem's negative theology" (Mosès, *Angel of History*, 157).

33. Benjamin, *Benjamin über Kafka*, 76.

34. Benjamin speaks here of the prophetic aspect of Kafka's "Aggadic" writing: "Die überaus präzisen Seltsamkeiten, von denen das Leben, mit dem es zu tun hat, so voll ist, sind für den Leser nur als kleine Zeichen, Anzeichen und Symptome von Verschiebungen zu verstehen, die der Dichter in allen Verhältnissen sich anbahnen fühlt, ohne den neuen Ordnungen sich selber einfügen zu können." [The precisely registered oddities that abound in the life it deals with must be regarded by the reader as no more than the little signs, portents, and symptoms of the displacements that the writer feels approaching in every aspect of life without being able to adjust to the new situation.] The most explicit reference to Kafka's vision of the situation that will become a reality in Benjamin's time is his insistence on "die fast unverständlichen Entstellungen des Daseins . . . die das Heraufkommen dieser Gesetze verraten" (Benjamin, *Benjamin über Kafka*, 41) [the almost incomprehensible distortions of existence that betray the emergence of these new laws] (Benjamin, *Selected Writings*, vol. 2, pt. 2: 496).

35. "Kafka's fixation on the sole topic of his work—namely the distortion of existence—may appear to the reader as obsessiveness" [Die Fixierung Kafkas an diesen seinen einen und einzigen Gegenstand, die Entstellung des Daseins, kann beim Leser den Eindruck der Verstocktheit hervorrufen]. Notably, Benjamin uses the word "Verstocktheit" when describing the aspect of Kafka's writings that reminds the reader of the Aggadah. At least since Luther, those seeking to discredit the Jews for refusing to acknowledge the truth of Christ have used this word.

36. Benjamin, *Benjamin über Kafka*, 78.

37. Benjamin, *Gesammelte Briefe*, 4: 458–65.

38. The seventeenth-century leader of an antinomian messianic sect.

39. Benjamin, *Benjamin über Kafka*, 75; letter from Scholem to Benjamin on July 17, 1934, in Benjamin, *Briefwechsel*, 158. In English: *Correspondence of Walter Benjamin*, 126.

40. Quoted by Benjamin in his letter to Scholem of March 28, 1933 (Benjamin, *Benjamin über Kafka*, 66).

41. Mosès, *Angel of History*, 154.

42. In his letter of July 7, 1934, Scholem accuses Benjamin of "regarding the law only from its most *profane* perspective" [die Terminologie des Gesetzes, die Du so hartnäckig nur von ihrer *profansten* Seite aus zu betrachten Dich versteifst] (emphasis by Scholem). He continues thus: "the moral world of the Halakhah and its abysses and dialectic must have been obvious to you" [Die moralische Welt der Halacha und deren Abgründe und Dialektik lagen Dir doch offenbar vor Augen] (Benjamin, *Benjamin über Kafka*, 75). Scholem believed that Benjamin's interpretation of the Halakhah lacked a theological dimension and disregarded the "abysses and dialectic" of the impossibility of fulfilling the Halakhah.

43. "What shall we say, then? Is the law sin? Certainly not! Indeed, I would not have known what sin was except through the law" (Romans, 7: 7).

44. In some respects, Scholem's view is clearly distinct from Agamben's—and Paul's: While considering the revealed law as unfulfillable, he obviously rejects the notion that Christ did fulfil the law. In his letter of August 1, 1931, he compares Kafka's writings to "the moral reflections of a Halakhist who tried putting into language a paraphrase of divine judgment" [die moralische Reflexion eines Halachisten, der die *sprachliche* Paraphrase eines Gottesurteils versuchen wollte]. But he adds, "Here, for once, a world is put into words, in which redemption cannot be assumed. Go and explain this to the Gentiles!" [Hier ist einmal die Welt zur Sprache gebracht, in der Erlösung nicht vorweggenommen werden kann—geh hin und mache das den Gojim klar! Benjamin, *Benjamin über Kafka*, 65.] For Scholem, the impossibility of fulfilling the Halakhah is part of his negative theology.

45. June 12, 38, 87.

46. Ibid., 87.

47. Ibid., 89.

48. Moshe Halbertal, "At the Threshold of Forgiveness," 34.

49. Benjamin, *Selected Writings*, 2: 496 (emphasis mine).

50. The English translation in *Selected Writings* 2, chooses "procrastination." "*Verzögerung*," however, has a more general meaning and is closer to deferral or postponement.

51. Benjamin: *Selected Writings* 2: 497.

52. Agamben writes, "The final sense of the legend is thus not, as Derrida writes, that of an 'event that succeeds in not happening' (or that happens in not happening: 'an event that happens not to happen,' *un évènement qui arrive à ne pas arriver*), but rather just the opposite: The story tells how something has really happened in seeming not to happen, and the apparent aporias of the story of the man from the country instead express the complexity of the messianic task that is allegorized in it." Agamben refers to Derrida, "Before the Law," 210; original in Derrida, "Préjugés," 359.

53. Kafka, "Das Dritte Oktavheft," 52; English: Kafka, *The Diaries*, 166 (translation slightly modified). Kafka's quote from *Tractate Baba Bathra* is somewhat distorted. The actual passage he refers to says: "Abaye said: A scholar [*talmid hakham*] who desires to betroth a woman should take with him an *am haaretz* [so that another woman] might [not] be substituted for her [who would be taken away] from him. [*Amar abaye: hai tsurba mi-rabanan de-azil likedoushe iteta nidbar am haaretz behedia, dilma michluphu lei minei*]." (See *Babylonian Talmud: Tractate Baba Bathra*, 2: 168a). I thank Eli Schönfeld for this reference.

## Chapter 6 Kafka's Other Job: From Susman to Žižek

1. Frye, *Great Code*, 195.

2. Donald M. Kartiganer, "Job and Joseph K.," 31.

3. Harold Fisch, *New Stories for Old.*, 98.

4. Susan E. Schreiner, *Where Shall Wisdom Be Found?*, 181.

5. Stuart Lasine, "The Trials of Job and Kafka's Josef K.," 187.

6. Fisch, *New Stories for Old*, 89.

7. Margarete Susman, "Das Hiob-Problem bei Kafka," 203. Further references to this essay are cited in the text as Hiob, page number.

8. Max Brod, "Franz Kafka's Fundamental Experience," 182–88. Further references to this essay are cited in the text as FK, page number.

9. Gershom Scholem to Walter Benjamin, August 1, 1931, in Benjamin, *Benjamin über Kafka*, 63–93, 64. Further references to this book are cited in the text as BK, page number.

10. Martin Buber, *Darko shel mikra*, 357; cited by Nahum Glatzer in *The Dimensions of Job*, 48.

11. Günther Anders, *Kafka Pro et Contra*, 91. Although there is no explicit evidence that Kafka actually read the Book of Job, he was doubtlessly familiar with it, not least through his reading of Søren Kierkegaard's *The Repetition*, as documented in his correspondence with Max Brod, and through plays by Yiddish theater troupes that Kafka attended and that referred to Job.

12. Kafka, *Tagebücher*, 757 (September 30, 1915). I would like to thank Stanley Corngold for making me aware of this parallel.

13. Franz Kafka, "A Little Fable," in Kafka, *The Complete Stories*, 445.

14. Jason Baker, "Introduction," in Kafka, *The Metamorphosis and Other Stories*, xvi.

15. Stanley Corngold, *Lambent Traces*, 125.

16. Anna Glazova, "Franz Kafka: Oszillierende Negationen," 2008.

17. Martin Walser, *Beschreibung einer Form*, 84.

18. Anders, *Kafka Pro et Contra*, 82.

19. For a recent, very different discussion of Susman's association of Job with Kafka, see Mark Larrimore, *The Book of "Job,"* 236–39. Larrimore states that, "if we recognize Job and Kafka as prophets, there is still hope in human life" (238). This hope, messianic in nature, comes at the price—more Christian than Jewish—of an affirmation of suffering.

20. Susman, *Das Buch Hiob und das Schicksal des jüdischen Volkes*.

21. "Als Glied eines Volkes ohne Land kann man nicht richtig leben" (FK, 184).

22. For an outstanding discussion of the correspondence between Scholem and Benjamin on Kafka, see Robert Alter, *Necessary Angels*, 3–23.

23. Mosès, *The Angel of History*, 151. Further references to this book are cited in the text as *Angel*, page number. Scholem's statement and the translation of Scholem's poem discussed in this chapter come from this book.

24. Benjamin, "Franz Kafka: On the Tenth Anniversary of His Death," in *Selected Writings*, 2: 794–818, and Benjamin, "Franz Kafka: Beim Bau der Chinesischen Mauer," in *Selected Writings*, 2: 495–500.

25. Benjamin, *The Correspondence of Walter Benjamin 1910–1940*, 449.

26. Benjamin, "Franz Kafka: Beim Bau der Chinesischen Mauer," 496.

27. "But what Kafka enjoys about these interminable reflections is the very fear that they might come to an end" (Benjamin, "Franz Kafka: Beim Bau der Chinesischen Mauer," 496–97). Benjamin in fact wrote: "Was sich aber bei Kafka in dieser Endlosigkeit gefällt ist eben doch *die Angst vor dem Ende*" [But what Kafka enjoys about these interminable reflections is, after all, the fear of the end] (BK, 42; emphasis mine).

28. Scholem read these theses, probably written in 1918, to Benjamin and his wife during a stay in Switzerland in October of the same year (Scholem, *Tagebücher 1917–1923*, 533–35). Further references to this book are cited in the text as *Tagebücher*, page number.

29. See Walter Benjamin, *Sämtliche Briefe* 1: 422.

30. Franz Kafka to Robert Klopstock, Matliary, June 1921, in Kafka, *Letters to Friends, Family, and Editors*, 285. Further references to this book are cited in the text as *Letters*, page number.

31. Kierkegaard, *Fear and Trembling*, 46.

32. Kafka, "The Burrow," in *Kafka's Selected Stories*, 162–89.

33. Kafka, "The Burrow," 169.

34. Ibid., 185.

35. I would like to thank Paula Schwebel for this important insight.

36. Judaism is not entirely devoid of explanations of human suffering in such terms, but this tendency is not central to its practices and beliefs.

37. Slavoj Žižek, *The Puppet and the Dwarf*, 129.

38. Ibid.
39. Ibid., 124.
40. Ibid.
41. Ibid.
42. Ibid., 125.
43. Slavoj Žižek, *Looking Awry*, 147.
44. Ibid., 148.

## Chapter 7 Pure Languages: Benjamin and Blanchot on Translation

1. Facsimiles of Blanchot's notes have been published in Hoppenot, *Maurice Blanchot et la tradition juive*, 461–63.
2. Even though a note at the beginning of Blanchot's essay refers to Maurice de Gandillac's translation of Benjamin (Benjamin, *Oeuvres choisies*), Blanchot's translation in his notes on the passages that he selected from Benjamin's essay does not resemble Gandillac's at all. Blanchot clearly translated these passages from the German himself, with an eye to writing his own essay on translation (Blanchot, "Traduire"). Further references to the English version of this essay will appear in the text as "Translating" with the page number.
    In this chapter, texts will be given in the original French or German when doing so is essential for the discussion.
3. Nouss, "La Réception de l'essai sur la traduction dans le domaine français," 81–82. My translation.
4. Irving Wohlfarth writes, "Der Sprachaufsatz beschreibt dessen Aufgabe vor dem Sündenfall. . . . Der Übersetzeraufsatz beschreibt die entsprechende Aufgabe danach" ("Das Medium der Übersetzung," 93). [The essay on language describes its task before the fall. . . . the essay on the translator describes the corresponding task after it].
5. Benjamin, "Aufgabe des Übersetzers," *Gesammelte Schriften*, vol. 4, pt. 1: 15. Further references to this essay will appear in the text as "Aufgabe" with the page number.
6. Walter Benjamin, "The Task of the Translator," 254. Further references will appear in the text as Translator, page number.
7. Benjamin repeatedly calls this idea of language "bourgeois" (Benjamin, "Über die Sprache überhaupt und über die Sprache des Menschen," *Gesammelte Schriften* vol. 2, pt. 1: 140–57).
8. In Gandillac's translation of Benjamin's essay into French, he speaks of "les portes d'un langage si élargi et si imprégnée [impregnated, *durchwaltet*]" (275) [in the English translation: "the gates of a language thus expanded and modified" (262)]. *Durchwaltet* is virtually untranslatable: one speaks of the presence of a divine sovereignty as "Walten Gottes," which would make of "durchwaltet" an adjective qualifying "language," i.e., a language impregnated by this divine presence.

## Chapter 8 Ideas of Prose: Benjamin and Agamben

1. Giorgio Agamben, *Idea of Prose*, 34.
2. Todorov, *Poétique de la Prose*, 87.
3. This renders the sense of the passage cited in full at the end of this chapter from Franz Kafka, *Nachgelassene Schriften und Fragmente* 2: 141. See footnote 41.
4. Walter Benjamin, "The Storyteller," *Selected Writings*, 3: 155.

5. Agamben, *Potentialities*, 171.

6. Agamben, "Language and History," in Agamben, *Potentialities*, 48–62; originally, *Walter Benjamin: tempo storia linguaggio*, 65–82.

7. Agamben, *Potentialities*, 56; Gadamer, *Truth and Method*, 458; Gadamer, *Wahrheit und Methode*, 523–34.

8. Agamben, *Potentialities*, 57.

9. Benjamin, "Theologico-Political Fragment," in *Selected Writings*, 3: 305. In German, *Gesammelte Schriften* 2: 203–04.

10. Gershom Scholem, *Über einige Begriffe des Judentums*, 166.

11. Compare Max Weber's notion of *Entzauberung* [disenchantment]—a term he borrowed from Friedrich Schiller—as a primary feature of modernity. This describes the inclination of modern society to reject traditional society's view of the world as an "enchanted garden." This new society adopts a secular, rational approach to life, valuing scientific understanding over belief.

12. Benjamin, *Selected Writings*, 4: 402; *Gesammelte Schriften*, vol. 1, pt. 3: 1232.

13. Benjamin, "The Storyteller," *Selected Writings*, 3: 143–66; "Der Erzähler," *Gesammelte Schriften*, vol. 2, pt. 2: 438–65.

14. Die messianische Welt ist die Welt allseitiger und integraler Aktualität. Erst in ihr gibt es eine Universalgeschichte. Was sich heute so bezeichnet, kann immer nur eine Sorte von Esperanto sein. Es kann ihr nichts entsprechen, eh die Verwirrung, die vom Turmbau zu Babel herrührt, geschlichtet ist. Sie setzt die Sprache voraus, in die jeder Text einer lebenden oder toten ungeschmälert zu übersetzen ist. Oder besser, sie ist diese Sprache selbst. Aber nicht als geschriebene, sondern vielmehr als die festlich begangene. Dieses Fest ist gereinigt von jeder Feier. Es kennt keine Festgesänge. Seine Sprache ist integrale Prosa, die die Fesseln der Schrift gesprengt hat und von allen Menschen verstanden wird wie die Sprache der Vögel von Sonntagskindern (Benjamin, *Gesammelte Schriften*, vol. 1, pt. 3: 1239; quoted in translation in Agamben, *Potentialities*, 48).

15. Benjamin, *Selected Writings*, 4: 404; *Gesammelte Schriften*, vol. 1, pt. 3: 1235.

16. Benjamin, *Selected Writings*, 4: 406; *Gesammelte Schriften*, vol. 1, pt. 3: 1238. For further versions, see *Gesammelte Schriften*, vol. 1, pt. 3: 1234 and 1235.

17. See also Wohlfarth, "Krise der Erzählung."

18. Benjamin, *Selected Writings*, 1: 62–74; *Gesammelte Schriften*, vol. 2, pt. 1: 140–57.

19. Benjamin, *Selected Writings*, 1: 253–66; *Gesammelte Schriften*, vol. 4, pt. 1: 9–21.

20. Benjamin, *Selected Writings*, 1: 116–200; *Gesammelte Schriften*, 1, pt. 2: 7–123.

21. Benjamin, *Selected Writings*, 4: 406; *Gesammelte Schriften*, vol. 1, pt. 3: 1238.

22. Benjamin, *Selected Writings*, 3: 152 (trans. modified); *Gesammelte Schriften*, vol. 2, pt. 2: 451.

23. Benjamin, *Selected Writings*, 3: 152; *Gesammelte Schriften*, vol. 2, pt. 2: 451.

24. Wenn nämlich . . . die Geschichtsschreibung die schöpferische Indifferenz der verschiedenen epischen Formen darstellt (wie die große Prosa die schöpferische Indifferenz zwischen verschiedenen Massen des Verses), so schließt deren älteste Form, das Epos, kraft einer Art von Indifferenz die Erzählung und den Roman ein (Benjamin, *Selected Writings*, 3: 154; *Gesammelte Schriften*, vol. 2, pt. 2: 453). Benjamin refers and implicitly criticizes Hegel's discussion of the relationship between poetic genres in his *Aesthetics*, particularly the section on the epic forms. See G.W.F. Hegel *Vorlesungen über die Ästhetik* vol. 3, pt. 3: 2, http://www.textlog.de/5775.html (last consulted July 3, 2016).

25. *Gesammelte Schriften*, vol. 1, pt. 1: 87.

26. Benjamin, *Selected Writings*, 1: 174; *Gesammelte Schriften*, vol. 1, pt. 1: 101.

27. Benjamin, *Selected Writings*, 1: 174; *Gesammelte Schriften*, vol. 1, pt. 2: 102.

28. Benjamin, *Selected Writings*, 3: 162; *Gesammelte Schriften*, vol. 2, pt. 2: 464.
29. Giorgio Agamben, *Idea of Prose*, 39–41.
30. Ibid., 39.
31. Ibid.
32. Benjamin, *Selected Writings*, 1: 340–41; *Gesammelte Schriften*, vol. 1, pt. 1: 181; Friedrich Hölderlin, "Anmerkungen zum Oedipus," 310.
33. Agamben, *Idea of Prose*, 27.
34. Heidegger, *On the Essence of Language*.
35. Agamben, *Language and Death*, 86.
36. Agamben, *Potentialities*, 59.
37. Agamben, *Idea of Prose*, 37.
38. Ibid. (trans. modified).
39. Kafka, *Nachgelassene Schriften und Fragmente*, vol. 2, pt. 5, 141.
40. Ibid.
41. Ibid.

## Chapter 9 Reading Scholem and Benjamin on the Demonic

1. Gershom Scholem, "95 Thesen über Judentum und Zionismus," in Peter Schäfer and Gary Smith, *Gershom Scholem: Zwischen den Disziplinen*, 295. My translation. References to this volume henceforth appear as Schäfer and Smith, page number.
2. Giorgio Agamben, "Walter Benjamin and the Demonic," in *Potentialities*, 138–59. Further references to this volume appear as *Potentialities*, page number.
3. Walter Benjamin, "Agesilaus Santander," in Scholem, "Walter Benjamin und sein Engel," 40–43.
4. Benjamin, "Über den Begriff der Geschichte," in *Gesammelte Schriften*, vol. 1, pt. 2: 697–98.
5. Moshe Idel, *Old Worlds, New Mirrors*, 6. Further references to this volume appear as Old Worlds, page number.
6. Benjamin, *Gesammelte Schriften*, vol. 1, part 2, 698.
7. See the discussion in Gershom Scholem, "Walter Benjamin und sein Engel," 66, 71.
8. Benjamin, "Über den Begriff der Geschichte," 697.
9. Benjamin, "Theologisch-politisches Fragment," in *Gesammelte Schriften*, vol. 2, pt. 1: 203–4.
10. Benjamin, "Karl Kraus," in *Gesammelte Schriften*, vol. 2, pt. 1: 345.
11. Ibid., 349.
12. As an example of this destructive impulse, Agamben cites Benjamin's comparison of Kafka's writings with the Aggadah, the narrative dimension of the Talmud, and he concludes: "The two Jewish categories of Halakhah (which designates the law in itself, truth insofar as it is separated from all narration) and Aggadah (that is, truth in its transmissibility) are played off against each other such that each abolishes the other" (*Potentialities*, 153). As evidence for this claim, Agamben quotes the passage from Benjamin's letter to Scholem that compares Kafka's stories to an Aggadah that would "not simply lie at the feet of doctrine as Aggadah lies beneath Halakhah, but unexpectedly raise a mighty paw against it." (*Potentialities*, 154) As shown in Chapter 5, Agamben's interpretation of this image, which, he believes, suggests a mutual destruction of the two dimensions of the Talmud, is a fundamental misreading of Benjamin's words.

13. For the similarities and difference between Scholem and Benjamin in this respect, see my essay "Kafka's Other Job."

14. See chapter 8 herein, "Ideas of Prose," for a further discussion of the topic.

15. "Mitokh hirhurim 'al ḥokhmat yisra'el" [Reflections on the Science of Judaism], published in *Luah Haaretz*. For details about this essay, see Peter Schäfer, "Gershom Scholem und die Wissenschaft des Judentums," in Schäfer and Smith, 123–24.

16. Peter Schäfer translates these words from Scholem's Hebrew essay into German as "die Entfernung des irrationellen Stachels und der dämonischen Glut" (Schäfer and Smith, 130).

17. "Ein harmloser Dummkopf, der die Gewohnheiten eines fortschrittsgläubigen Bürgers pflegt, und jeder brave jüdische Hausvater darf ihn auf den Straßen des Städtchens grüßen, des sauberen Städtchens des 19. Jahrhunderts." The English translation is taken from Biale, *Gershom Scholem*, 6.

18. Ibid., 4.

19. Quoted from Biale, *Gershom Scholem*, 4.

20. Aramaic term used in the Kabbalah to refer to the other side of the divinity, dark or evil forces.

21. See my critique of Idel on this point in my essay "On Getting It Right."

22. Benjamin calls messianism the core of Romanticism (Benjamin, *Briefe*, 1: 208).

## Chapter 10 Paradoxes of Exemplarity: From Celan to Derrida

1. "Man kann zum Juden werden, wie man zum Menschen werden kann; Man kann verjuden. . . . Ich [halte] das für empfehlenswert" (Paul Celan, *Der Meridian*, 130). The English translation is quoted from Paul Celan, *The Meridian: Final Version—Drafts—Materials (Meridian: Crossing Aesthetics)*, 131.

2. Steven Aschheim, "'The Jew Within': The Myth of Judaization in Germany," in *The Jewish Response to German Culture*, 212–24.

3. Aschheim, *Culture and Catastrophe*, 45.

4. For an excellent discussion of this reversal in French postmodern thought, see Sarah Hammerschlag, *The Figural Jew*. She notes the differences in the situation when the figural identification with the Jew occurs in a self-conscious literary mode and involves "comparison, performance and irony" (23).

5. Dana Hollander, *Exemplarity and Chosenness*.

6. Ibid., 103.

7. Ibid., 103–4.

8. Ibid., 112.

9. Ibid., 113–14.

10. Derrida, *The Other Heading*, 12.

11. Derrida, "Abraham l'autre," in *Judéités*, 12.

12. Ibid.

13. Derrida, "Interpretations at War: Kant, the Jew, the German," in *Acts of Religion*, 150.

14. Ibid., 135–88.

15. Ibid., 138.

16. See the discussion in Hollander, *Exemplarity and Chosenness*, 123.

17. Aschheim, *Culture and Catastrophe*, 59.

18. Sigmund Freud, "Ansprache an die Mitglieder des Vereins B'nai B'rith (1926)," in S. Freud, *Gesammelte Werke*, 17: 52.

19. Jacques Derrida, "Zeugnis, Gabe," 65. Quoted in English in Hollander, *Exemplarity and Chosenness*, 134.

20. Jonathan Boyarin, *Thinking in Jewish*.

21. Ibid., 67.

22. Yosef Hayim Yerushalmi, *Freud's Moses*.

23. Hollander, 198.

24. Yerushalmi, *Freud's Moses*, 95.

25. Hollander, *Exemplarity and Chosenness*, 198.

26. Jacques Derrida, *Archive Fever*, 76–77.

27. Ibid., 67.

28. Celan, *Der Meridian*, 130–31.

29. Ibid.

30. This note, as I understand it here, refutes Derrida's critique in "Abraham l'autre" that "even Celan" surrendered to "the formidable temptation of exemplarism" (Derrida, "Abraham l'autre," 32).

31. Derrida, *Schibboleth pour Paul Celan*, 98–105.

## Chapter 11 Two Kinds of Strangers: Celan and Bachmann

1. *Frankfurter Algemeine* http://www.faz.net/aktuell/feuilleton/buecher/rezensionen/belletristik/briefwechsel -celan-bachmann-wer-bin-ich-fuer-dich-wer-nach-so-vielen-jahren-1683095.html (last accessed July 17, 2016).

2. Ingeborg Bachmann, "Das schreibende Ich," 61.

3. Paul Celan, "Der Meridian," 196.

4. "Ich bin du, wenn ich ich bin," in "Lob der Ferne" [In praise of distance], in Celan, *Gesammelte Werke*, 1: 33.

5. Theodor Adorno, "Rede über Lyrik," 50.

6. Ingeborg Bachmann and Paul Celan, *Correspondence*, 13; emphasis by Celan. Further references appear in the text as *Correspondence*, page number.

7. Celan, *Gesammelte Werke*, 1: 33.

8. Ibid., 37.

9. Ruven Karr explains that Celan objected to Bachmann's description of their relationship "as exemplary" because he saw it as a "threat to his individuality." His interpretation does not, however, adequately account for Celan's insistence on seeing only "with his own eye" (Ruven Karr, "Ménage à trois," 172). Karr's volume includes a remarkable essay by Barbara Wiedemann that highlights Bachmann's attempt to present herself as victim while accusing Celan of purposely claiming victim status for himself. She quotes from Bachmann's unsent letter: "You want to be the victim, but it is only up to you, to stop being one" [Du willst das Opfer sein, aber es liegt nur an Dir, es nicht zu sein]. Wiedemann correlates Bachmann's attitude with the general postwar atmosphere in Germany (Barbara Wiedemann, "'Du willst das Opfer sein,'" 45).

10. Significantly, the translator, by mistake, put "relationship" in the plural. He may have been unconsciously misled by Bachmann's actual statement that the exemplarity concerns their lives—their two, distinct, *lives* in the plural—rather than, as Celan misreads Bachmann's passage, their *relationship* in the singular. The translator's error thus betrays his justified intuition that there were, indeed, two relationships because of the two lovers' disparate views.

11. The German original is from Bachmann and Celan, *Herzzeit—Briefwechsel Ingeborg Bachmann–Paul Celan*, 64.

## Chapter 12 Exile as Experience and Metaphor: From Celan to Badiou

1. Martin Buber with Franz Rosenzweig, *Die Schrift*, 5: 111.
2. See Arnold Eisen, "Exile," 220–21.
3. Gershom Scholem, "Kabbala und Mythos," 156.
4. See Steven Aschheim, *Culture and Catastrophe*, 47.
5. Franz Rosenzweig, *Der Stern der Erlösung*, 333.
6. Rosenzweig is, of course, neither the only one nor the first to regard the Jews as the extraterritorial people *par excellence* and to consider their rootlessness a way of preserving the unique Jewish spirituality. Major historians such as Simon Dubnow adhered to this view, and it was at the core of his debate with the cultural Zionist Ahad Ha'am. Fascinating examples of modifications of this view triggered by the Holocaust can be found in Margarete Susman's *Das Buch Hiob und das Schicksal des jüdischen Volkes* (1948) and the epilogue that Jizchak Fritz Baer added to the postwar version of his work *Galut* (first published in 1936, then again in 1947).
7. For recent examples from German-Jewish literary studies, see Bernd Witte, *Jüdische Tradition und literarische Moderne: Heine, Buber, Kafka, Benjamin*; and Anne Kuhlmann, "Das Exil als Heimat," 198. For a discussion of recent references to the motif of the Jews as the "people of the book," see Andreas B. Kilcher, "Volk des Buches."
8. George Steiner, "A Kind of Survivor," in *George Steiner: A Reader*, 232. For a more elaborate discussion of this quote, see Liska, *When Kafka Says We*, 111.
9. Moshe Idel, *Old Worlds*, 65.
10. Ibid., 68.
11. Steiner, "Heidegger's Silence," in *George Steiner: A Reader*, 263. See also Martin Heidegger, ". . . dichterisch wohnet der Mensch . . ."
12. Emmanuel Levinas, *Difficult Freedom*.
13. Ibid., 231–34.
14. Ibid., 137.
15. Ibid., 232.
16. Ibid., 232–33.
17. Ibid., 137–38.
18. Jean Paul Sartre, *L'Être et le néant*, 138.
19. Jean Paul Sartre, *Réflexions sur la question juive*.
20. Sartre retracted this position years later, but this reversal of his views remains contentious.
21. For a radical critique of Sartre's approach to the "Jewish Question," see Pierre Birnbaum, *Sur la corde raide*. See also Jonathan Judaken's *Jean-Paul Sartre and the Jewish Question*.
22. Maurice Blanchot, *L'Espace littéraire*, 91–92.
23. For an excellent discussion of the similarities and differences between Levinas and Blanchot on Jews, place, and exile, see Sarah Hammerschlag, *The Figural Jew*, esp. 173–75 and 187–96. See also my review of Hammerschlag's book in *European Journal of Jewish Studies* 6, no. 2 (2012), 303–8.
24. Maurice Blanchot, *L'Entretien infini*, 195.
25. Hammerschlag, *The Figural Jew*, 189.
26. Ibid.
27. Blanchot, *L'Entretien infini*, 18.
28. Jean-François Lyotard, *Heidegger et les "juifs,"* 152.
29. Blanchot endorsed Lyotard's position except for one point: He reacted critically to the quotation marks around "juif" because, in order to function as a self-canceling trope, there

can be no distinction between real and metaphorical *juifs*, as otherwise there would remain a referential reminder to the "real" (see Hammerschlag, *The Figural* Jew, 196).

30. See Rony Klein, "Une Rencontre inattendue entre la pensée française contemporaine et le Juif."

31. Paul Celan and Peter Szondi, *Briefwechsel*, 40.

32. Paul Celan, *Die Gedichte*, 268.

33. My translation.

34. Celan, *Die Gedichte*, 526.

35. See Gianni Vattimo and Michael Marder, *Deconstructing Zionism*.

36. Judith Butler, *Parting Ways*.

37. Butler, "Who Owns Kafka?"

38. Ibid., 4.

39. Alain Badiou, *Polemics*, 207 (emphasis added). Originally published in French in 2005 as *Circonstances 3: Portées du mot " juif."* These statements are made in the context of Badiou's discussion of Udi Aloni's film *Local Angels* and have been republished in Badiou's collection *Polemics*.

40. Badiou, *Polemics*, 205.

41. Ibid., 194; *Circonstances 3*, 65.

42. Badiou adds: "in other words, he anticipates Paul." Ibid.

43. Badiou, *Polemics*, 207; *Circonstances 3*, 86.

## Chapter 13 Winged Words and Wounded Voices: Geoffrey Hartman on Midrash and Testimony

1. Geoffrey Hartman, *The Third Pillar*, 86.

2. Hartman, *The Eighth Day*, 11.

3. Ralph Waldo Emerson, *Nature and Selected Essays*, 39.

4. Emerson, *The Heart of Emerson's Journals*, 267. Quoted in *Third Pillar*, 86.

5. Franz Kafka, *Nachgelassene Schriften und Fragmente*, 2: 141. See Chapter 8 for a further discussion of Kafka's remarks on a near-death experience.

6. Hartman, *Scars of the Spirit*, 88. Further references appear in the text as *Scars*, page number.

7. Primo Levi, *The Drowned and the Saved*, 83–84.

## Epilogue

1. Walter Benjamin, *Selected Writings*, 4: 392 (translation slightly modified).

2. Walter Benjamin to Gershom Scholem, June 12, 1938, in Benjamin and Scholem, *The Correspondence of Walter Benjamin and Gershom Scholem*, 225.

3. Most interpreters such as Stéphane Mosès and Irving Wohlfarth use the term "allegory" to describe Benjamin's "angel of history." For an interesting but contestable critique of this designation in relation to the Jewish tradition, see http://www.cms.fu-berlin.de /geisteswissenschaften/v/drehmomente/content/1-Weigel/ (last accessed February 13, 2016). See also Sigrid Weigel, *Walter Benjamin, die Kreatur, das Heilige, die Bilder*, 272–77.

4. Geoffrey Hartman notes, somewhat sarcastically, that Klee's *Angelus Novus* has been "so often reproduced that it has become, retroactively, Benjamin's logo." In Geoffrey Hartman, *Criticism in the Wilderness*, 79.

5. Benjamin's Kraus essay concludes with the image of the new angel, "perhaps one of those who, according to the Talmud, are at each moment created anew in countless throngs, and who, once they have raised their voices before God, cease and pass into nothingness" (in Benjamin, *Selected Writings*, vol. 2, pt. 2: 457).

6. In this text, Benjamin makes specific references to kabbalistic beliefs in a personal angel representing a secret self (Benjamin, "Agesilaus Santander," in Scholem, "Walter Benjamin und sein Engel," 40–3; all translations from this book are mine).

7. Giorgio Agamben is explicitly critical of Scholem's blindness to other possible references underlying Benjamin's allegory (Agamben, "Benjamin and the Demonic," 145).

8. Scholem, "Walter Benjamin und sein Engel," 35.

9. In the course of its reception, the angel inspired fantastic interpretations with various degrees of plausibility. Geoffrey Hartman believes that the angel's paper-thin curls are really Torah scrolls (Hartman, *Criticism in the Wilderness*, 79). For Otto Karl Werckmeister, the angel's wish to "reawaken the dead" was inspired by Benjamin's reading of Blaise Cendrars's novel *Moravagine*. In the novel, a filmmaker records, and then plays backward, the destruction of Paris as announced by angels above the portal of Notre Dame: reeling backward, the buildings return to wholeness and the dead arise (Otto Karl Werckmeister, "Walter Benjamin's angel of history," 242). Criticizing the disjunction between Klee's *Angelus Novus* and Benjamin's "angel of history," Carl Djerassi calls Benjamin's commentary on the painting "naively absurd" (Carl Djerassi, "Walter Benjamin's Angel and Hitler"). See also Johann Conrad Eberlein, *"Angelus Novus," Paul Klees Bild und Walter Benjamins Deutung*, 32–6. Both Djerassi and Eberlein interpret Klee's angel as a representation of Hitler.

10. Ariella Azoulay, *Once Upon a Time: Photography in the Footsteps of Walter Benjamin* (Heb.).

11. Azoulay's theoretical reflections introduce her own remarkable use of Benjamin's angel in the context of her critique of Zionism. For a more elaborate discussion that emphasizes her political stance, see my essay, "Die Reproduzierbarkeit des *Angelus Novus*," 287–89.

12. Udi Aloni, *Local Angel*.

13. Slavoj Žižek, "What Does a Jew Want?" in Aloni, *Local Angel*, 27. The book accompanies the DVD of the film.

14. Ibid. In Christian dogma, however, Christ cannot be an angel (see http://www.askelm .com/news/n040110.htm, last accessed December 9, 2015).

15. Alain Badiou, "Angel for a New Place," in Aloni, *Local Angel*, 22. Badiou's text is reprinted in Badiou, *Polemics*, 202–7.

16. Ibid.

17. Ibid., 23.

18. Judith Butler, *Parting Ways*, 75.

19. Ibid., 92.

20. Ibid., 94.

21. Moshe Idel, *Old Worlds*, 105.

22. Benjamin, "On the Concept of History," in *Selected Writings* 4: 400.

# Bibliography

Adorno, Theodor. 1974. "Rede über Lyrik und Gesellschaft." In *Noten zur Literatur*, 49–68. Frankfurt am Main: Suhrkamp.

Agamben, Giorgio. 1970. "L'Angelo malinconico." *Nuovi argomenti* 9: 153–65.

———. 1999. "Benjamin and the Demonic." In *Potentialities: Collected Essays in Philosophy*. Translated by Daniel Heller-Roazen. 138–59. Stanford, CA: Stanford University Press.

———. 1998. *Homo Sacer: Sovereign Power and Bare Life*. Translated by Daniel Heller-Roazen. Stanford, CA: Stanford University Press.

———. 1995. *Idea of Prose*. Translated by Michael Sullivan and Sam Whitsitt. Albany, NY: SUNY Press.

———. 1996. *Infancy and History: The Destruction of Experience*. Translated by Liz Heron. London: Verso.

———. 1991. *Language and Death*. Translated by Karen Pinkus with Michael Hardt. Minneapolis: University of Minnesota Press.

———. 1982. *Il Linguaggio e la morte*. Turin: Einaudi.

———. 1999. *The Man without Content*. Translated by Georgia Albert. Stanford, CA: Stanford University Press.

———. 1999. *Potentialities: Collected Essays in Philosophy*. Translated by Daniel Heller-Roazen. Stanford, CA: Stanford University Press.

———. 2005. *Profanierungen*. Frankfurt am Main: Suhrkamp (Available in English as 2007. *Profanations*. Translated by Jeff Fort. Cambridge, MA: MIT Press).

———. 2005. *State of Exception*. Translated by Kevin Attell. Chicago: University of Chicago Press.

———. 2005. *The Time That Remains: A Commentary on the Letter to the Romans*. Translated by Patricia Dailey. Stanford, CA: Stanford University Press.

———. (1970) 1994. *L'Uomo senza contenuto*. Milan: Rizzoli. Macerata, Italy: Quodlibet.

———. 1983. *Walter Benjamin: tempo storia linguaggio*. Edited by Lucio Belloi and Lorenzina Lotti. Rome: Reuniti.

Aloni, Udi. 1999. *Local Angel: Theological Political Fragments*. London: Institute of Contemporary Arts. (CD and book).

Alter, Robert. 1991. *Necessary Angels: Tradition and Modernity in Kafka, Benjamin, and Scholem*. Cambridge, MA: Harvard University Press.

Anders, Günther. 1951. *Kafka Pro et Contra*. Munich: C. H. Beck.

Arendt, Hannah. 1963. *Eichmann in Jerusalem: A Report on the Banality of Evil*. New York: Viking.

———. 1968. "The Gap between Past and Future." In *Between Past and Future*, 3–15. New York: Viking.

———. 2007. *Hannah Arendt: The Jewish Writings*. Edited by Jerome Kohn and Ron H. Feldman. New York: Schocken.

———. (1958) 1988. *The Human Condition*. Chicago: University of Chicago Press.

———. 1978. *The Jew as Pariah: Jewish Identity and Politics in the Modern Age*. Edited by Ron H. Feldman. New York: Grove.

———. 2007. "Jewish History, Revised." In *Hannah Arendt: The Jewish Writings*. Edited by Jerome Kohn and Ron H. Feldman, 304–12. New York: Schocken.

———. 1978. *The Life of the Mind*. San Diego: Harcourt.

———. 1991. *On Revolution*. London: Penguin.

———. 1997. *Rahel Varnhagen: The Life of a Jewess*. Edited by Liliane Weissberg and translated by Richard and Clara Winston. Baltimore, MD: Johns Hopkins University Press.

———. 2006. *Vom Leben des Geistes*. Munich: Piper.

———. (1968) 1995. "Walter Benjamin, 1892–1940." In *Men in Dark Times*. Translated by Harry Zohn, 153–206. New York: Harcourt Brace.

———. 2000. *Zwischen Vergangenheit und Zukunft: Übungen im politischen Denken I*. Munich: Piper.

Arendt, Hannah, and Gershom Scholem. 2010. *Der Briefwechsel*. Frankfurt am Main: Jüdischer Verlag Suhrkamp.

Arendt, Hannah, and Karl Jaspers. 1992. *Correspondence, 1926–1969*. Edited by Lotte Kohler and Hans Saner and translated by Robert Kimber and Rita Kimber. New York: Harcourt Brace Jovanovic.

Asad, Talal. 2000. "Agency and Pain: An Exploration." *Journal of Culture and Religion* 1, no. 1: 29–60.

Aschheim, Steven. 2007. *Beyond the Border: The German-Jewish Legacy Abroad*. Princeton, NJ: Princeton University Press.

———. 1996. *Culture and Catastrophe: German and Jewish Confrontations with National Socialism and Other Crises*. New York: New York University Press.

Aschheim, Steven, ed. 2001. *Hannah Arendt in Jerusalem*. Berkeley: University of California Press.

Azoulay, Ariella. 2007. *Once Upon a Time: Photography in the Footsteps of Walter Benjamin,* Ramat-Gan: Bar-Ilan University Press (In Hebrew). English translation in an unpublished manuscript; in the possession of V. L. by courtesy of the author.

Bachmann, Ingeborg. 1990. *Malina*. Translated by Philip Boehm. New York: Holmes and Meier.

———. 1980. "Das schreibende Ich." In *Frankfurter Vorlesungen: Probleme zeitgenössischer Dichtung*, 41–61. Munich: Piper.

Bachmann, Ingeborg, and Paul Celan. 2010. *Correspondence*. Translated by Wieland Hoban. Calcutta: Seagull.

———. 2008. *Herzzeit—Briefwechsel Ingeborg Bachmann–Paul Celan*. Frankfurt am Main: Suhrkamp.

Badiou, Alain. 2005. *Circonstances 3: Portées du mot 'juif'*. Paris: Léo Scheer.

——— 2006. *Polemics*. Translated by Steve Corcoran. London: Verso.

——— 2003. *Saint Paul: Foundation of Universalism*. Translated by Ray Brassier. Stanford, CA: Stanford University Press.

Baer, Jizchak Fritz. 1936. *Galut*. Berlin: Schocken.

Baker, Jason. 2003. "Introduction." In Franz Kafka, *The Metamorphosis and Other Stories*. New York: Barnes and Noble Classics.

Benhabib, Seyla. 2003. *Arendt's Reluctant Modernism.* Lanham, MD: Rowman and Littlefield.

———. 1995. "The Pariah and Her Shadow: Hannah Arendt's Biography of Rahel Varnhagen." *Political Theory* 23, no. 1: 5–24.

Benjamin, Walter. 1992. *Benjamin über Kafka.* Edited by Hermann Schweppenhäuser. Frankfurt am Main: Suhrkamp.

———. 1966. *Briefe,* 2 vols. Edited by Gershom Scholem and Theodor W. Adorno. Frankfurt am Main: Suhrkamp.

———. 1980. *Briefwechsel.* Edited by Gershom Scholem. Frankfurt am Main: Suhrkamp.

———. 1994. *The Correspondence of Walter Benjamin 1910–1940.* Edited and annotated by Gershom Scholem and Theodor W. Adorno and translated by Manfred R. Jacobson and Evelyn M. Jacobson. Chicago: University of Chicago Press.

———. 1996–2000. *Gesammelte Briefe,* 6 vols. Frankfurt am Main: Suhrkamp.

———. 1972–91. *Gesammelte Schriften,* 7 vols. Edited by Rolf Tiedemann and Hermann Schweppenhäuser. Frankfurt am Main: Suhrkamp.

———. 1968. *Illuminations: Essays and Reflections.* Translated by Harry Zohn. New York: Schocken.

———. 1959. *Oeuvres choisies.* Translated by Maurice de Gandillac. Paris: Julliard.

———. 2003. *Selected Writings,* 4 vols. Edited by Howard Eiland and Michael W. Jennings and translated by Edmund Jephcott, et al. Cambridge, MA: Belknap.

———. 1996. "The Task of the Translator." In *Selected Writings,* vol. 1: *1913–1926,* 253–63. Edited by Marcus Bullock and Michael Jennings and translated by Harry Zohn. Cambridge, MA: Harvard University Press.

Benjamin, Walter, and Gershom Scholem. 1989. *The Correspondence of Walter Benjamin and Gershom Scholem, 1932–1940.* Edited by Gershom Scholem and translated by Gary Smith and Andre Lefevre. New York: Schocken.

Bernstein, Richard J. 1996. *Hannah Arendt and the Jewish Question.* Cambridge, MA: MIT Press.

Biale, David. 1979. *Gershom Scholem: Kabbalah and Counterhistory.* Cambridge, MA: Harvard University Press.

Birnbaum, Pierre. 2002. *Sur la corde raide: Parcours juifs entre exile et citoyenneté.* Paris: Flammarion.

Birns, Nicolas. 2010. *Theory after Theory: An Intellectual History of Literary Theory from 1950 to the Early Twenty-First Century.* Buffalo, NY: Broadview.

Blanchot, Maurice. 1969. *L'Entretien infini.* Paris: Gallimard.

———. 1955. *L'Espace littéraire.* Paris: Gallimard.

———. 1993. *The Infinite Conversation.* Translated by Susan Hanson. Minneapolis: University of Minnesota Press.

———. 2015. "Notes." In Eric Hoppenot. *Maurice Blanchot et la tradition juive,* 461–63. Paris: Kimé.

———. 2010. "A Rupture in Time: Revolution." *Political Writings: 1953–1993.* Translated by Zakir Paul. New York: Fordham University Press.

———. 1971. "Traduire." In *L'Amitié,* 69–73. Paris: Gallimard.

———. 1997. "Translating." In *Friendship.* Translated by Elizabeth Rottenberg, 57–61. Stanford, CA: Stanford University Press.

Blanton, Ward, and Hent de Vries, eds., 2013. *Paul and the Philosophers.* New York: Fordham University Press.

Bollack, Jean. 2000. *Poetik der Fremdheit*. Translated by Werner Wögerbauer. Vienna: Zsolnay.

Boyarin, Jonathan. 1996. *Thinking in Jewish*. Chicago: University of Chicago Press.

Brod, Max. 1931. "Franz Kafkas Grunderlebnis." *Die Weltbühne* 27: 696–699.

———. 1974. *Über Franz Kafka*. Frankfurt am Main: Fischer.

Buber, Martin. 1964. *Darko shel mikra* (the Bible and its styles: Hebrew). Jerusalem: Mosad Bialik.

Buber, Martin, with Franz Rosenzweig. 1927. *Die Schrift: Die fünf Bücher der Weisung*. Berlin: Schneider.

Butler, Judith. 2013. *Parting Ways: Jewishness and the Critique of Zionism*. New York: Columbia University Press.

———. 2011. "Who Owns Kafka?" *London Review of Books* 33, no. 5: 3–8.

Caputo, John D., and Linda M. Alcoff. 2009. *St. Paul among the Philosophers*. Bloomington: Indiana University Press.

Celan, Paul. 2003. *Die Gedichte*. Edited by B. Wiedermann. Frankfurt am Main: Suhrkamp.

———. 1997. "Der Meridian." In *Gesammelte Werke in fünf Bänden*, 3: 187–202. Frankfurt am Main: Suhrkamp.

———. 1999. *Der Meridian. Endfassung – Entwürfe – Materialien*. Edited by Bernhard Böschenstein and Heino Schmull. Frankfurt am Main: Suhrkamp.

———. 2011. *The Meridian: Final Version – Drafts – Materials*. Edited by Bernhard Böschenstein and Heino Schmull and translated by Pierre Joris, Stanford, CA: Stanford University Press.

Celan, Paul, and Ilani Shmueli. 2004. *Paul Celan–Ilana Shmueli: Briefwechsel*. Edited by Thomas Sparr. Frankfurt am Main: Suhrkamp.

Celan, Paul, and Peter Szondi. 2005. *Briefwechsel*. Frankfurt am Main: Suhrkamp.

Corngold, Stanley. 2004. *Lambent Traces: Franz Kafka*. Princeton, NJ: Princeton University Press.

Derrida, Jacques. 2003. "Abraham l'autre." In *Judéités: Questions pour Jacques Derrida*. Edited by Joseph Cohen and Raphael Zagury-Orly, 11–42. Paris: Galilée.

———. 2002. *Acts of Religion*. Edited and with an introduction by Gil Anidjar. New York: Routledge.

———. 1996. *Archive Fever: A Freudian Impression*. Chicago: University of Chicago Press.

———. 1992. "Before the Law." In *Acts of Literature*. Edited by Derek Attridge, 183–220. London: Routledge.

———. 2005. "*Fichus*: Frankfurt Address." In *Paper Machine*. Translated by Rachel Bowlby, 164–81. Stanford, CA: Stanford University Press.

———. 2002. "Interpretations at War: Kant, the Jew, the German." In *Acts of Religion*. Edited by Gil Anidjar, 137–188. New York: Routledge.

———. 1992. *The Other Heading*. Bloomington: Indiana University Press.

———. 1985. "Préjugés – Devant la loi." In *La faculté de juger*, 87–139. Paris: Minuit.

———. 1994. *Specters of Marx: The State of the Debt, the Work of Mourning and the New International*. Translated by Peggy Kamuf. London: Routledge.

———. 1986. *Schibboleth pour Paul Celan*. Paris: Galilée.

———. 2004. "Zeugnis, Gabe." In *Jüdisches Denken in Frankreich*. Edited by Elisabeth Weber, 63–90. Frankfurt am Main: Suhrkamp.

Dikeç, Mustafa. "Space as a Mode of Political Thinking," *Geoforum* 43 (2012): 669–676.

Djerassi, Carl. 2014. "Walter Benjamin's Angel and Hitler." *New York Review of Books*, September 25. Accessed December 3, 2015. http://www.nybooks.com /articles/2014/09/25/walter-benjamins-angel-hitler/.

Eberlein, Johann Conrad. 2006. *"Angelus Novus," Paul Klees Bild und Walter Benjamins Deutung*. Freiburg im Breisach: Rombach Wissenschaft.

Eisen, Arnold. 1988. "Exile." In *Contemporary Jewish Religious Thought*. Edited by Arthur A. Cohen and Paul Mendes-Flohr, 219–225. New York: Free Press.

Emerson, Ralph Waldo. 1982. *Nature and Selected Essays*. Edited by Larzer Ziff. New York: Penguin.

———. 1958. *The Heart of Emerson's Journals*. Edited by Bliss Perry. New York: Dover.

Fenves, Peter. 2001. "Die Unterlassung der Übersetzung." In *Übersetzen: Walter* Benjamin. Edited by Christiaan L. Hart-Nibbrig, 159–73. Frankfurt am Main: Suhrkamp.

Finkelde, Dominik. 2007. *Politische Eschatologie nach Paulus: Badiou, Agamben, Žižek*. Vienna: Turia + Kant.

Fisch, Harold. 1998. *New Stories for Old: Biblical Patterns in the Novel*. Houndmills, Basingstoke: Macmillan.

Freud, Sigmund. 1941. "Ansprache an die Mitglieder des Vereins B'nai B'rith (1926)." In *Gesammelte Werke*. Edited by A. Freud, et al. 17:51–53. London: Fischer.

Frye, Northrop. 1982. *The Great Code: The Bible and Literature*. London: Routledge and Kegan Paul.

Gadamer, Hans-Georg. 1993. *Truth and Method*. Translated by Joel Winsheimer and Donald G. Marshall. New York: Continuum.

———. 1960. *Wahrheit und Methode*. Tübingen: J. C. B. Mohr.

Gasché, Rodolphe. 2011. *The Stelliferous Fold: Toward a Virtual Law of Literature's Self-Formation*. New York: Fordham University Press.

Geulen, Eva. 2008. "Gründung und Gesetzgebung bei Badiou, Agamben und Arendt," In *Hannah Arendt und Giorgio Agamben: Parallelen, Perspektiven, Kontroversen*. Edited by E. Geulen, K. Kaufmann, and G. Mein, 59–74. Münster: Fink.

Glatzer, Nahum. 1969. *The Dimensions of Job: A Study and Selected Readings*. New York: Schocken.

Glazova, Anna. 2008. "Franz Kafka: Oszillierende Negationen." Accessed November 14, 2013. http://www.kafka.org/index.php/icqlist/index.php?id=194,229,0,0,1,0.

Glen, Patrick J. 2011. "Franz Kafka, Lawrence Joseph, and the Possibilities of Jurisprudential Literature." *Southern California Interdisciplinary Law Journal* 21, no. 1: 47–94.

Goldschmidt, Lazarus, trans. 2002. Der babylonische Talmud. Frankfurt am Main: Jüdischer Verlag Suhrkamp.

Hahn, Barbara. 1990. *"Antworten Sie Mir": Rahel Levin Varnhagens Briefwechsel*. Basel: Stroemfeld/Roter Stern.

Halbertal, Moshe. 2011. "At the Threshold of Forgiveness: A Study of Law and Narrative in the Talmud." *Jewish Review of Books* 7: 33–34.

———. 2007. *Concealment and Revelation: Esotericism in Jewish Thought and Its Philosophical Implications*. Princeton, NJ: Princeton University Press.

Hamacher, Werner. 1998. *Entferntes Verstehen*. Frankfurt am Main: Suhrkamp.

Hamburger, Käte. 1983. "Rahel und Goethe." In *Rahel Varnhagen Gesammelte Werke*. Edited by Konrad Feilchenfeldt, Uwe Schweikert, und Rahel E. Steiner, 10: 179–204. Munich: Mattes and Seitz.

Hammerschlag, Sarah. 2014. "Bad Jews, Authentic Jews, Figural Jews." In *Judaism, Liberalism, and Political Theology*. Edited by Randi Rakover and Martin Kavka, 220–40. Bloomington: Indiana University Press.

———. 2010. *The Figural Jew: Politics and Identity in Postwar French Thought*. Chicago: University of Chicago Press.

Handelman, Susan A. 1991. *Fragments of Redemption: Jewish Thought and Literary Theory in Benjamin, Scholem, and Levinas*. Bloomington: Indiana University Press.

Harink, Douglas, ed. 2010. *Paul, Philosophy, and the Theopolitical Vision: Critical Engagements with Agamben, Badiou, Žižek, and Others*. Eugene, OR: Wipf and Stock.

Hartman, Geoffrey. 1980. *Criticism in the Wilderness: The Study of Literature Today*. New Haven, CT: Yale University Press.

———. 2013. *The Eighth Day: Poems Old and New*. Lubbock: Texas Tech University Press.

———. 2002. *Scars of the Spirit*. New York: Palgrave.

———. 2011. *The Third Pillar: Essays in Judaic Studies*. Philadelphia: University of Pennsylvania Press.

Heidegger, Martin. 1954. "…dichterisch wohnet der Mensch…." *Akzente* 1: 57–71.

———. 2004. *On the Essence of Language: The Metaphysics of Language and the Essencing of the Word; Concerning Herder's Treatise on the Origin of Language*. Albany: SUNY Press.

———. 1992. *Parmenides*. Bloomington: Indiana University Press.

———. 2003. *Plato's Sophist*. Bloomington: Indiana University Press.

Heller, Agnes. 2001. "Hannah Arendt on Tradition and New Beginnings." In *Hannah Arendt in Jerusalem*. Edited by Steven Aschheim, 19–33. Berkeley: University of California Press.

Hertz, Deborah. 2007. *How Jews Became Germans: The History of Conversion and Assimilation in Berlin*. New Haven, CT: Yale University Press.

Hölderlin, Friedrich. 1992. "Anmerkungen zum Oedipus." In *Sämtliche Werke und Briefe*. Edited by Michael Knaupp, 2: 309–316. Munich: Hanser.

Hollander, Dana. 2008. *Exemplarity and Chosenness: Rosenzweig and Derrida on the Nation of Philosophy*. Stanford, CA: Stanford University Press.

Hoppenot, Eric. 2015. *Maurice Blanchot et la tradition juive*. Paris: Kimé.

Idel, Moshe. 2010. *Old Worlds, New Mirrors: On Jewish Mysticism and Twentieth Century Thought*. Philadelphia: University of Pennsylvania Press.

Ivanovic, Christine. 1998. "All Poets Are Jews: Paul Celan's Readings of Marina Tsvetayeva." *Glossen* 6. Accessed December 30, 2015. http://www2.dickinson.edu/glossen/heft6/celan.html.

Jacobitti, Suzanne. 1988. "Hannah Arendt and the Will." *Political Theory* 1, no. 16: 53–76.

Jacobson, Eric. 2005. "Ahavat Yisrael: Nationhood, the Pariah and the Intellectual." In *Creation and Recreation in Jewish Thought*. Edited by Rachel Elior and Peter Schäfer, 401–15. Tübingen: Mohr Siebeck.

Judaken, Jonathan. 2009. *Jean-Paul Sartre and the Jewish Question*. Lincoln: University of Nebraska Press.

Kafka, Franz. 1998. *The Castle*. New York: Schocken.

———. 1971. *The Complete Stories*. Edited by Nahum Glatzer and translated by Willa Muir and Edwin Muir. New York: Schocken.

———. 1976. *The Diaries: 1910–1913*. Translated by Joseph Kresh. New York: Schocken.

———. 2002. *Drucke zu Lebzeiten*. Frankfurt am Main: Fischer.

———. 2007. *Kafka's Selected Stories*. Edited and translated by Stanley Corngold. New York: Norton.

———. 1977. *Letters to Friends, Family, and Editors*. Translated by Richard Winston and Clara Winston. New York: Schocken.

———. 1990. *Letters to Milena*. New York: Random House.

———. 2002. *Nachgelassene Schriften und Fragmente*. 2 vol. Frankfurt am Main: Fischer.

———. 2002. *Der Prozeß*. Frankfurt am Main: Fischer.

———. 2002. *Tagebücher*. Frankfurt am Main: Fischer.

———. 1991. "The Third Notebook." In *The Blue Octavo Notebooks*. Edited by Max Brod and translated by Ernst Kaiser and Eithne Wilkins, 13–40. Cambridge, MA: Exact Change.

———. 1992. *The Trial*. New York: Schocken.

Karr, Ruven. 2014. "Ménage à trois: Die Liebesbeziehung als biographischer Ausgangspunkt des dialogischen Totengedenkens." In *Ingeborg Bachmann und Paul Celan: Historisch-poetische Korrelationen*. Edited by Gernot Wimmer, 171–91. Berlin: De Gruyter.

Kartiganer, Donald M. 1962. "Job and Joseph K.: Myth in Kafka's *The Trial*." *Modern Fiction Studies* 8: 31–43.

Kierkegaard, Søren. 1986. *Fear and Trembling*. London: Penguin Classics.

Kilcher, Andreas B. 2009. "'Volk des Buches.' Zur kulturpolitischen Aktualisierung eines alten Topos in der jüdischen Moderne." *Münchner Beiträge zur jüdischen Geschichte und Kultur* 2: 43–58.

Klein, Rony. 2009. "Une Rencontre inattendue entre la pensée française contemporaine et le Juif: le cas de Jean-François Lyotard." *Controverses* 11: 302–16.

Kuhlmann, Anne. 1999. "Das Exil als Heimat: Über jüdische Schreibweisen und Metaphern." In *Exil im 20. Jahrhundert* (*Exilforschung: Ein internationales Jahrbuch* 17). Edited by Claus-Dieter Krohn, Erwin Rotermund, Lutz Winckler, and Wulf Koepke, 198–213. Munich: Text und Kritik.

Lacoue-Labarthe, Philippe, and Jean-Luc Nancy. 2003. "From Where Is Psycho-analysis Possible?" Translated by Brian Holmes. *JEP—European Journal of Psychoanalysis* 17: 3–20.

Larrimore, Mark. 2013. *The Book of "Job": A Biography*. Princeton, NJ: Princeton University Press.

Lasine, Stuart. 1990. "The Trials of Job and Kafka's Josef K." *German Quarterly* 63, no. 2: 187–98.

Levi, Primo. 1986. *The Drowned and the Saved*. New York: Summit Books.

Levinas, Emmanuel. 1990. *Difficult Freedom: Essays on Judaism*. Translated by Seán Hand. Baltimore, MD: Johns Hopkins University Press.

Lévy, Bernard-Henry. 1979. *Le Testament de Dieu*. Paris: Grasset.

Liska, Vivian. 2012. "On Getting It Right: Moshe Idel's *Old Worlds, New Mirrors*." *Jewish Quarterly Review* 102, no. 2: 297–302.

———. 2015. "Kafka's Other Job." In *The Book of Job: Aesthetics, Ethics and Hermeneutics* (Perspectives on Jewish Texts and Contexts). Edited by Leora Batnitzky and Ilana Pardes, 121–43. Berlin: De Gruyter.

———. 2011. "Die Reproduzierbarkeit des *Angelus Novus* im Augenblick der Gefahr: Walter Benjamins Engel der Geschichte in Israel." In *Gedächtnisstrategien und*

*Medien im interkulturellen Dialog*. Edited by Bernd Witte, 283–89. Würzburg: Königshausen und Neumann.

———. 2012. Review of *The Figural Jew: Politics and Identity in Postwar French Thought* by Sarah Hammerschlag. *European Journal of Jewish Studies* 6, no. 2: 303–8.

———. 2009. *When Kafka Says We: Uncommon Communities in German-Jewish Literature*. Bloomington: Indiana University Press.

Litowitz, Douglas E. 2002. "Franz Kafka's Outsider Jurisprudence." *Law and Social Inquiry* 27, no. 1: 103–37.

Lyotard, Jean-François. 1988. *Heidegger et les "juifs."* Paris: Galilée.

Marty, Eric. 2015. "Saint Paul among the Moderns: Symbolic Universal or Mimetic Universal? History and Metahistory." In *Radical French Thought and the Return of the "Jewish Question,"* 80–96. Bloomington: Indiana University Press, 2015.

Meinecke, Dietlinde. 1970. *Wort und Name bei Paul Celan: Zu Paul Celan; Zur Widerruflichkeit des Gedichts*. Bad Homburg: Verlag Gehlen.

Meschonnic, Henri. 1973. *Pour la Poétique II: Épistémologie de l'écriture, poétique de la traduction*. Paris: Gallimard.

Mosès, Stéphane. 2009. *The Angel of History: Rosenzweig, Benjamin, Scholem*. Stanford, CA: Stanford University Press.

———. 2002. "Le Fil de la tradition est-il rompu? Sur deux formes de modernité religieuse." In *Laïcité et religions: Revue des deux mondes*. 102–14.

Muir, Willa, and Edwin. 1946. *The Great Wall of China*. New York: Schocken.

Neiman, Susan. 2001. "Theodicy in Jerusalem." In *Hannah Arendt in Jerusalem*. Edited by Steven Aschheim, 65–69. Berkeley: University of California Press.

Nouss, Alexis, ed. 1997. "La Réception de l'essai sur la traduction dans le domaine français." In *Walter Benjamin: traductions critiques / Walter Benjamin's Essay on Translation: Critical Translations*. Special issue of *TTR: Traduction, Terminologie, Rédaction* 10, no. 2: 71–85.

Reuss, Roland. 2011. "Running Texts, Stunning Drafts." In *Kafka for the Twenty First Century*. Edited by Stanley Corngold and Ruth Gross, 24–48. Rochester, NY: Camden House.

Rose, Gillian. 1993. *Judaism and Modernity. Philosophical Essays*. Oxford: Blackwell.

Rosenzweig, Franz. (1921) 1988. *Der Stern der Erlösung*. Frankfurt am Main: Suhrkamp.

Ruderman, David B. 2007. "Introduction." In *Simon Dubnow Institute Yearbook*, vol. 6 (Special Issue: *Early Modern Culture and Haskalah*). Edited by Dan Diner, 17–21. Munich: Deutsche Verlags-Anstalt.

Sartre, Jean Paul. 1943. *L'Être et le néant*. Paris: Gallimard.

———. 1946. *Réflexions sur la question juive*. Paris: Paul Morihien.

Schäfer, Peter. 1995. "Gershom Scholem und die Wissenschaft des Judentums." In *Gershom Scholem: Zwischen den Disziplinen*. Edited by Peter Schäfer and Gary Smith, 122–56. Frankfurt am Main: Suhrkamp.

Schatz, Andrea. 2007. "Peoples Pure of Speech: The Religious, the Secular, and Jewish Beginnings of Modernity." In *Simon Dubnow Institute Yearbook*, vol. 6 (Special Issue: *Early Modern Culture and Haskalah*). Edited by Dan Diner, 169–87. Munich: Deutsche Verlags-Anstalt.

Schmitt, Carl. 1991. *Political Romanticism*. Translated by G. Oakes. Cambridge, MA: The MIT Press.

————. 2005. *Political Theology: Four Chapters on the Concept of Sovereignty*. Translated by George Schwab. Chicago: University of Chicago Press.

Scholem, Gershom. (1960) 1973. "Kabbala und Mythos." *Zur Kabbala und ihrer Symbolik*. Frankfurt am Main: Suhrkamp.

————. (1945) 1995. *Major Trends in Jewish Mysticism*. New York: Schocken.

————. 1971. *The Messianic Idea in Judaism*. New York: Schocken.

————. 1995. "95 Thesen über Judentum und Zionismus." In *Gershom Scholem: Zwischen den Disziplinen*. Edited by Peter Schäfer und Gary Smith, 287–95. Frankfurt am Main: Suhrkamp.

————. 2000. *Tagebücher 1917–1923*. Frankfurt am Main: Jüdischer Verlag Suhrkamp.

————. 1980. *Über einige Begriffe des Judentums*. Frankfurt am Main: Suhrkamp.

————. (1972) 1983. "Walter Benjamin und sein Engel." In *Walter Benjamin und sein Engel: Vierzehn Aufsätze und kleine Beiträge*. Edited by Rolf Tiedemann, 35–72. Frankfurt am Main: Suhrkamp.

Schreiner, Susan E. 1994. *Where Shall Wisdom Be Found? Calvin's Exegesis of Job from Medieval and Modern Perspectives*. Chicago: University of Chicago Press.

Siegelberg, Mira. 2005. "Arendt's Legacy Usurped: In Defense of the (Limited) Nation State." In *Columbia Current* (Fall): 33–41.

Simmel. Georg. 1906. "The Sociology of Secrecy and of Secret Societies." *American Journal of Sociology* 11, no. 4: 441–98.

Slotki, Israel W., trans. 1976. Babylonian Talmud: Tractate Baba Bathra, vol. 2. London: Soncino.

Smith, Graham M. Smith. 2008. "Reading Kafka's Trial Politically. Justice. Law. Power." In *Contemporary Political Theory* no. 7: 8–30.

Starn, Randolph. 2002. "The Early Modern Muddle." In *Journal of Early Modern History* 6, no. 3: 296–307.

Steiner, George. 1984. *George Steiner: A Reader*. Harmondsworth, Middlesex: Penguin.

Susman, Margarete. 1946. *Das Buch Hiob und das Schicksal des jüdischen Volkes*. Zürich: Steinberg.

————. 1992. "Das Hiob-Problem bei Kafka." *Das Nah- und Fernsein des Fremden: Essays und Briefe*. Edited by Ingeborg Nordmann, 183–203. Frankfurt am Main: Suhrkamp.

Sutcliffe, Adam. 2007. "Imagining Amsterdam—the Dutch Golden Age and the Origins of Jewish Modernity." In *Simon Dubnow Institute Yearbook*, vol. 6 (Special Issue: *Early Modern Culture and Haskalah*). Edited by Dan Diner, 79–97. Munich: Deutsche Verlags-Anstalt.

Taubes, Jacob. 2003. *The Political Theology of Paul*. Translated by Dana Hollander. Stanford, CA: Stanford University Press.

————. 2003. *Die politische Theologie des Paulus*. Munich: Fink.

Tewarson, Heidi T. 1998. *Rahel Levin Varnhagen: The Life and Work of a German-Jewish Intellectual*. Lincoln: University of Nebraska Press.

Todorov, Tzvetan. 1971. *Poétique de la Prose: Nouvelles Recherches sur le Récit*. Paris: Seuil.

Twellmann, Marcus. 2008. "Lex, nicht nomos. Hannah Arendts Kontraktualismus." In *Hannah Arendt und Giorgio Agamben: Parallelen, Perspektiven, Kontroversen*. Edited by Eva Geulen, Kai Kauffmann, and Georg Mein. Munich: Fink.

Vattimo, Gianni, and Michael Marder. 2014. *Deconstructing Zionism: A Critique of Political Metaphysics*. New York: Bloomsbury.

Waldstein, Edith. 1989. "Identity as Conflict and Conversation in Rahel Varnhagen (1771–1833)." In *Out of Line—Ausgefallen*. Edited by Ruth-Ellen B. Joeres and Marianne Burkhard, 95–113. Amsterdam: Rodopi.

Walser, Martin. 1999. *Beschreibung einer Form: Versuch über Kafka*. Frankfurt am Main: Suhrkamp.

Weigel, Sigrid. "Angelus Novus—Engel der Geschichte und Bote des Glücks." Accessed February 13, 2016. http://www.cms.fu-berlin.de/geisteswissenschaften/v /drehmomente/content/1-Weigel/.

———. 2008. *Walter Benjamin, die Kreatur, das Heilige, die Bilder*. Frankfurt am Main: Fischer.

Weissberg, Liliane. 1995. "Schreiben als Selbstentwurf: Zu den Schriften Rahel Varnhagens und Dorothea Schlegels." *Zeitschrift für Religions—und Geistesgeschichte* 47, no. 4: 231–53.

———. 1991. "Stepping Out: The Writing of Difference in Rahel Varnhagen's Letters." *New German Critique*, no. 53: 149–62.

Werckmeister, Otto Karl. 1996. "Walter Benjamin's Angel of History, or the Transfiguration of the Revolutionary into the Historian." *Critical Inquiry* 22, no. 2: 239–67.

Wiedemann, Barbara. 2014. "'Du willst das Opfer sein': Bachmanns Blick auf Celan in ihrem nicht abgesandten Brief vom Herbst 1961." In *Ingeborg Bachmann und Paul Celan: Historisch-poetische Korrelationen*. Edited by Gernot Wimmer, 42–70. Berlin: De Gruyter.

Witte, Bernd. 2007. *Jüdische Tradition und literarische Moderne: Heine, Buber, Kafka, Benjamin*. Munich: Hanser.

Wohlfarth, Irving. 1981. "Krise der Erzählung, Krise der Erzähltheorie: Überlegungen zu Lukacs, Benjamin und Jauss." In *Erzählung und Erzählforschung im 20. Jahrhundert*. Edited by R. Klopfer and G. Janetzke-Dillner, 269–88. Stuttgart: Kohlhammer.

———. 2001. "Das Medium der Übersetzung." In *Übersetzen: Walter Benjamin*. Edited by Christiaan L. Hart-Nibbrig, 80–130. Frankfurt am Main: Suhrkamp.

Yerushalmi, Yosef Hayim. 1993. *Freud's Moses: Judaism Terminable and Interminable*. New Haven, CT: Yale University Press.

Young-Bruehl, Elisabeth. 1982. *Hannah Arendt: For the Love of the World*. New Haven, CT: Yale University Press.

Ziolkowski, Theodore. 1997. *The Mirror of Justice: Literary Reflections of Legal Crisis*. Princeton, NJ: Princeton University Press.

Žižek, Slavoj. 1992. *Looking Awry: An Introduction to Jacques Lacan through Popular Culture*. Cambridge, MA: MIT Press.

———. 2003. *The Puppet and the Dwarf: The Perverse Core of Christianity*. Cambridge, MA: MIT Press.

Zornberg, Avivah Gottlieb. 1995. *The Beginning of Desire: Reflections on Genesis*. New York: Random House.

# Index

Abraham, 80–83, 85, 150

Adorno, Theodor W., 43, 104, 130, 138

Agamben, Giorgio, 5–6, 25–38, 41–53, 56–60, 62, 64, 103–105, 109–112, 115–119, 122–124, 160, 166; *Homo Sacer,* 43–46, 57; *Idea of Prose,* 45, 48, 50, 109, 111–112; *Language and Death,* 111; *Language and History,* 104–105; *The Melancholy Angel,* 26–27, 32, 37; *Profanations,* 52; *State of Exception,* 43; *The Time That Remains,* 42, 46; "Walter Benjamin and the Demonic," 115

Aggadah, 51, 60–65, 76

Aloni, Udi, 167; *Local Angel,* 167

American Jewish Committee, 19

angel(s), 31, 35, 115–119, 124, 161, 164–168

antinomian, 4, 21, 32, 35, 42, 62–64, 118–119

antisemitism, 89, 133

Arendt, Hannah, 2–4, 7, 13–38, 129–130, 147; *Between Past and Future,* 26–27; *The Human Condition,* 34; *Jewish History, Revised,* 17–23; *Jewish Writings,* 25; *On Revolution,* 29; *Rahel Varnhagen: The Life of a Jewess,* 13–17

Aristotle, 158; Aristotelian, 157–158

art, 27, 30–32, 35, 37

Aschheim, Steven, 127, 129, 134

assimilation, 3, 11–15, 19, 71, 119, 121, 135

Auschwitz, 137

Azoulay, Ariella, 166

Babel, tower of, 93, 97, 106

Bachmann, Ingeborg, 7, 46–47, 137–144; *The Writing Self,* 138

Badiou, Alain, 6, 154–155, 167

Benjamin, Walter, 2–4, 5–7, 17–19, 23–25, 27–29, 31, 35, 37–38, 43–46, 50–52, 56–64, 66, 73–81, 89–119, 122–124, 130–131, 147, 165–169; "Agesilaus Santander," 115–118, 166; Angel of History, 31, 116–119, 165–167; *Critique of Violence,* 59; "On the Concept of History," 105–106, 115–116, 118, 166; *Origins of German Tragedy,* 31; "The Storyteller," 106–107, 109–110; "The Task of the Translator," 89–90, 107

Biale, David, 120

Bible, 23, 102, 145, 157

Blanchot, Maurice, 5, 89–102, 128, 148, 150–152; *The Infinite Conversation,* 89; *Political Writings,* 89; "Translating," 89–92, 95–97, 101

Boyarin, Daniel, 128

Boyarin, Jonathan, 128, 130–131, 153; *Thinking in Jewish,* 130

Brod, Max, 61, 66, 68, 71–74, 76

Buber, Martin, 66, 145–147; *Die Schrift,* 145

Butler, Judith, 154–155, 167–168; *Parting Ways,* 154

Celan, Paul, 2–4, 7, 127–128, 130, 133–144, 153–154; "Corona," 140–141; "In Egypt," 140; "Meridian" speech, 127, 134; "Praise of Distance," 139–140

Cervantes, Miguel de, 51–53; *Don Quixote,* 51–53

Christ, 47, 53, 57, 62, 70, 83–84, 118, 157, 167

Christianity, 6, 13, 16, 22, 43, 82–84, 130, 150

Cohen, Hermann, 3, 22, 129; *Deutschtum und Judentum,* 129

concealment. *See* hiddenness

conflict, Israeli-Palestinian, 167

demonic, 114–124

Derrida, Jacques, 5, 43, 49, 56–58, 64, 104–105, 128–136, 148, 153; *Archive Fever,* 132; *Interpretations at War: Kant, the German, the Jew,* 129; *The Other Heading,* 128

Diaspora, 20–22

Eichmann, trial, 19

election, 2–3, 5–6, 70–71, 73, 83–84, 128–129

emanation, 23, 25, 158

emancipation, 11–12, 14–15, 119

Emerson, Ralph Waldo, 157–158

Enlightenment, 4, 11–12, 14–16, 22–23, 25, 129; Jewish, 11

Esperanto, 104, 106

exception (state of), 34–35, 41–46, 48–49, 57, 60

exemplarity, exemplarism, 6–7, 129–133, 137, 141–143, 155; paradox of exemplarity, 128–129, 131, 133, 135

exile, 2–3, 5–7, 22, 69, 119, 71, 145–155

**VIVIAN LISKA** is Professor of German literature and Director of the Institute of Jewish Studies at the University of Antwerp, Belgium. In addition, since 2013, she is Distinguished Visiting Professor in the Faculty of the Humanities at The Hebrew University of Jerusalem. She has published extensively on literary theory, German modernism, and German-Jewish authors and thinkers. Liska's recent books include *Giorgio Agambens leerer Messianismus Messianism* (2008); *When Kafka Says We: Uncommon Communities in German-Jewish Literature* (2009); and *Fremde Gemeinschaft: Deutsch-jüdische Literatur der Moderne* (2011). She is the editor of numerous books, most recently, *What Does the Veil Know?* (with Eva Meyer, 2009); *The German-Jewish Experience Revisited* (with Steven Aschheim, 2015); and *Kafka and Universalism* (with Arthur Cools, 2016). She is the editor of the book series Perspectives on Jewish Texts and Contexts (De Gruyter, Berlin), coeditor of the *Yearbook of the Society for European-Jewish Literature*, and *arcadia: International Journal of Literary Studies*. In 2012, she was awarded the Cross of Honor for Sciences and the Arts from the Republic of Austria.

CPSIA information can be obtained
at www.ICGtesting.com
Printed in the USA
BVHW081334220419
546159BV00008B/781/P